W9-AFD-451

MASTER CLASS

MASTER CLASS

LESSONS WITH THE WORLD'S GREATEST CHEFS

DIANE HOLUIGUE

E. P. Dutton
New York

Copyright © 1988 by Diane Holuigue

All rights reserved. Printed in Hong Kong.

No part of this publication may be reproduced or transmitted in any
form or by any means, electronic or mechanical, including photocopy,
recording, or any information storage and retrieval system now known
or to be invented, without permission in writing from the publisher,
except by a reviewer who wishes to quote brief passages in connection
with a review written for inclusion in a magazine, newspaper, or
broadcast.

Published in the United States by E.P. Dutton,
a division of NAL Penguin Inc.,
2 Park Avenue, New York, N.Y. 10016

Published simultaneously in Canada by
Fitzhenry and Whiteside, Ltd., Toronto.

Originally published in Australia.

Library of Congress Catalog Card Number: 88–70786

ISBN: 0-525-24695-9

10   9   8   7   6   5   4   3   2   1

First American Edition

Contents

Acknowledgements

To Wendely Harvey, who commissioned this book, really encouraged me, trekked around the world to bring its international sales into being, and then saw the company change hands before seeing it to fruition;

To Fiona Hardie who sat with me and slogged through the many details; in three books and years of magazine editing and writing, the first editor I've ever worked with so closely, needed so much, demanded as much of, and appreciated as much;

To the photographers, many of whom I've worked with and grown to love over many years, and whose work is so vital it needs separate accreditation;

To Tony Hitchin, Editor of *Epicurean* and his successors Dulcie Boling and Eric Page, and to the team at Southdown Press, particularly Jeremy Vincent, who gave great technical assistance to the project;

To Penny Smith and Anita Hughes, writers and stunning food stylists for *Epicurean*, from whom I begged photography to complement my own;

To Sharon Carr for a difficult job well done in designing the book;

To the staff at the cooking school, who keep the French Kitchen flag flying despite the never-ending work, the absence of the chief, or her exhaustion;

And to my family, who supported me adding the book work to my already crazy load, and who coped yet again with the nights at 4.30 am, the lack of breakfasts, the never-ending clack of the computer, and my interminable absences on yet another mission;

And of course, to all the chefs who've made the book such a challenge and such a pleasure...

My grateful thanks

Introduction

Diane Holuigue

What a joy it is to have the passion of your life become your job. In eighteen years of teaching French cooking, this wonderful profession has made of me a journalist, an incessant traveller, and an international tablehopper as I strive to taste the unusual and the traditional, the regional and the way-out in order to explore the trends and flavours of the world of food. Not the least of these pleasures has been to make a veritable who's who of friends among the world's greatest cooking personalities.

Many I encountered in my work as Food Editor for *Epicurean* magazine by bursting in upon them with a camera and an angle for an article. I'd smile my way through a door too often beaten down by over-enthusiastic journalists who knew nothing about food, and stay to have the luck to find the right phrase, or show just that glimmer of knowledge that made the chef stick around and the door stay open. Many came to our far-off country to launch books or tour for the press and stayed to do a cooking class before my enthusiastic students at The French Kitchen; and some I just rang, with trepidation, to say I'd enjoyed their work — and that phone call to a stranger made me a lifetime friend.

This book represents the fruit of those years of work, fun and wonderful friendships. For you it creates the unique opportunity to see gathered together the world's greatest chefs, sharing their recipes and helping you work step by step through some of the marvellous dishes that have made them famous. Interestingly, the dishes they make for you are not all that difficult, and sometimes I wonder if what the truly great chefs have in common is that their dishes are so often simple but always perfectly cooked, beautifully presented and unique in style.

The recipes span a wide range: from traditional Italian to innovative modern French; from appetisers to desserts; and from easy seafood dishes to the techniques of making your own pasta and croissants.

This is a book for amateur and professional cooks alike; a book too for the armchair gourmet, who has read or heard about the cooking celebrities, their accomplishments, their restaurants and the food of the areas they represent.

INTERNATIONAL WEIGHTS AND MEASURES

This book was originally compiled with metric measurements, although due to its unique nature in dealing with chefs from many countries, some of the metric was 'worked back' from other measuring styles, depending on the origin of the chef. The imperial scale appears alongside for British readers with (Br.) beside it, and volume measurements (where practicable) have been added for North American readers with (U.S.) beside them. Wherever a weight is more practical than a volume — usually when food is bought from a butcher, fruiterer or supermarket in the correct amount, or when it is large, uncut, or unpeeled — the pounds and ounces are meant for both British and North American readers. The weight measurements of pounds and ounces are the same in these two scales, therefore if ever the bracketed forms (Br.) and (U.S.) do not appear, it is understood that the pounds and ounces should be read for the two.

However, the imperial liquid measures are not the same as the North American, and fluid ounces and pints (Br.) **must not be read for** fluid ounces and pints (U.S.). (The former has 20 fl oz to the pint; the latter 16 fl oz to the pint.) Similarly the metric and North American cup volumes differ. The former

1

is slightly larger than the latter and again these **must not be interchanged**. Imperial and North American tablespoons are also different. This is hardly detectable in small measures, hence if only one tablespoon is needed, there is no separation into (Br.) and (U.S.), although when two or more are used the differentiation appears. The teaspoon measurements are the same.

Translations, unfortunately, are never totally accurate, because they don't multiply exactly, and translating from one base to another yields ridiculous measurements, impossible to read off a scale. If I appear inconsistent, it is usually in the interest of a rounded and intelligible compromise. Thus sometimes you will read 'use 2lb', or 'a good cup', or 'a scant cup'.

* Follow only one style of stated measurements, never a mixture.

* All good cooks need a reliable set of scales and a measuring jug. This is certainly so when trying to cook with these top chefs, and particularly in pastry, where accuracy and carefully balanced ratios are vital. Most pastrysmiths weigh even egg yolks and whites, milk and cream, because of the inaccuracy of volume measurements. The cost of scales is minimal when so much of your cooking depends on it. Many modern digital scales give both metric and imperial weights at the touch of a button. Don't even bother to understand them — simply use them: put the scales on zero, add the ingredients and read off the totals. It is quicker than spooning out butter, easier than working out what is two-fifths of a cup, and the results are always reliable. There is not a chef in this book who works without them.

TEMPERATURES

Temperatures are written in Centigrade (Celsius) and Fahrenheit throughout. However, if you have only a gas regulo (numbering system), hang a little oven thermometer inside the oven, as a 'hot' or 'medium' oven is really not accurate enough.

* Always preheat an oven unless you are reheating food. Other than in a convection oven, when it is slightly less, the time an oven takes to heat can be up to 15 minutes, and this will affect your recipe timing. Only high heat will seal the juices into meat; lukewarm ovens draw the blood to the exterior. Worse,

only high heat will spring yeast and raising agents into action before crusting inhibits cakes, soufflés and breads from rising. With reheating however, the reverse is true. There is something to be said for heating the mass gradually rather than bringing the sauce to the boil, where it will bubble, skin, evaporate and even curdle before the meat or other ingredients heat through.

WHEN IS A MINCER NOT A MINCER? A WORD ON NOMENCLATURE AND INGREDIENTS.

Multi-national editions are somewhat tricky to write. Although we are all reading this book in English, even where the language is clear for one nation, it cannot be taken for granted that it works for another. In my own country, Australia, one state calls spinach 'spinach', and in another, spinach means silver beet (chard) and has to be specified as 'English spinach'. And that's without even crossing national borders.

For many years I have worked a lot in the French language, and now I find that English, my own language, is wonderfully confusing. In Australia we call summer squash 'zucchini', a fine old Italian word because we have Italian greengrocers. The Americans also say zucchini, but the British use courgette, a French word. A true shallot is never a spring onion or a green onion, and the champignon is a cultivated mushroom, never a wild one. Are red peppers, 'bell peppers', 'sweet peppers', or just plain 'capsicums' in your country; is icing sugar 'confectioner's sugar', and when is a mincer a 'meat grinder'?

Many words that can confuse — technical terms, ingredients, specialised equipment, etc. are in the glossary. I have also tried to accommodate what I can of English changes in nomenclature by giving alternatives in brackets. But however we try, even phrasing and expressions are sometimes going to be different. I hope to have been detailed enough in expression to guide you well through the recipes, but sometimes will require your patience and insight.

Cream

Australian cream is sold with 24% milk fat content (reduced cream), 35% milk fat content (with or without gelatine added, but either is suitable for whipping), and in some states 45% milk fat content. The latter is heavy, thick cream, ideal for sauces, as it is unctious and doesn't thin them out, and boils readily without risk of turning. However, it will not whip, as it turns to butter.

In Britain cream is sold as 'single cream' (with 18% milk fat), 'whipping cream' (around 35% milk fat) and 'double cream' (with 45 to 50% milk fat). The unique and wonderful 'clotted (scalded) cream' is cooked, and not used in cooking. **In Britain, where cream with 35% milk fat is called for, use 'whipping cream'; and where cream with 45% milk fat is preferred, use 'double cream'.**

In North America, the really heavy, thick cream is not generally available. The thickest cream widely available ('standard heavy cream') has 36% milk fat, although some states have 'heavy cream' with 40% milk fat. For these recipes, **where heavy cream is not available in North America, in all cases use cream with 36% milk fat.**

I hope the milk fat content acts as a guide, but have added the terms 'whipping' and 'heavy' as a second epithet to differentiate between the thicker and thinner varieties. Even if the creams in different countries are not identical in milk fat content, most cooks know which of their creams will whip and serve the purpose of the former, and which is the 'heaviest' that will do the best job in a sauce. If cream with 45% milk fat does not exist, simply use a lighter cream, with around 35% milk fat. The result will be less unctious, and in the case of a sauce, it will be thinner, but either the cream or the sauce can always be reduced to condense the sauce to a more suitable thickness.

Many a travelling food buff will have noted the comparatively different flavour of French cream. In fact there are two French creams, only the lighter one of which whips. Called 'fleurette', it is the equivalent of cream with 35% milk fat and whips well. But it is not readily available to the public at large, and thus many traditional French recipes speak of adding water to cream to be able to whip it (sweetened, this recipe is called 'Chantilly'). The better known cream in France sells under the name crème fraîche, and varies between 45% and 48% in milk fat content. The term, which simply means 'fresh cream' to the French, is now used internationally in cookbooks to suggest a formulated cream simulating this French flavour. It is somewhat more sour to our taste because it is left longer on the milk before skimming, and the lactic acid has had more time to work on it.

I have not specified crème fraîche in this book, however, if you aspire to achieving exactly the same results and tastes as the European, and particularly the French chefs, you may choose to make a simulated version of French cream yourself. It can be substituted throughout wherever cream with 45% milk fat is preferred, but is strictly better in sauces than desserts, unless a quantity of sweetener is added. The recipe is simple.

To make crème fraîche:
Add 1 tablespoon natural yoghurt or buttermilk to 300ml/½ pint (Br.)/1¼ cups (U.S.) cream with 35% milk fat. Leave out of the refrigerator overnight in a warm place (on top of the fridge is ideal) to mature, then refrigerate again and wait 2 or 3 days before using. The flavour is enhanced if the cream is first heated to blood temperature. Many cooks use a yoghurt maker to do this automatically. The result, after 5 to 7 hours in the yoghurt machine, pours readily when retrieved, but firms in the refrigerator. The resulting cream can be refrigerated for up to 10 days.

Dominique Bouchet

La Tour d'Argent
Paris, France

So famous is La Tour d'Argent in Paris that it is as much a landmark to the student of gastronomy as is the Tour Eiffel to the tourist. In fact the Tour Eiffel is a comparative upstart in terms of its age and history. Flanking the Seine on the Quai de la Tournelle and named for its beautiful, white mica-flecked Champenois stone which shimmers silver in the river's image, La Tour d'Argent has a visitors book which dates from 1582. With entries such as Henry III, it reads like a history of France, or even Europe, over the four hundred years of the restaurant's existence.

Through its doors there has been a constant parade of kings, queens, and courtiers: among them Tsar Alexandre 11, who feasted on peacock *aux amandes*, and Cardinal Richelieu, who had a roasted swan or two and the occasional partridge *au sucre* (roasted, sugared and stewed in verjuice and cinnamon). Louis XIV rarely ventured far from Versailles, but his courtiers loved la Tour, and although the Revolution forced the café underground, Napoleon brought back the dukes and princesses and one of his own imperial chefs became the proprietor. Through the centuries, the list of patrons broadened and the inclusion of presidents, ambassadors and millionaires tells an international story of change in politics, friendships and treaties. But the success of the restaurant continued and continues today.

Nearly all of this century La Tour d'Argent has been under the baton of the Terrail family. At first it was the formidable André Terrail, a contemporary and friend of Escoffier, and restaurateur extraordinaire. With his great business skill, culinary flair and ability to look beyond national boundaries (he had worked in England at the turn of the century), he made the rest of the world aware of the sacred Parisian haunt. In turn he handed over his treasure to his son Claude Terrail, the present owner.

It was Frederick, Maître d'Hôtel at the turn of the century, who made duck the centrepoint of La Tour d'Argent, and Frederick's invention too the celebrated recipe *canard au sang* (duck bled of its juice), for which the restaurant is famous. He inscribed the method in great detail — the 'rite' and the technique of this 'culinary sacrifice' — and from 1890 on, every duck served at La Tour d'Argent has been numbered and a card with the number on it given to the diner for whom the duck is destined.

So famous is the wonderful duckling dish with the sauce bound with the duck's own blood, that most first-time diners feel it is the dish that they should try — although perhaps less so if they saw it immortalised in the film *Who's Killing the Great Chefs of Europe?* One look at Philippe Moiret behind the renowned silver and brass duck press and everyone knew just how the chef of La Tour d'Argent must die! The dish has such a place in culinary history that it is worth becoming acquainted with its intricacies, and here, translated and paraphrased, is Claude Terrail's own description, taken from his autobiography *Ma Tour d'Argent*.[1]

Caneton Tour d'Argent

It is indispensable to choose a duck of 6-8 weeks old, taking extreme care to ensure it has a large, full body. Ours, grown in our own duck farms in the Vendée (south of Brittany) are particularly well looked after in the last fortnight before they're killed and are always killed by suffocation to ensure they keep their blood. First we make a good consommé from the carcasses, wing-tips, necks etc., then roast the meat in a very hot oven for about 20 minutes. It is thus cooked only superficially and still retains its blood. All this takes place in the kitchens.

Canard Marco Polo

The duck is then presented to the customer and afterwards taken to the 'duck chefs' (*les canardiers*), who create the theatrical drama in the dining room, where all can observe the ritual of finishing the dish.

The liver, chopped finely, is placed on a silver salver and a measure of old Madeira, a small glass of cognac and a touch of lemon juice are added to it. The chef then removes the legs, which return to the kitchen to be finished on the charcoal grill. With the aid of a very sharp knife, he then removes all the skin and cuts the breast into fine slices which are placed on the platter. The carcass, broken up, is then passed into the neck of the duck press and with the addition of a little cognac, is squeezed to extract all the blood and juices which run out onto the platter to join the liver and fillets. Over alcohol burners, this preparation, salted and peppered, is reduced for around 20 minutes. It is a work of extreme precision, during which the chef stirs and beats the sauce continually until it is reduced to the consistency of melted chocolate.

When served, the fillets and their sauce are accompanied by *pommes soufflées,* and a second service of the charcoal-grilled thighs and drumsticks is made with a tender green salad.

Nowadays the dining room at La Tour d'Argent is high on the rooftop of the building, the welcome and bar area on the ground floor and below, the cellar, one of the most famous in the world, with 130,000 bottles dating from the 1800s. Boarded up during the occupation of France, the cellar escaped unharmed and undetected and is now a virtual museum of wine, housing many great years and all the *grands crus*. The cellar may be visited for a digestif, during which time, as part of the overwhelming but understated Tour d'Argent service, ladies' shoulders will be covered with a sheepskin vest while they browse.

The 'new' dining room, with its glass walls, overlooks Notre Dame, the Ile de la Cité, the Seine and its barges and boats, and the magnificent illuminated skyline of Paris. It is probably the most romantic dining room in the world with the most discreet and old-fashioned service from white-aproned, dinner-suited waiters. The house has had three stars from the Michelin Guide for many years and the recent arrival (in 1978) of Dominique Bouchet and his second chef Jean Locussol has been an attempt to keep its food up with the trends of the moment. Despite this Dominique laments that the fame of the classic duck dishes means that his modern-style lighter cuisine takes second place. Both Dominique and Jean worked with Joël Robuchon of Jamin fame at Les Célébrités and yearn to have people try their creative dishes of the same ilk. Whichever way you go, you cannot fail to appreciate the grandeur and professionalism of La Tour d'Argent. It has been a hallmark of French cuisine now for four hundred years!

1 Claude Terrail, *Ma Tour d'Argent*, Stock, France, 1974, p 437

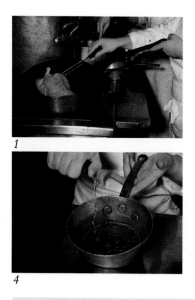

3

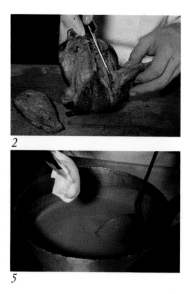

1

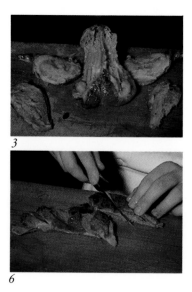

2

Canard Marco Polo
Duck Marco Polo

Serves 4, but if you roast two ducks, using the simpler roasting method below, the sauce can easily be doubled to serve 8.

2 kg/4½ lb duck*
2 tablespoons (Br.)/scant 3 tablespoons (U.S.) green peppercorns plus 20ml/1 tablespoon brine from the can
10ml/½ tablespoon cognac
20ml/1 tablespoon dry white wine
500ml/good ¾ pint (Br.)/2 good cups (U.S.) strong veal stock or demi glace
40g/1½ oz (Br.)/3 tablespoons (U.S.) butter
100ml/3 fl oz (Br.)/scant ½ cup (U.S.) cream, preferably with 45% milk fat (heavy cream)
salt and pepper

Vegetables to garnish the dish. In this presentation Dominique chose carrots and turnips 'turned' into pretty oval shapes, boiled in salted water ahead of time and then quickly sautéed in a little butter when needed. Allow about 4 pieces of each per person.

*In the restaurant, they serve half a duck each, serving first the underdone breast; then the legs, grilled over charcoal to finish their cooking, are served as a separate course with green salad. For the family situation, the chefs recommended roasting the bird until it is fully cooked, then serving it cut into 4 quarters to serve 4 persons (see **1** and **3** below).

To cook the duck:

1. Season the duck with salt and pepper, truss it so it holds its shape, then quickly brown it in a pan greased with a fine layer of butter. This is to ensure the bird colours well. When browned all over, place it breast up in a baking dish with the butter and roast in a 200ºC/400ºF oven for 40 to 45 minutes, basting it with its own juices. This should result in a rare duck, and the restaurant would now remove the legs to grill them and serve them separately.

You may prefer to roast the duck for 1 hour 10 minutes, and then the legs can be served at the same time as the breast, fully cooked through.

2. With a sharp knife, slit and pull away the strings, then remove the breast from the front of the bird. Now remove the breast fillet of the second side.

3. Remove the legs. You'll note that the legs are very rare with this cooking time, so they must be taken away and placed over the charcoal grill. Serve them as a second course on a small plate with green salad, after your guests have finished the main dish with the breast.

If you have roasted the dish until fully cooked, the simplest cutting method is to take carving shears or very sharp scissors and cut along the centre back on either side of the parsons nose and backbone, then cut along the centre front. With the bird divided into 2, cut each half into a wing and leg section, curving your scissors around the leg line to

allow a little extra breast meat to accompany the wings.

To prepare the sauce:

4. Put the brine from the green peppercorns, the cognac and the wine in a saucepan. Reduce to half its volume then add the green peppercorns. Allow to reduce again. When there is only a strongly flavoured base left in the pan, add the veal stock and reduce again, slowly over a period of 20 minutes.

5. Now add the cream, check the seasoning and reduce to sauce consistency (it should lightly coat the back of a spoon).

To serve:

6. Cut the breast into thin slices, usually called on a menu either the *magret* (from the word 'lean') or *aiguillettes*, meaning needle-like pieces.

7. Place the vegetables on the plate, then fanned-out slices of breast meat.

8. Coat with a little of the sauce. The rest goes into a sauceboat to serve at the table.

9. Close up of the finished product, about to be covered by the fabulous silver bell of La Tour d'Argent.

7

8

9

Pêche Blanche sur Granité de Pamplemousse

Poached White Peach on a Bed of Grapefruit and Champagne Granita

Serves 6
450ml/¾ pint (Br.)/2 scant cups (U.S.) grapefruit juice
150ml/good 5 fl oz (Br.)/scant ¾ cup (U.S.) champagne
150ml/good 5 fl oz (Br.)/scant ¾ cup (U.S.) sugar syrup at 30⁰ Baumé*, chilled
6 whole fresh peaches, preferably white fleshed, lightly poached in a syrup made in the ratio of 1 cup sugar to 2 cups water, then cooled and peeled
100g/3 oz (Br.)/¼ cup (U.S.) redcurrant jelly softened with a little kirsch
6 leaves fresh mint

*To make a syrup at 30⁰ Baumé, combine 1 litre/1¾ pints (Br.)/4¼ cups (U.S.) water and 1.35kg/use 3 lb (Br.)/6¾ cups (U.S.) sugar. Bring to the boil, ensuring that the sugar is dissolved totally prior to boiling point. Cool the liquid and store in the refrigerator until needed. Stores indefinitely.

Equipment:
6 large-bowled burgundy glasses or glass bowls

Combine the grapefruit juice, Champagne and sugar syrup. Set it to freeze in the freezing compartment of your refrigerator in either a plastic container or stainless steel bowl. During freezing, stir it several times with a fork to obtain the typical crystallised look of a granita.

To serve:
Place 3 or 4 tablespoons of granita in each glass. Put a poached peach in each glass over the granita. Brush each peach with the redcurrant jelly to give it a sheen. Top each peach with a mint leaf.

Gâteau au Chocolat Amer
Bitter Chocolate Cake

This cake, so extremely light that it is more like a mousse than a cake, sounds much easier to make than it is. Be warned to try it first when you are not awaiting important guests; but when you know how to do it, it is delicious as a cake or a very rich dessert for the table.

Serves 8 to 10
200g/7 oz dark (bittersweet) chocolate. Use the finest quality chocolate you can find.
500ml/good ¾ pint (Br.)/2 good cups (U.S.) cream with 35% milk fat (whipping cream)

The icing:
Either *pâté à glacer*, a commercially prepared icing made for pâtissiers, or 100g/use 4 oz dark (bittersweet) chocolate mixed with 40g/1½ oz (Br.)/3 tablespoons (U.S.) unsalted butter.

Equipment:
16cm/use 6 in cake circle (i.e. straight-sided walls without a base). The cake is easier to make in individual sizes (see **Variations** below), in this case 8 circles with a width of about 7cm/use 3 in and a height of about 2.5 cm/1 in.

The cake:
Melt the chocolate in a double boiler, or in a basin sitting over hot water in a second basin or saucepan. Stir only occasionally so it doesn't disturb the brilliance of the chocolate, but make sure there are no grains in it before removing from the double boiler. Allow to cool, but it must remain liquid.

Whip the cream until firm enough to hold soft peaks only.

Now the cream and chocolate must be folded together, the trickiest part of the operation. To do this successfully, check first that there is not enough heat in the chocolate to melt the cream, then take about 1 good cup of the cream and with a whisk, stir it very quickly into the chocolate. Then with a rubber spatula, scrape all the chocolate mixture into the cream bowl and, also with a whisk, and working fast and stirring firmly, blend the chocolate mixture into the remaining cream in the bowl. If you have done this swiftly and successfully, you have a smoothly blended mixture; if not, some of the chocolate will have set in the cool of the cream, and you will have a graininess in the end product.

You may now use the whisk to thicken the mixture a little more by continuing to stir. Transfer the mixture into the cake circle, placed firmly onto the plate on which you wish to serve the cake. The plate must be a type that is able to be refrigerated. The mousse mixture should come to just a fraction below the rim of the mould, thus leaving room for a thin coating of icing. Refrigerate overnight or for a minimum of 3 hours before icing.

The icing:
At La Tour d'Argent, like many French pâtissiers, they use a pre-prepared chocolate mix called *pâte à glacer*, which runs on very easily and does not need to be tempered. Alternatively you may temper the chocolate and then mix it with up to 40% bland oil (peanut or safflower) or clarified unsalted butter; or, in the domestic kitchen, you may even choose to use compound chocolate, which does not need to be tempered.

Whichever the choice, melt the *pâte à glacer*, chocolate and oil or clarified butter, or compound chocolate in a basin over hot water again, and when cool but still liquid, pour a thin layer in the height remaining between the rim and the mousse. In fact, La Tour d'Argent ices the whole cake, but this is extremely difficult to do without *pâte à glacer*.

Note: Watch that the mousse is very cold at the time of application, and that the chocolate is still runny but has no heat in it or it may melt the mousse underneath.

Return to the refrigerator to set. To unmould, place a warm, well rung out damp teatowel around the edge for a moment, and the cake circle can be easily lifted off the cake.

Variations:
La Tour d'Argent serves small individual-sized cakes which are much easier to make than the one in our photograph. Use moulds with a width of 7cm/use 3 in and a height of about 2.5cm/1 in. Similarly, you can also make a version which covers the top with sieved Dutch cocoa rather than icing. This works easily as a very functional and very tasty dessert. Another alternative it to add a little grated zest of orange and a touch of Grand Marnier to the mousse.

Madeleine Kamman

Chef. Teacher. Author
Annecy, France. Napa Valley, U.S.A.

Paul Bocuse called her former restaurant 'the greatest in the U.S.A.'; *Cuisine* magazine referred to her as 'a major creative force in the food world'; and *Bon Appétit*, on the magazine's cover no less, declared her Annecy (Haute Savoie) cooking classes to be 'France's best cooking school' and coined for her the term 'professeur de cuisine extraordinaire'. In the introduction to her latest book James Beard wrote 'Madeleine has a gift for instilling in others her love for food, her feeling for ingredients, her sense of the rightness of one flavour or texture with another...to read her books is an adventure.'[1]

Great chef, great teacher, great author...She is Madeleine Kamman, a small, hyperactive Frenchwoman born in Paris in 1930, but whose heart soars somewhere around the mountains and the kitchens of Annecy, her spiritual home. Married for twenty-five years to an American, she also has one foot in American kitchens where, since 1961, she has run two restaurants and taught a legion of devoted students all she can of her French culinary heritage.

Madeleine's classes are just about the liveliest around. She is a great communicator, offering a forthright, dare-I-say dogmatic stream of evocative language as she cooks. 'I have the reputation of being a tough lady,' she says. 'It isn't enough to be a "born" cook; you have to be disciplined too.' Her classes are a combination of demonstration, philosophy, history, childhood reminiscences of France and above all her beloved bourgeois cuisine, chit chat, chemistry and even tongue-wagging. 'Recipes are only like learning the ABC. The class can be a wonderful forum for learning technique, technique and technique.' Madeleine is at once a stern teacher and an inspiring entertainer, and she has a lot to impart.

Madeleine's long course, for which a tiny group of eight was chosen each year, and for which students paid US$10,000, no longer exists, for she has retired from her restaurant and now devotes her time to writing and guest demonstrating around the world. In its day, however, her course was accredited by the U.S. Board of Education as a chef's training course, and Madeleine is very proud of this. She is an ardent women's liberationist, if not a militant one, and hers was the first school opened by a woman to receive official accreditation.

At her school, Madeleine didn't believe in prerequisites. She has even turned lawyers into chefs, and many of her students are now doing well in some of the best restaurants in the States. She believes in hard work; exposure to the tasks involved, by placing the students directly in a restaurant kitchen; and love and dedication. As part of the course she used to take everyone to France for two weeks, believing that learning in a country where the whole population is steeped in a strong gastronomic heritage added inestimable dimensions to the programme even in the small amount of time she had them under instruction there. They visited markets, restaurants, the kitchens of important chefs, cheese factories and shop after shop to compare, evaluate and buy produce. Back in America, they themselves prepared restaurant meals, for Madeleine believes that in the long run, training is seventy-five per cent practice.

When she stopped running her courses, those aspiring to follow in her footsteps needed to steep themselves in her writings, but the retired Madeleine coped only two years before heading back to the profession she was born for, and nowadays, professionals who care to study in depth with Madeleine will find her based eight months of the year at Beringer's Winery in the Napa Valley giving two-week seminar

Marinated Tenderloin Steak Viking Style

programmes. Equally demanding in style perhaps, but Madeleine 'feels' retired, in that Beringer's allow only four people to attend each programme.

So far there have been five books, plus many articles in the well-known food magazines, and even a few specialised volumes that she has translated from French into English. The book that first made her name as a cookbook writer, and the one that expounds her skills as a teacher and a gifted trouble shooter who can answer all her students' questions, is *The Making of a Cook*. It not only has a wealth of technical information to help you understand good French cooking techniques, but it is written with the usual Kamman romantic flair.

When French Women Cook is Madeleine's most eloquent work. She describes with great love and nostalgia the France of her youth and the wonderful earthy women who set in motion her romance and life-long obsession with good food. The book is a trove of recipes, but also a tribute to the women who nourished her — an aunt, the keeper of a boarding house, an aged friend, and others, each an evocative portrait better than the one before it. It is at once a plea to restore what was, and a firm statement on feminism. Madeleine has a friendly feud going with Paul Bocuse. He maintains that women don't belong in the professional kitchen. She believes they are ultimately the better cooks. So the dedication of *When French Women Cook* is written to Bocuse's mother and grandmother!

Madeleine's latest book is *In Madeleine's Kitchen*. It is an anthology of her more recent recipes and the development of her *'cuisine personelle'*, the modern, creative style of cookery which she derived from fielding her traditional French techniques with American ingredients. This is Madeleine at the peak of her creativity. Her wealth of knowledge is incredible, for she has been in the restaurant business since she was nine, when she was taken from Paris to her aunt's country restaurant to escape the horrors of war. It is also a tribute to her extraordinarily inquisitive mind, which refuses to take any habit or technique for granted just because it is in place. It sends her back to her books — even science and medical books — to find out why things should be so, or if there's a better way.

Currently, Madeleine is spending her free time holed up in Annecy writing *Between Heaven and Earth — the Land, People and Food of the Savoie*, to be released in 1989. Knowing how beautiful her writing can be, one can only guess that this may well be the most poetic of her books, as she is talking of the land where her heart truly lies.

The steak dish you find here is a simple dish that is typical of Madeleine's work in that it uses one of her favourite techniques for creating good sauces. She creates a strong base 'essence', much stronger than stock and much more related to the dish, being made on the parings of the main ingredient. It is typical of her also in that it combines unusual flavours to give an exciting, up-market presentation of what could be just a simple steak dish. I hope it will force you back into the bookshelves to delve into her books, for there is much to learn from this inspiring woman.

1 Madeleine Kamman, *In Madeleine's Kitchen*, Atheneum, New York, 1984, Introduction.

1

2

3

4

5

6

Marinated Tenderloin Steak Viking Style

Serves 6 to 8
This recipe can be recreated with a whole fillet marinated overnight then roasted at 200ºC/400ºF to rare or medium-rare.

1 large fillet (tenderloin) of beef 'peeled' of any thick loin fat by the butcher
1 tablespoon caraway seeds
about 3 tablespoons aquavit
butter as needed
use 1 litre/1¾ pints (Br.)/4 cups (U.S.) quality jellied veal stock
175 ml/6 fl oz (Br.)/good ¾ cup (U.S.) cream, preferably with 45% milk fat (heavy cream)
½ teaspoon grated lemon zest
about 3 tablespoons chopped fresh dill weed
1 red bell pepper (capsicum), peeled, cut into small oval confetti shapes and sautéed lightly in butter

Trim the tenderloin so that it is totally fat free. Cut it into steaks 1.5cm/5/8 in thick. You may serve 2 per person or only 1, depending on your taste and on the width of the fillet. From the 'chain' and the 'tail' of the tenderloin completely de-fat and cut 300 to 350g/11 to 12 oz of meat into 1cm/½ in cubes. (About 1½ cups [U.S.]). Set aside.

1. In a small mortar or mill, powder the caraway seeds. Brush each side of each steak with aquavit and sprinkle with caraway powder. Let stand 2 hours on a stainless steel rack. In hot climates keep refrigerated, then bring to room temperature before cooking.

2. Meantime, cut the red bell pepper (capsicum) into the tiny oval decorative confetti shapes for the garnish, and pan fry them in butter. Set them aside between plates in the oven to stay warm.

The beef essence:

3. Brown the cubes of meat very well in about 3 tablespoons of butter. Discard the browning fat, then cover with the veal stock.

4. Simmer slowly until it reduces to approximately 1 cup of single essence. If you used rich enough stock, it should now glaze the back of the spoon; if not, add more veal stock and reduce again. This part of the base sauce may be made in advance. Strain into a saucepan, add the cream and reduce by one third. Add the lemon zest and dill and blend together. Set aside.

5. Pan fry the steaks to your taste. Season them well and discard the cooking fat. Madeleine has a neat trick to keep the waiting steaks warm while she deglazes the pan: they are arranged along a cranked spatula and set over the sauce, so that any juice that falls, drops into the sauce. De-glaze the pan with about 3 tablespoons of aquavit. Add the resulting liquid to the prepared sauce. Place the steaks in the centre of your dinner plates, coat each with a little sauce and sprinkle with the red bell pepper (capsicum) confetti.

6. Serve surrounded by the wilted spinach and cucumber vegetable prepared as follows.

Cucumber Strips on Wilted Spinach

Serves 6

6 small cucumbers, peeled
500g/use 1 lb spinach (English spinach) in leaves, whole, washed and still slightly wet
butter as needed
salt and pepper

Using a potato peeler with swivel blade, remove thin strips of cucumber from the whole length of each vegetable. To obtain the uniform width, turn each cucumber a bit before you remove the next strip. Separate the leaves of the spinach, pluck free of thick stems, wash well and dry well in a spinner or teatowel to ensure easy frying.

Heat some butter in a very large skillet and quickly toss the spinach leaves in until they heat through and slightly wilt. Do not cook too much at once, or it loses water and packs. Work quickly in small batches, each time arranging some on each of the heated dinner plates in turn.

Add more butter and stir fry the cucumber strips very quickly. Salt and pepper and remove quickly. Plate the spinach in a nest and weave a few cucumber strips around the spinach leaves.

Cardamom and Macerated Pineapple Mousse Cake

Serves 12 to 14

For the meringue:
butter as needed
1 tablespoon flour
3 eggwhites
85g/3 oz (Br.)/scant ½ cup (U.S.) sugar
125g/4½ oz (Br.)/⅔ cup (U.S.) ground macadamia nuts
125g/4½ oz (Br.)/⅔ cup (U.S.) ground almonds

For the frozen mousse:
4 sun-dried pineapple rings (available from healthfood shops) diced and soaked overnight in bourbon or dark rum
10 egg yolks
180g/6½ oz (Br.)/1 scant cup (U.S.) sugar
pinch of salt
3 leaves or 3 teaspoons granulated unflavoured gelatine
3 eggwhites
1 teaspoon ground cardamom powder
500ml/good ¾ pint (Br.)/2 good cups (U.S.) cream with 35% milk fat (whipping cream), whipped until barely mounted
icing (confectioner's) sugar

To prepare the cake tin:
Dab a few pieces of butter on the bottom and around the sides of a 24cm/10 in springform cake tin. Fit a layer of baking (parchment) paper on the cake tin and all around the edge.

To prepare the meringue:
Butter and lightly flour an unbendable baking tray. Pre-heat the oven to 170ºC/325ºF. Beat the eggwhites until they are **very** firm. Mix the sugar and nuts and fold into the eggwhites. Spread the mixture onto a baking tray and bake for approximately 20 minutes or until uniformly brown. Remove to a rack, break into pieces and crumble very finely. Process this for a few seconds in a food processor to make the texture uniform, then line the bottom of the prepared cake tin with 5mm/¼ in of meringue powder.

Drain whatever bourbon or rum is left after macerating the dried pineapple overnight. Keep 125ml/4 fl oz (Br.)/½ cup (U.S.) for the mousse. Cream together the egg yolks, sugar and a pinch of salt in an electric beater until the mixture forms a heavy ribbon. While the mixture ribbons, soften and melt the gelatine in a tablespoon of water in a small saucepan over heat. Add some of the ribboning mixture to the gelatine. Blend well and then reverse the process, adding the gelatinised egg mixture back into the bulk of the base. Continue to whip in the electric beater while you beat the eggwhites. Add half the bourbon or rum to the egg yolk base as well as the cardamom. Whip the cream, slowly adding the rest of the alcohol, but keep it only very lightly whipped — it needs to be only barely mounted.

Fold successively the eggwhites, then the cream, into the yolk base. Spoon half the mousse into the prepared cake tin. Then put it in the freezer until it is semi-solid. Top it with the diced pineapple, the remainder of the mousse and another 5mm/¼in layer of meringue crumbs. Wrap the tin in plastic wrap and freeze for at least 4 hours. Dust with icing (confectioner's) sugar before serving.

Aiguillettes of Lamb Mechoui Style

A delightfully inventive barbecue recipe using fillets of lamb with the aromatic herbs of North Africa.

Serves 6 or 12 if using 1 fillet for 2 people
6 'fillets' of lamb. These are in fact not the true fillet, which is very tiny, but the eye, or larger side of the loin chop. Have your butcher bone them from the loin and remove all fat and sinew. Use the scraps, or any extra meat to obtain, as well, 200g/7 oz of extra lamb meat.
120g/4½ oz each chopped parsley, mint and coriander (cilantro) leaves (**not** coriander seeds), or 1 large bunch of each
4 medium garlic cloves, finely chopped
1 teaspoon cumin powder
60ml/scant 2 fl oz (Br.)/3 tablespoons (U.S.) olive oil
50g/scant 2 oz (Br.)/3 tablespoons (U.S.) unsalted butter
1.5 litres/2½ pints (Br.)/6 cups (U.S.) well-jellied veal stock
¼ teaspoon fennel seeds, whole
salt and freshly ground black pepper

Mix two-thirds of the chopped parsley, mint and coriander (cilantro) with two-thirds of the garlic and cumin powder. Spread the mixture evenly on all sides of the meat and allow to marinate for at least 2 hours.

The sauce:
The sauce may be prepared in advance, and is built upon the 200g/7 oz of extra lamb, cut in small pieces. Madeleine would prefer the meat that is used in the sauce to be char-grilled to pick up the barbecued flavour, but if the barbecue is not alight, pan fry them in butter in a heavy-based skillet until well browned. Discard any burnt butter or rendered fat. To the skillet add 250ml/ 8 fl oz (Br.)/1 good cup (U.S.) of veal stock and reduce until 2 to 3 tablespoons are left. (For preparation of a good 'essence', see the Viking Steak recipe page 13.) Repeat the operation 2 or 3 more times to obtain approximately 350ml/ 11 fl oz (Br.)/1½ cups (U.S.) of excellent lamb essence. During the last 2 additions, add the whole fennel seeds. Strain into a clean saucepan.

Cream the butter with the remaining chopped parsley, coriander (cilantro), mint etc. Salt and pepper this, and add to the lamb essence, stirring it in on either very low heat or on full boil.

To cook the lamb:
Heat the barbecue grill very well. Brush a thin layer of oil over each piece of meat and grill to the degree of cooking you prefer, preferably keeping it pink in the centre (around 3 minutes each side). There will be 1 fillet per person, or 1 for 2 if you prefer. For preference cut the fillet into fine slices and fan over the plate. Serve with Mushroom Kibbe (see recipe below).

Mushroom Kibbe

Serves 6 to 8
500g/1 lb 2 oz (Br.)/4 cups (U.S.) cracked wheat (bourghul)
100g/3½ oz (Br.)/½ cup (U.S.) butter
100g/3½ oz (Br.)/¾ cup (U.S.) finely chopped onions
2 cloves garlic, crushed
500 to 600ml/up to 1 pint (Br.)/about 2½ cups (U.S.) water or vegetable broth
250g/use ½ lb (Br.)/scant 3 cups (U.S.) fresh mushrooms, cleaned and sliced
25g/1 oz (Br.)/½ cup (U.S.) dried boletus or *cèpe (porcini)* mushrooms, rehydrated in water
1 egg
400ml/⅔ pint (Br.)/1¾ cups (U.S.) cream with 35% milk fat (whipping cream)
1½ teaspoons cornflour (cornstarch)
1 clove garlic, whole

Heat 60g/2 oz (Br.)/¼ cup (U.S.) butter in a large frying pan with some depth (*sauteuse*), and sauté the onions and the crushed garlic until translucent. Add the cracked wheat (bourghul) and toss until the mixture gains heat. Add the water or vegetable broth, bring to the boil then reduce heat to a simmer. Block the top of the pan completely with several layers of paper towels and the lid, and cook slowly until all the moisture has been absorbed (about 15 minutes). The time varies with the quality and type of cracked wheat (bourghul).

Heat the remaining butter in a skillet and add the fresh and the rehydrated mushrooms, retaining the water of the latter. Toss the butter quickly in then cover to allow the moisture to fall from the mushrooms. Drain in a colander placed over a bowl; retain the liquid. Rub a rectangular baking dish with the whole clove of garlic. Spread one half of the cracked wheat (bourghul) on the bottom of the dish. Top with the mushrooms, then cover with a second layer of the remaining cracked wheat.

Beat a whole egg with the mushroom juices and the water from the dried mushrooms, and the heavy cream. Sift the cornflour (cornstarch) over the mixture and beat again. Season to taste with salt and pepper, and pour this mixture over the cracked wheat (bourghul). Bake in a 190°C/375°F oven until it sets (about 30 minutes).

Giuliano Bugialli

Teacher. Author
U.S.A. Florence, Italy

When prize-winning author, teacher, television cook and fine old Italian patriot Giuliano Bugialli first found himself standing in, of all places, a cooking school by the name of 'The French Kitchen', he vowed to 'clear away some myths, and rock this temple to French gastronomy'. As luck would have it, there was a terrible thud in the room above the kitchen, hearts fell, Giuliano grinned at me to show his vow had authority and the class burst out laughing.

For charm and good humour, coupled with the most pig-headed Italian chauvinism one can imagine, is what makes this man one of the most loved cooking teachers in the world.

Giuliano loves to dispel myths about Italian cooking, laughing at foreign pseudo-Italian restaurants with their clichéd versions of supposedly classical dishes. He sets the record 'straight' with his ideas on the Italian origins of International cuisine, and above all, of French cuisine, which 'everyone knows' was picked up holus-bolus and taken to France by Caterina di Medici when she married Henri II. And, French cooks beware, for if you argue too much, Giuliano has photos of 14th Century manuscripts with recipes for *quinquinelle* (the original *quenelles*), or *savore per paparo* (a type of foie gras), and his stories of Caterina putting *salsa balsamella* (*béchamel* sauce) on her face as beauty cream are an epicurean's nightmare!

Giuliano's first book, *The Fine Art of Italian Cooking*, is an authoritative work which also gives a clue to his background, for Giuliano was not a cook by training, but a professor of history and languages in his hometown Florence. In the course of his work he began researching old manuscripts and documenting the traditional cookery of his beloved Tuscan province. His mother, recounts Giuliano, was 'an original

women's libber': she was very innovative and worked in fashion design, something most uncommon for women of her class at that time. She was not at all at home in the kitchen. Conversely, as Giuliano grew in his love for architecture, history and the finer things of life, he began to want to eat well, and so he started to put his academic research into practice in the kitchen.

Giuliano soon became an accomplished cook and one very keen on the old traditions. At that time, as now, these traditions were mostly only kept up in the homes of certain Italian families who still took care to pass them down from generation to generation. 'By scrupulously comparing one's own experience with that of the old families, as well as with old manuscripts and early books, it is possible to arrive at generalisations about techniques, spicing, and so on, and to produce authentic recipes that remain gastronomically very valid indeed', he wrote in the preface to his first book, which gained him the 1980 Caterina di Medici Award for the most outstanding contribution to Italian cooking in the Medici anniversary year. Most claim this to be Giuliano's best book, although many would opt for his third, *Giuliano Bugialli's Foods of Italy*, whose rich tapestry of photography and regional recipes has helped it appeal to a much broader audience, and which earned America's prestigious Tastemaker Award.

Giuliano started teaching his native cuisine first in Italy, and then in the United States, after arriving there as an Italian language teacher. Before long he was teaching full-time, first in his New York apartment, then as a sought-after guest demonstrator in cooking schools around the country. But it was in Florence in 1973 that he began, when he founded Italy's first English-speaking school of Italian cookery, primarily for an American audience. It was a summer school, set in a wonderful old monastery, which he rented from the nuns. Eventually, Giuliano revamped the format

Fettucine alla Panna

of the school, and it is now situated in the roomy kitchen of his Florentine apartment, where he lives for several months of the year. The apartment has a wonderful view overlooking the ochre tones of the buildings of Florence, the domes of old churches, a nearby Jewish synagogue, and the terracotta rooftops of the nearby villas.

Visitors from all over the world attend a variety of weekly classes that run regularly from May to October, excluding August. Giuliano's demonstrations break after the initial instruction into practical sessions, and the students learn to cook up wonderful meals on a series of little marble benches nestled in wrought-iron trolleys placed strategically in the spacious room. It is a glorious setting, the room furnished with Italian understatement — an old oak bread-proving coffer and oak wall shelving housing antique plates; and with colourful overstatement — a wall lined with huge shelves of fine white crockery, elegant glassware and speckled green-splattered terracotta pottery.

Apart from Florentine and Tuscan cooking, there are special classes in the cuisine of other regions, Italian tradition, the wonderful 'Autumn Game and Truffle' classes, a class especially for professionals wanting to further their knowledge of Italian cuisine, and one in which Giuliano works only with pasta — covering an exceedingly disparate gamut of techniques from the hard-style Sicilian pasta with few eggs and higher water ratios to the finest tagliatelle, wholemeal doughs, 'stamped' disc-shaped doughs, and doughs embossed with parsley. Some classes tour other regions, as in the spa town of Montecatini. All are supplemented with special dinners, visits to the opera or to concerts, excursions to nearby historic Tuscan and Umbrian towns, or walking tours of local markets. Giuliano

also often takes foreign press on tours of the various regions of Italy, introducing them to the authentic sights, smells, flavours and market places of his beloved country.

Giuliano turns his hand to just about anything **authentically** Italian — no forays into *nuova cucina* for him — and he is a fund of information for all the trivia and techniques that help students put what they've learnt into practice. None the less, people are still most fascinated when he teaches the art of making home-made pasta. Years of experience have made him like a great circus performer — kneading and pushing, gathering the dough between his fingers and balling it speedily and with aplomb, then flipping the enormous lengths of dough he pulls from his hand-cranked machine (**never**, but **never** an extruder) through the flour and into the air like a Chinese ribbon swirler, finally extracting no less than fourteen people from his audience to help hold the thirty-metre lengths of tissue-fine pasta he churns from the tiny machine. The end result is a fine tagliatelle that cooks for only one second, and I defy you ever to taste a lighter pasta. It's all in the kneading, Giuliano will tell you, and the light handling of the dough. Only a bad worker blames the flour, he says, for Giuliano has worked all over the world, and never travels with his flour, never insists on imported durum wheat. He simply feels two or three of the local varieties and works with the one his instinct and experience tells him will yield the best results.

In the hope that some of this can rub off on us lesser mortals, here is Giuliano describing for us his own fine technique.

1 Giuliano Bugialli, *The Fine Art of Italian Cooking*, Times Books, New York, 1977, p.xii.

1

2

3

FINE PASTA

In his books, Giuliano gives the ratio of ingredients for pasta rather than absolute quantities: 1 egg for each (U.S.) cup of flour (1 egg for each 130g/4½ oz [Br.] flour). The method given here is for making tagliatelle but this is only a size and shape of cut, and the dough is suitable for other cuts. (You may choose to make it thicker — one less notch — for some of the differing shapes.) Giuliano uses a hand-cranked pasta machine that is widely available in cookware or department stores and in many Italian delicatessens. Like most fine cooks, he will not use the modern electric extruder-style pasta machine, noting that it compresses the pasta rather than kneading it into a natural, springy dough. The resulting taste difference is enormous. When completed, the dough may be cut into many shapes: taglierini, tagliatelle (fettuccine), pappardelle, farfelle, spaghetti, or penne to be eaten with sauces; taglierini or vermicelli for soups; or it can be cut into large sheets for lasagne or cannelloni.

Basic Fresh Pasta Recipe

1 cup basic recipe

Serves 2 people, depending on how the pasta is to be used, and should be multiplied for larger quantities
130g/4½ oz (Br.)/1 cup (U.S.) plain (all-purpose) flour, preferably unbleached
1 extra large egg, at least 65g/2 oz
1 teaspoon olive oil
pinch salt

For red pasta, puréed cooked beetroot is added; for green pasta, puréed spinach (English spinach), but due to the extra moisture content, 1¾ (U.S.) cups of flour is the ratio to the egg and oil instead of 1 cup (use 230g/scant 8 oz [Br.] flour for each egg). The tablespoon of purée (per egg) is incorporated in the well (hole) in the beginning.

Note:
*Unbleached flour is preferable. Giuliano works world-wide and uses local, plain (all-purpose) flour almost everywhere. He has used baker's flour for a stronger gluten content, but finds the myth that this is better quite unfounded. However, it is important to avoid finely sifted flours, which are too aerated. If unavoidable, weigh and leave them to rest out on the bench for an hour or so before starting.

*Use a large egg, at least 65g/2 oz, preferably larger. If using under a 65g/2 oz egg, you will need an extra egg for every 5 or 6. Flour absorbs less egg in damp weather, so you may need more.

*If you do not use olive oil, be sure that the vegetable oil is safflower or peanut, which does not have a strong taste.

1. Place the flour in a mound on a board. Make a well (hole) in the centre and put in the egg, olive oil and salt. With a fork, first mix together the egg, oil and salt, and then begin to incorporate the flour from the inner rim of the well (hole), always incorporating fresh flour from the lower part, and pushing it under the dough to keep the ball of dough attached.

2. When half the flour has been absorbed, start kneading, always using the palms of your hands, not the fingers. Continue absorbing the flour until almost all of it has been incorporated. Try to add flour from the underneath of the ball, with the left hand if you're right handed, and roll the ball over and away from you with the right hand.

3. The amount of flour that remains unabsorbed should be passed through a sifter to remove bits of dough, then used to re-flour the table.

4. Recommence kneading the dough until most of the flour is incorporated and the dough is elastic. If you are working with a mixture larger than 2 eggs, cut the dough into 3 or 4 pieces before passing through the machine.

5. Attach the pasta machine to the table with its clamp. First you use the roller side for kneading to a finer texture. Start by setting the wheel for the rollers at the widest rollers. Flatten a piece of dough a little by hand so that it enters the machine readily, then pass it through the rollers.

6. Fold the resultant length into 3 and press together firmly with your fingertips. Sprinkle with flour and repeat the rolling and folding about 8 to 10 times. Then move the wheel to the next notch and pass once, not folding. Narrow the rollers each time and each time sprinkle the dough with a little flour. The more a pasta is kneaded through the rollers, the lighter it becomes to digest.

4

5

6

7

8

7. Re-pass until the pasta is as fine as desired. Giuliano prefers to go to the finest notch, except for spaghetti and linguine, which he cuts at the second finest notch. Place each length on a floured teatowel and proceed with the next ball of dough.

8. Now the set of cutting rollers comes into play. Place the crank handle into the notch on the cutting side, and pass each length of dough in turn through either the tagliatelle (fettuccine) — the thicker — or the linguine — the thinner — set of cutters, as desired. Collect the lengths as they come through and lay them on a floured board, without layering, until needed. The amount of time they are left to dry will affect the amount of cooking time they need, as will their thickness. They may be used after a short time (say 10 minutes) if preferred; they may be left an hour or overnight; and they may even be frozen.

Fettuccine alla Panna
Fettuccine with Cream

The recipe is known as *'alla panna'* (with cream) in Florence and Bologna; *'doppia burro'* (double butter) in Rome.

Serves 6
600g/1 lb 6 oz fettuccine
200g/7 oz (Br.)/1 scant cup (U.S.) unsalted butter
250ml/8 fl oz (Br.)/1 good cup (U.S.) cream with 35% milk fat (whipping cream)
200g/7 oz (Br.)/2 cups (U.S.) freshly grated parmesan cheese
salt and freshly ground pepper
nutmeg (optional)

Heat a large stockpot of salted water. When the pot is giving off steam, but not yet boiling, place the butter in a large frying pan or sauteuse and place it over the pan to melt, without heating too much.

When the water is boiling vigorously, remove the pan, keep it warm and add the pasta to the pot. The pasta will rise almost immediately to the top and is cooked in a matter of 2 or 3 seconds if the pasta has just been made, or 15 seconds if it has been allowed to dry for an hour or so. Drain it immediately.

Place the pan containing the butter over a low heat and add the cooked pasta. Toss it gently with the cream, unheated, and the parmesan cheese. Add salt, lots of freshly ground pepper and nutmeg, if you like it.

Variation:
If you like champignons (baby mushrooms), fry them sliced, in a little butter (separately, for they give up grey juices). Add them just as you place the butter on the stove to add the pasta. In Rome this is commonly known as fettuccine Alfredo, a wonderfully picturesque name, as fettuccine is Roman slang for the laces of an old-fashioned, lady's corset.

Osso Buco alle Verdure
Osso Buco in a Vegetable Sauce

Serves 6
2 zucchinis (courgettes), ends trimmed
2 carrots, peeled
1 red onion, peeled
1 stalk celery
20 sprigs Italian parsley, leaves only
6 ossi buchi (veal shank cut into 3.5cm/1½ in slices, with bone and marrow)
65g/good 2 oz (Br.)/good ½ cup (U.S.) flour
5 tablespoons (Br.)/6 tablespoons (U.S.) butter
1 to 2 tablespoons (Br.)/1 to scant 3 tablespoons (U.S.) tomato paste
1 to 2 tablespoons (Br.)/1 to scant 3 tablespoons (U.S.) olive oil
60ml/scant 2 fl oz (Br.)/3 tablespooons (U.S.) home-made chicken or beef broth
475ml/good ¾ pint (Br.)/2 cups (U.S.) dry white wine
salt and freshly ground black pepper
1 teaspooon dried thyme

The vegetable garnish:
350g/good ¾ lb (Br.) fresh peas, shelled (about 1 cup [U.S.] shelled peas)
350g/good ¾ lb string beans, ends and the string removed
350g/good ¾ lb carrots
350g/good ¾ lb celery
coarse-grained salt
5 tablespoons (Br.)/6 tablespoons (U.S.) butter
1 to 2 tablespoons (Br.)/1 to scant 3 tablespoons (U.S.) olive oil
salt and freshly ground black pepper
pinch freshly grated nutmeg

Cut the zucchinis (courgettes), carrots, onion and celery into small lengths and put them into a bowl of cold water until needed.

Tie each osso buco around the side with string, to compact its shape. Lightly flour the ossi buchi on both sides but not on the edges.

In a casserole, over a medium heat, heat the butter and oil. Sauté the meat until golden brown on both sides. Combine

the tomato paste and the chicken or beef broth, then add to the casserole and allow it to cook for 2 minutes. Add 120ml/4 fl oz (Br.)/½ cup (U.S.) white wine and allow to simmer for 10 minutes to evaporate the alcohol.

Drain the vegetables and add them to the casserole with the parsley leaves. Cover and cook over a medium heat

for 20 minutes. Check for seasoning. Turn the meat over, add the remaining wine and the thyme, and cook for a further 35 minutes or until tender. When the meat is tender, check again for seasoning. Remove the meat to a bowl, and cover with a plate.

Pass the sauce remaining in the pan through a food mill, using the disc with

the finest holes. Return to a casserole and cook over a medium heat for 15 minutes, or until a thick, smooth sauce is formed. Return the meat. Up to this point, the dish may be made in advance.

The garnish vegetables:
Cut the garnish vegetables into lengths of about 10cm/4 in to give them a similar appearance. Soak each in separate

bowls of cold water for at least 30 minutes. In separate pots of boiling salted water, cook each vegetable until tender but still firm — about 15 minutes. Drain and set aside. When required, heat the butter and oil and gently sauté the vegetables for 5 minutes. Season with salt, pepper and nutmeg.

To serve:
Reheat the meat in the casserole with the reduced sauce, allowing it to absorb some of the sauce itself. Remove the strings from the ossi buchi and serve them on individual serving plates. Coat each osso buco with some of the sauce, and arrange with the sautéed vegetables in piles alongside.

Fagiolini alle Nocciole

String Beans with a Cream-Hazelnut Sauce

Serves 6 as a starter
500g/use 1 lb string beans
coarse-grained salt
1 lemon
60g/2 oz (Br.)/¼ cup (U.S.) shelled hazelnuts
80ml/2½ oz (Br.)/⅓ cup (U.S.) cream, preferably with 45% milk fat (heavy cream)
salt and freshly ground black pepper

Clean the string beans and soak them in a large bowl of cold water for 30 minutes. In a large pot of boiling salted water add the coarse-grained salt to taste. Cook the beans for about 12 minutes, if they are thin and young. If they are very large, they may require up to 25 minutes to cook. Drain them, and cool under cold running water. Transfer the beans to a serving dish and pour the juice of a lemon over them.

Finely chop half of the hazelnuts and coarsely chop the other half. In a bowl, combine the cream and the chopped nuts, and add salt and pepper to taste.

Pour this over the beans and toss them well with 2 spoons. Cover and refrigerate for at least 15 minutes before serving.

The garnish:
500ml/good ¾ pint (Br.)/2 good cups (U.S.) cream with 35% milk fat (whipping cream)
3½ tablespoons (Br.)/4 tablespoons (U.S.) sugar
2 to 3 tablespoons icing (confectioner's) sugar
2 amaretti biscuits (cookies), coarsely crumbled

Peel the pears, rub them with lemon and transfer each to the acidulated water to prevent browning while peeling the rest. Place in a casserole with the wine, sugar and clove. Cover with cold water, place a lid on the pan and simmer until the pears are cooked but firm (about 20 minutes, depending on ripeness). Transfer to a plate and cool.

To make the stuffing:
Mix the mascarpone with the sugar, icing (confectioner's) sugar and brandy or marsala. A little grated zest of the lemon may be added.

From the bases of the pears remove the cores with a small paring knife and a teaspoon, taking care to leave the stalks intact. Fill a pastry bag with the mascarpone stuffing and pipe it into the cavities.

To make the garnish:
Whip the cream with the sugars until stiff, and place in a pastry bag fitted with a large star nozzle.

To serve:
Place the stuffed pears on a large serving dish. Pipe the whipped cream around the pears and sprinkle with the coarsely crumbled amaretti crumbs.

Pere al Mascarpone
Poached Pears with Mascarpone

Serves 8
8 large pears (*Beurre Bosc* or other brown cooking pears), ripe but not overripe
2 lemons, to acidulate about 1 litre/1¾ pints (Br.)/4¼ cups (U.S.) water
1 litre/1¾ pints (Br.)/4¼ cups (U.S.) white wine
3½ tablespoons (Br.)/4 tablespoons (U.S.) sugar
1 whole clove

The stuffing:
250g/9 oz (Br.)/1¼ cups (U.S.) mascarpone cheese or, if unavailable, ricotta
3½ tablespoons (Br.)/4 tablespoons (U.S.) sugar
1 to 2 tablespoons (Br.)/1 to scant 3 tablespoons (U.S.) icing (confectioner's) sugar
1 to 2 tablespoons (Br.)/1 to scant 3 tablespoons (U.S.) brandy or dry marsala
grated zest of 1 lemon (optional)

Gérard Boyer

Restaurant les Crayères
Reims, France

I t is correct to say that Gérard Boyer comes from Reims, but it would not just be grander to say he comes from Champagne, it is also the compliment that is his due. For Gérard Boyer is the chef who gave Champagne a name for fine food. This northern province of France is sleety and cold, and sits upon a chalky soil that yields its wonder drink precisely because the grapes eke their way out, acidic and deprived of richness, promising little until the wine is corked, dosed with sugar, the pressure builds, and pop! out comes champagne! The only other thing that grows in the district is rape-seed for oil and beetroots; and the undulating hills, pretty in the misty light, are generally low slung and mundane. Champagne, the district, attracts its visitors for the golden liquid and the wealth of its history rather than for its food.

Peasant food abounds, and the local specialities are *maroilles* cheese, *potées* and stews, and the famous *pieds paquets* (stuffed pig's trotters) of Saint Menhouold — scarcely comparable with the lightness, brightness and magic synonymous with the wondrous beverage.

Then along comes Boyer. First Gaston Boyer, Gérard's father. From Auvergne in the truly barren centre of France, Gaston migrated to Paris, where he had an unpretentious bistro in Vincennes, in the suburbs just outside the city. The family later migrated further north and in 1961 Gaston opened his first restaurant in Reims, the capital of Champagne and famous for its Cathedral where historically the Kings of France were crowned. (It was also to Reims that Joan of Arc lead Charles VII through the battlefields to be crowned King.) Called La Chaumière, the restaurant was simple in décor and in its philosophy, but after Gérard had done some training with the three-star restaurant Lasserre in Paris, and came back to work with his father, he pushed his father to refine its cuisine.

Already they had found their major patrons were the heads of the champagne houses, who entertained their famous international clients on a grand scale. Gérard knew he needed a cuisine that was light in flavour to match the fact that few of their clients rarely drank anything but champagne throughout the meal. As a result, his cuisine never drowns the basic flavour of the natural products he chooses. Saucing is generally with light *jus*, sometimes a dash of champagne; most often if they are enriched, it is with a plethora of truffles and cream. The Boyers won their first Michelin star in 1966, and by the early 1970s La Chaumière had the coveted rating of three stars. The Boyers became the pride of the region.

An offer to install a restaurant in the château in the grounds of the champagne-making company Pommery gave Gérard the chance to have the optimum surroundings for the grandeur and importance his restaurant had obtained. The château is situated on top of a huge underground maze of caves, known as les Crayères, that date from Roman times and extend for miles underneath the township of Reims. Pommery has probably the largest holding of these, and hundreds of steps take you deep into the chalky ground to admire the thousands upon thousands of bottles of champagne fermenting on their sides there.

Les Crayères gave the restaurant its name and the family has now developed the rooms of the wonderful beige stone mansion into a small hotel with beautifully decorated rooms, conservatories and lounge-rooms that extend the atmosphere of the restaurant and make it one of the most elegant small hotels in France.

Gérard's wife Eliane is one of the most elegantly dressed and charming hostesses, and extends her warmth throughout the restaurant to complement the

Fruits Rouges Gratinées

fine food of the brigade, which has now extended to fifteen. Gérard makes sure he has every brand of champagne on hand, and numerous vintages at that. His restaurant boasts over 190 choices!

A visit to Les Crayères is possible even for those who go to Paris without plans to tour the provinces, for Reims is only three-quarters of an hour from Paris, and there are regular trains — if you have no car.

The restaurant is closed for lunch on Mondays and Tuesdays, but otherwise a day trip is possible. If you wish to stay, the hotel boasts only sixteen suites; but however long your stay there, splurge on your meal and wallow in champagne, for that is the reason one goes. Here in Reims is the absolute luxury of 'la vie de Château' that books talk of. A night here feeds the memories of a lifetime.

Fruits Rouges Gratinées
Gratiné of Strawberries

Serves 4
500g/use 1 lb strawberries. In summer the dish may be done with other red berries or a mixture of various berries.
250ml/9 fl oz (Br.)/scant 1¼ cups (U.S.) milk
225g/7 oz (Br.)/1 good cup (U.S.) castor (superfine) sugar
70g/good 2 oz (Br.)/⅓ cup (U.S.) cornflour (cornstarch)
2 egg yolks
200ml/scant 7 fl oz (Br.)/1 scant cup (U.S.) cream with 35% milk fat (whipping cream)
icing (confectioner's) sugar

1. Soak the strawberries in a bowl of water to remove any grit, then hull them and transfer them to a teatowel to blot up any excess moisture.

2. Bring the milk to the boil with the castor (superfine) sugar, stirring.

3. Beat together the cornflour (cornstarch) and the 2 egg yolks. Add the hot milk to the yolks mixture, stirring to blend them, then return to the saucepan and allow to boil, stirring continuously. When it begins to boil, immediately remove from the heat.

4. Transfer to a bowl to cool.

5. Whip the cream. When the milk custard has cooled, gently fold in the whipped cream. Fold the two mixtures carefully so as to keep the cream light and airy.

6. Ladle the custard into shallow soup bowls.

7. Cut the strawberries in two unless they are small. Arrange the berries on top of the custard.

8. Sprinkle with icing (confectioner's) sugar, then gratiné (glaze).

9. In the restaurant the strawberries are gratinéed (glazed) under the salamander. A domestic grill (broiler) should yield a similar result when preheated well before use. Failing that, a blow-torch does it beautifully.

Pigeonneau à l'Ail Douce et au Persil
Squab with Garlic and Parsley

Serves 4
4 squabs, trussed
4 garlic cloves per person. In season you can use the large new-season garlic that is sweeter (even the whole tiny heads with their unifying green stalk).
250ml/8 fl oz (Br.)/1 good cup (U.S.) oil
12 tablespoons (Br.)/15 tablespoons (U.S.) butter
60g/2 oz foie gras, sieved to obtain a purée
50ml/1½ fl oz (Br.)/¼ cup (U.S.) cognac or port, depending on whether you like the sweetness or the strength
300ml/½ pint (Br.)/1¼ cup (U.S.) veal stock, as jellied as possible
1 teaspoon sugar
salt and freshly ground pepper

The accompanying vegetable:
500g/use 1 lb parsley, cleaned, washed and the stalks picked off
3 tablespoons (Br.)/3½ tablespoons (U.S.) cream with 35% milk fat (whipping cream)

To prepare the garlic:
Peel the garlic cloves. Place in a saucepan and cover with cold water. Bring to the boil then immediately rinse the garlic under cold water. Repeat the operation, drain the blanched garlic cloves then place them in a saucepan and cover with olive oil. Bring to the boil and cook for 3 minutes. Drain and set aside.

To cook the squabs:
Heat 3 tablespoons (Br.)/3½ tablespoons (U.S.) butter in a heavy, ovenproof skillet and brown the squabs on all sides (4 to 5 minutes). Season to taste and transfer to a 240⁰ C/475⁰ F preheated oven for 15 minutes. Baste often during cooking.

Remove cooked squabs to a plate and keep warm. De-grease the casserole and de-glaze the pan with port or cognac, stirring to pick up all the sediment. Add the veal stock and cook until reduced by half. Away from the flame add the sieved foie gras and whip in 3 tablespoons (Br.)/3½ tablespoons (U.S.) butter with a wire whisk. Season to taste. Do not allow the sauce to boil any more.

Fry the garlic cloves in butter with a little sugar until browned.

To cut and serve the squabs:
Remove the legs (not the wings), then hold the squab breast up on the board. With a strong downward motion, free the breast and wing from one side of the carcass by cutting downward from the point of the breastbone, easing the breast and wing from the bone. Repeat for other side. Reconstruct each squab in its true shape as you transfer it to the serving plate. Serve with the garlic on one side of the plate, the parsley as a vegetable on the other. Spoon the sauce over the meat.

The parsley:
Blanch the washed parsley in the boiling water for about 3 minutes. Drain and dry well on a towel. Heat 3 tablespoons (Br.)/3½ tablespoons (U.S.) olive oil in a saucepan and sauté the parsley to warm it, then add 3 tablespoons (Br.)/3½ tablespoons (U.S.) cream and stir it through.

Pigeonneau à l'Ail Douce et au Persil

Saumon en Papillotte
Salmon 'en Papillotte' with Ginger and Lime

This dish is suitable for salmon or the new ocean-run trout that is now being bred in some countries. If you cannot find this stronger tasting trout, make it with river trout fillets (cooked less, for they are fragile), John Dory (St. Pierre), or pieces (cutlets) from larger lobed, white-fleshed fish like turbot, barramundi or ling.

Serves 2
4 pieces of salmon or chosen fish, each weighing about 100g/4 oz
2 limes (one for slicing, one for sauce)
10g/⅓ oz fresh ginger
6 tablespoons (Br.)/7 tablespoons (U.S.) cream with 35% milk fat (whipping cream), whipped
50g/scant 2 oz (Br.)/3 tablespoons (U.S.) butter
salt and pepper
3 tablespoons (Br.)/3½ tablespoons (U.S.) white port

Take a piece of foil and smear a little butter on half of its surface. Place the fillets on the butter and add small slices of lime (removing the skin before using), and a small amount of very finely chopped ginger. Season with salt and pepper.

Fold the foil over and roll the edges together tightly. Inflate the *'papillotte'* by leaving a little hole and blowing through it. Place in a hot oven about 220ºC/425ºF for 8 minutes. The flesh of the fish must remain very smooth and moist, and just opaque when it is cooked. Any more, and it is stringy.

The sauce:
Combine the white port and 1 tablespoon of lime juice. Reduce. Add grated ginger to taste and then add the whipped cream and let it boil for a few minutes. Whisk in the remaining butter swiftly with a wire whisk and it's ready to serve. The ginger may be left in or strained out, to taste.

To serve:
Take the foil package directly from the oven to serve. In the restaurant it is taken to the table to show the balloon-like inflated package, where a silver-service waiter opens it on a side table, serves each fillet onto a plate, and spoons the sauce over for each guest. At home, the package should be opened by the dinner guest, allowing the full aroma of the fish to be appreciated as the package is opened. The sauce may be passed in a sauceboat.

Prue Leith

Leith's Restaurant
Leith's School of Food and Wine
London, England

There's a wonderful touch of spontaneity to a cookery class taken by Prue Leith. Full of confidence, sure of herself and her skills, she is so relaxed in a classroom that there's time for a joke, time for chatter, time for her mischievous grin and natural warmth to come through. In contrast to some of the more pretentious chefs, nothing could be more encouraging, and Prue's enthusiasm fires many an amateur cook to set to and try something a little more difficult.

Of all the personalities in the food world, few have done as well or established such an international reputation as Prue. Born in South Africa, she developed an interest in food when she spent a year as an *au pair* in France, while trying to further her studies in French history. She then migrated to London and in 1961 started her first food company from a bed-sitter in Earls Court.

From catering to running her own restaurant, and teaching a new generation of up-and-coming chefs in the much-quoted Leith's School of Food and Wine, Prue has made her mark in most aspects of food service in Britain. Having built up the business acumen to run a series of businesses spanning different parts of the city, she now turns over upwards of £1 million per annum. The restaurant seats ninety to one hundred people in *grande luxe* and the catering business, now in large commercial kitchens in the city, is busy with board-room lunches, society dinners, lunches and teas aboard the English section of the famed *Orient Express* and is the appointed caterer of the Government's Queen Elizabeth II Conference Centre in London's Parliament Square. The ability on Prue's part to delegate work and to inspire dedication from her staff is not the least of the keys to her success.

Among her more 'public' skills, Prue writes a regular column for the London newspaper, the *Guardian*. She has a serious food column and, as well, a personality column, full of fun and a bit of mockery at herself and her chosen field. Prue also contributes regularly on food-related topics to BBC Radio and from time to time, to the *Daily Telegraph*, *The Sunday Times* and the *Sunday Express* (other London newspapers). In the past she has had her own twenty-six-part television series and been a member of the Boards of British Rail and the government-sponsored Economic Development Committee for the Leisure Industries; and she is currently a Fellow of the Royal Society of the Arts and a Council Member of the Museum of Modern Art in Oxford, where she spends her 'spare' time with her family on their farm . . . which, not incidentally, grows herbs and unusual vegetables for the Leith's businesses!

Does this leave time for writing books? Prue has just released her tenth, *Entertaining with Style* (co-authored with Polly Tyrer), after a run of best sellers. Among them is the three volume *Leith's Cookery Course* and the equally successful *Leith's Cookery School* (both co-authored with Caroline Waldegrave, the principal of Leith's School of Food and Wine). These books have unselfishly placed much of the school's programme in the hands of the general public and have had enormous influence in helping amateur cooks and aspiring chefs alike to understand the basics of good cuisine. The expansive Prue is as generous with her information as she is with her time.

For us, Prue cooks her very elegant cold buffet dish, Boned Chicken Stuffed with Leeks, which bears witness to what is written of her above: When Prue takes the reigns to pass on her skills, the guidance is very deft. If you take her advice, she'll prove to you that even a dish that requires some complicated techniques, you can master like an old hand!

Boned Chicken Stuffed with Leeks

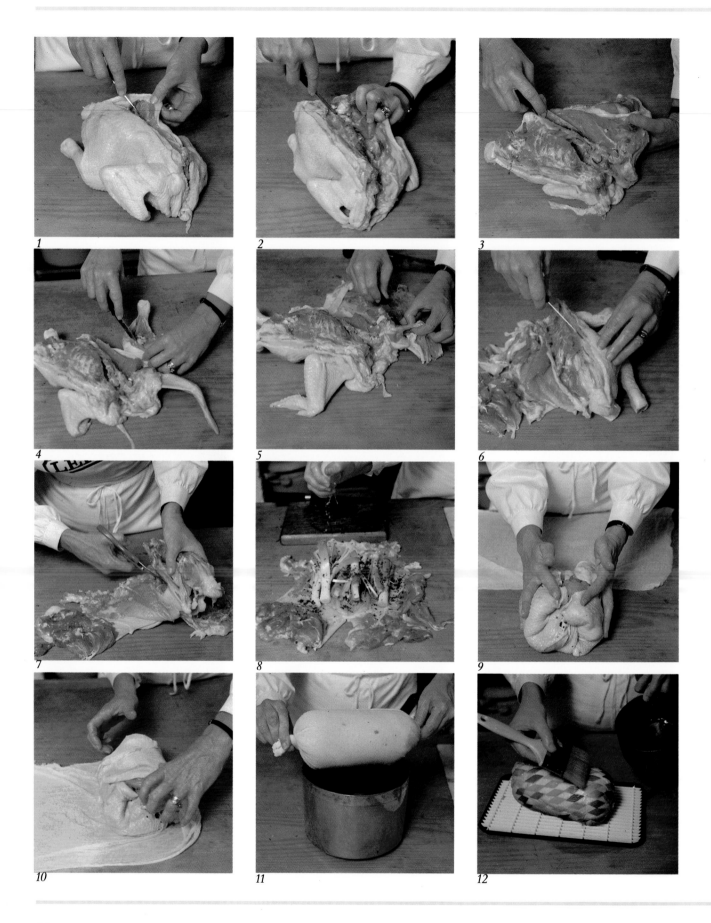

Boned Chicken Stuffed with Leeks

Serves 8
1.5kg/3 lb 5 oz chicken
1½ tablespoons (Br.)/2 tablespoons (U.S.) chopped, fresh thyme mixed with marjoram or oregano
8 baby leeks, as small and thin as you can buy (halve this if they are larger)
4x15cm/6 in sticks celery
6 juniper berries
water
salt, pepper, lemon juice

The garnish:
The blanched green of some leek
300ml/½ pt (Br.)/1¼ cups (U.S.) of the resulting chicken stock
1 leaf or 1 scant teaspoon granulated unflavoured gelatine to make a better aspic of the stock (optional)

The sauce:
The remaining vegetables and stock
200g/good 7 oz (Br.)/¾ cup (U.S.) quarg (quark) or ricotta or cottage cheese
salt, pepper, lemon juice to taste

Equipment:
Large piece muslin or cheesecloth; string

To bone the chicken:
1. Cut the flesh along the length of the backbone. Starting from the fleshy little section known as the oyster, cut and scrape the flesh free from the chicken carcass with a sharp, small pointed knife held as close as possible to the bone.

2. Move from this central section around the carcass in both directions at first, so you can see what you are doing. Then, when you have reached the limbs, work one side before the other. When you get to the limbs (wings, drumsticks and thighbones), release the little tendons, pull the limbs back until they are exposed at the joint, and sever the knuckles, allowing the limbs to stay with the fleshy part, thus continuing to expose more and more of the cylindrical section of the carcass.

3. Continue to work around the bird until you get to the breastplate. Use a scraping motion with the knife to remove the flesh from the breastplate, and when you've reached the point of the breastplate, you have reached the halfway mark.

4. To remove the leg and wingbones, start by placing the skin back over the legbone. Cut through the flesh along the length of the bone. Chop off the knuckle. Scrape the flesh off the two legbones (the drumstick and thighbone) until they are severed from the meat. Remove the bones.

5. Chop the tip off the wing and, as for the legbone, slice the flesh along the length of the wing and scrape free the bone.

6. Turn the bird around totally to put the flesh on your left and repeat the procedure for the other half of the bird.

7. Cut the carcass free from the flesh, starting from both the neck and tail ends so you can see better what you're doing. The last area is the centre of the breast area — the area where you are closest to the skin, and the area where a mistake (piercing a hole) will most show. Using the falling weight of the carcass to better expose the breastplate, scrape free the flesh to the very point of the breastbone, then cut (with scissors if it's easier) along the edge of the breastplate's length to free the flesh completely.

To arrange the stuffing:
8. Lay the chicken flesh out on the benchtop, like a baby's vest. Trim off any bits of fat, but retain all the skin, even the raggy edges. Trim, peel and wash the leeks, and cut to the approximate length of the chicken, leaving a little flesh at either end to fold over and enclose them. It is probable only 6 or 7 will fit, leaving some over for the stock. Alternate the leeks top to tail so all the green, thinner ends are not down one end. Sprinkle with the chopped marjoram and thyme, ground black pepper and lemon juice.

9. First fold in the neck and tail ends, then roll the sides inwards.

10. Place on a piece of wet muslin, and roll as tightly as you can. Screw the ends like a cracker, and tie with string.

11. Place the diced celery, a leek (if there is one remaining) or a little of its green and the juniper berries in the base of a saucepan. The saucepan must be just wide enough to fit the chicken snugly if it's to keep its shape well. Cover with water, but not much above the height of the chicken. Cook for approximately 1¼ to 1½ hours. Exactly how long will depend on the thickness of the leeks. Test by piercing with a skewer. The skewer must pass fairly readily right to the core. Remove the chicken from the liquid. Re-wrap in order to firm the roll and refrigerate until cold (at least 6 hours, so the leeks firm).

To decorate:
12. Blanch some of the green of the leek, slice it, cut it into diamond shapes, and arrange decoratively on the top of the chicken. Brush with some of the chicken stock. It should have just enough natural gel to hold and give a sheen. If not, take a cupful and melt in a little gelatine.

The sauce:
After removing the juniper berries, purée the vegetables in a food processor. Add the quarg (quark) or cheese and blend to a thick, mayonnaise-like consistency, adding just enough of the remaining stock to obtain the desired consistency. Season and serve as a cold sauce.

Tarte Normande aux Poires
Pear Tart, Normandy Style

The original of this recipe was made with apples, and incorporates the apple and cream produce so typical of Normandy, the area of France that gave it its name. Naturally, the pears may be substituted with apples, but it is delicious too in this lesser-known version, when the pear season is at its height.

Serves 8 to 10

The shortcrust pastry:
200g/good 7 oz (Br.)/½ cup (U.S.) plain (all-purpose) flour
120g/4½ oz (Br.)/⅔ cup (U.S.) unsalted butter
pinch salt
1 egg yolk
very cold water

The almond cream:
120g/4½ oz (Br.)/⅔ cup (U.S.) unsalted butter
120g/4½ oz castor (superfine) sugar
1 whole egg plus 1 egg yolk
60g/2 oz (Br.)/½ cup (U.S.) flour
120g/4½ oz (Br.)/⅔ cup (U.S.) ground almonds

2 tablespoons (Br.)/3 tablespoons (U.S.) cream, preferably with 45% milk fat (heavy cream)

The filling:
5 to 6 small ripe eating pears
5 tablespoons (Br.)/6 tablespoons (U.S.) smooth apricot jam (failing that, the jam should be passed through a sieve)
1 tablespoon water or lemon juice

Equipment:
26 to 28cm/10 to 11 in flan ring or skillet

The pastry:
Sift the flour together with the salt. Place in a bowl. In the centre, add the butter, cut into pieces, and the egg yolk, mixed together with one tablespoon of water. Use a knife to 'cut' together the mixture, then continue to work with the fingers until it amalgamates into a firm dough. Add more water if necessary; how much will depend on the humidity already present in the room and the flour. The pastry should remain somewhat pliable, as a crumbly pastry is always shorter and more tender. Refrigerate the pastry for about 30 minutes so that it will be easier to roll,

then roll it out and line the flan tin. Allow to rest a further 30 minutes before baking.

The almond cream filling:
Cream the butter and sugar until white and well blended. Add the whole egg and egg yolk, the flour, almonds and cream. Beat together well, then spread into the base of the pastry crust.

The pears:
Peel the pears, halve them and then remove their cores carefully. Slice the pear halves, keeping the slices together, then fan them out slightly and arrange the halves in the pastry case, pressed into the almond cream so that it raises up a little to encompass the pears. Melt the jam carefully, diluting it with a little water if too thick, and flavouring it with lemon juice. Spoon about half of it over the pears. Bake the flan in a 220ºC/425ºF oven for about 15 minutes, then decrease the heat to 180ºC/350ºF and continue baking for a further 20 minutes. Remove from the oven when the pastry is crisp, the pears cooked, and the almond cream has risen and browned. Brush with the rest of the apricot jam and return to the oven for 10 minutes. Serve lukewarm.

Hearts and Flowers Pudding

Serves 6

The hearts:
5 eggs
110g/4 oz (Br.)/scant ⅔ cup (U.S.) castor (superfine) sugar
50ml/1½ fl oz (Br.)/¼ cup (U.S.) advocaat
150g/6 oz (Br.)/1½ cups (U.S.) coarsely grated toasted almonds
¼ teaspoon salt
icing (confectioner's) sugar

The filling:
85g/3 oz (Br.)/scant ⅓ cup rose-hip or redcurrant jelly
250ml/8 fl oz (Br.)/1 good cup (U.S.) cream with 35% milk fat (whipping cream)

leave in a warm room and/or near a heater or boiler for 24 hours or so, until they go brittle and dry. Store between waxed paper sheets in a box until needed.

To make the sauce:
In a saucepan, gently heat the fruit juice and jelly together, stirring gently until smooth. Boil to a thin syrup. Pour into a plastic jug and allow to cool. Cold, the consistency should still be able to be poured.

Make the *crème anglaise* (see recipe page 177). Pour it into a plastic jug, cool, and store it in the refrigerator until needed. If storing for more than an hour, put plastic wrap on the surface to prevent a skin from forming.

To make the sponge hearts:
Separate the eggwhites and yolks and set the eggwhites aside. Put the egg yolks, castor (superfine) sugar and advocaat in a bowl and whisk over a saucepan of simmering water until the mixture is pale and mousse-like and the whisk leaves a thin ribbon trail when lifted in the air.

Sift in the coarsely grated almonds and salt. Whisk the eggwhites to a firm snow and fold them into the egg base mixture gently, with a wooden spatula.

Pour into the greaseproof (parchment) paper lined tin and bake in a 190°C/375°F oven for 15 minutes. When ready, turn out onto a sheet of greaseproof (parchment) paper, lightly sugared with castor (superfine) sugar. Allow to cool. Stamp into heart shapes with a small cutter.

Spread half the hearts lightly with rosehip (or redcurrant) jelly. Whip the cream and pipe onto the jelly-covered surfaces. Top with the remaining hearts, smooth (browned) side up, and dredge with icing (confectioner's) sugar.

To serve:
Use dinner plates or large dessert plates. From either side of the plate, pour a little of the *crème anglaise* and a little of the jelly sauce, forming two pools of colour on the plates. Add a heart sandwich at the junction of the colours, and decorate with 1 or 2 crystallised petals.

The sauce:
140g/5 oz (Br.)/½ cup (U.S.) rose-hip or redcurrant jelly
150ml/good 5 fl oz (Br.)/scant ¾ cup (U.S.) apple juice or juice from stewed rhubarb
300ml/½ pint (Br.)/1¼ cups (U.S.) *crème anglaise* (see recipe page 177)

The flowers:
dark red rose petals
2 eggwhites, beaten with a fork
castor (superfine) sugar

Equipment:
shallow Swiss roll (jelly roll) tin, buttered and lined with greaseproof (parchment) paper

At least the day before, crystallise the rose petals:
Brush each petal on either side with eggwhite. Holding the petals above a bowl of castor (superfine) sugar, sprinkle the sugar over them to coat them evenly. Put them on waxed paper to dry, and

Stephanie Alexander

Stephanie's Restaurant
Melbourne, Australia

One of the great chefs of our times once explained to me how he had spent the latter part of his career trying to shed the mantle of chef and 'cook like a woman'. Charles Barrier, one of the most respected chefs in France since the War, said simply, 'A woman uses her brains, her intuition and the available ingredients — not just the rule book. To do this well is the ultimate achievement.'

Stephanie Alexander 'cooks like a woman'. Which is not to lay in doubt any of the recent accolades she has gained as one of the great chefs of Australia, nor the 1987 award from the Australian Tourist Bureau which acclaimed her restaurant as the Best Restaurant in Australia; but Stephanie is a self-taught, impassioned food buff turned restaurateur, not a traditionally trained chef.

Years ago, it was sometimes her greatest humiliation, but actually it's her greatest asset, for in these times when restaurants throughout the world are serving up a tremendously similar round of trendy dishes, it is a joy to eat at the restaurants of those few who have a genuinely creative talent.

In any case, ten years on, Stephanie's knowledge and practice has made her an expert in all forms of her art; even a highly respected judge in international competitions. As the founders of the Hong Kong Food Festival acknowledged when they first set up an international panel of judges to award their prizes, Stephanie's knowledge of international cuisine in all its ethnic forms, proved to be much greater than those from countries with a very strong culinary basis.

Stephanie will turn her hand to every aspect of the culinary arts, because her interest is phenomenal. She pickles, she preserves, she crystallises things; she has experimented in cheese-making; she grows her own sorrel, lemon verbena, spearmint geraniums, and other edible flowers and rare herbs that she cannot obtain commercially. Styrofoam boxes filled with soil and sprouting shoots produce much of the tiny mixed salad greens for her *mesclun* salads, and the beautifully kept garden around the restaurant provides all the flowers for Stephanie's. She also begs the produce of her friends' gardens. A crop of guava turns up as sorbet or ice-cream; crab apples pickled and sliced become a crunchy garnish for a salad of pigeon breasts; elderberry flowers turn up in crêpes or as fritters; preserved redcurrant leaves are garnish, while the berries are served fresh in season, and in jellies, jams and sauces the rest of the year.

Stephanie's background is an overwhelming factor in all this interest. Her father was a wine buff, her mother wrote for various gourmet magazines, and the kitchen and dining table were the focal point of their family life. Stephanie and her mother were very close and built their tremendous interest in food together. The spiced cumquats, the vinegar made from raspberries, the idea for a certain dish — and much of her passion — stems from her mother. Woe betide a man without an interest in food, who might have wandered into Stephanie's life! Luckily such was not the case . . . Maurice was a barrister 'without wild enthusiasm' when she met him. Stephanie was originally a secondary teacher and librarian. 'But I was so passionate about a restaurant that we decided to give it a go.'

Stephanie first opened a small, bring-your-own-liquor establishment in a shop front with bare brick walls. It was quite short on charm, but Stephanie gayed it up with Liberty-print tablecloths and fresh flowers and soon it became a haven for Melbourne's food buffs. From the beginning she chose a fixed price limited menu, which to this day she feels is vital to being

Macadamia Nut Tart with Honey and Lavender Ice-cream

able to buy the produce of the season, serve it in a few well-chosen dishes to reflect her personal style, and help the diner. She is very articulate — even imposing — about her beliefs, and feels this way she can give the meal a beginning, a middle and an end, while guiding her guests through a succession of tastes.

She recalls that the first years were like working in a repertory company, practising by day, serving by night, and changing the menu often daily, definitely weekly. Nowadays, the menus are seasonal, changing only four times a year, and giving her the rest of the year to invent, compose and perfect. The result is more professional, but interestingly, the food buffs love to go on a Friday lunch (her only lunchtime meal), for they know the new dishes, the possible dishes and the dishes threading their way through her thought processes are on the line-up then.

There are five choices in each course, for Stephanie insists the menu be broad enough for people to choose a light meal or a heavy meal, or avoid things they don't like. The 'bill of fare' style of menu has full descriptions of the dishes rather than flamboyant titles, helping you to choose wisely rather than accidentally find yourself with an imbalanced progression. The overall effect is thoughtful, highly personal, and represents some of the best cooking in the country.

Stephanie loves detail and spends a lot of time on little throw-away gestures like preserving, making or growing all her own garnishes, chocolates and petits fours. Every day the restaurant makes up to four kinds of bread for the main serving baskets, and also olive bread, walnut bread, brioches and brown rye for toast if a special dish requires it. I have seen Stephanie spend hours cutting out the skins of rockmelons and pear halves which she re-forms into whole fruit with the appropriate ice-cream or sorbet made from the pulp. Twenty-four bunches of violets go into her litre of violet sorbet, painstakingly served with a bouquet of three or four fresh ones tied together alongside. There is also an equivalent with rose petals, and a junket lovingly made with spearmint geranium.

Stephanie's restaurant is a very personal statement. Early on, there were some who liked to label her a nouvelle cuisine chef, noting the pink-fleshed duck, the undercooked vegetables, the pretty arranging of food on the plate. But Stephanie would thwart them all by serving a *pot au feu*, stuffed braised pork trotters, or a perfect cassoulet with home-made *confit* and sausages to show her love of the provincial. 'I see no need to categorise,' she says. 'I find nouvelle cuisine very interesting, and have been very much influenced by it, but I'm also strongly influenced by fine regional dishes, and attracted by some great classic preparations. And I have a continuing interest in the cuisine of Asia. I don't want to feel I have to be fashionable to be thought of as a good cook.'

Curiosity made Stephanie bone out oxtails, until she became so perfect at it that she could bone one in nine minutes and dared to put it on the menu stuffed with a minced meat and orange rind filling in a brown-braised *jus*. Lately, the boning is of rabbits (one every three minutes), and they are stuffed with a pork and chestnut filling and served with *char siu bao* (Chinese pork buns) and a sauce of Chinese subtleties. But don't count on it being that way next week, for I've also recently had her boned rabbits stuffed with spinach and fresh morel mushrooms.

Exciting you about her dishes is not really wise, for Stephanie casts dishes aside as soon as she has satisfied herself with them, and while they then appear on other people's menus, or in her writings, they will not be on her menu. Her creativity is such that she is always onto the next thing.

With time have come the accolades and a form of stardom. Stephanie has written two successful books, *Stephanie's Menus for Food Lovers* and *Stephanie's Feasts and Stories*, and she writes regular columns for two magazines—full of reflections, opinions, her travels, and happenings in the food world. Highly articulate, she is sought after on the radio, as a guest speaker and a judge, and is on the Board overseeing food-related events at the Australian Bicentenary and the Board of the Australian Symposium of Gastronomy.

But most often you'll find Stephanie in her kitchen. Exploring, inventing, and directing her own large, highly competent staff. Cooking is very much her life, particularly the craft of it.

Charles Barrier would agree she is the ultimate, excellent, woman cook. It's possible he might even envy her.

Macadamia Nut Tart

Serves 8

The pastry:
50g/scant 2 oz (Br.)/3 tablespoons (U.S.) butter
100g/3½ oz (Br.)/good ¾ cup (U.S.) plain (all-purpose) flour
50g/scant 2 oz (Br.)/¼ cup (U.S.) castor (superfine) sugar
1 teaspoon grated orange zest

The filling:
3 eggs
75g/2½ oz (Br.)/good ⅓ cup (U.S.) sugar
180ml/6 fl oz (Br.)/good ¾ cup (U.S.) light corn syrup
30g/1 good oz (Br.)/2 tablespoons (U.S.) unsalted butter
½ teaspoon grated orange zest
200g/7 oz (Br.)/2 cups (U.S.) macadamia nuts

Equipment:
26cm/10 in tart mould

The pastry:

1. Place the flour on a marble slab or cool work area, and in the centre place the butter. Using a pastry scraper, Stephanie cuts the (firm) butter continually until it picks up much of the flour and begins to incorporate. (The more conventional way would be to place softened butter in the centre of the flour and gradually blend together with the fingertips. If you have no scraper, proceed in this manner. It is because the orange juice makes it sticky and fragile, that Stephanie prefers to make her pastry this way.)

2. When the butter is only partially cut in, scoop the flour back into a pile with a hollow in the centre, and add the orange juice.

3. Continue the cutting action with the scraper until the mixture is well brought together and ready to form into a ball. If it feels too wet, you may add a little further flour. The pastry has thus gathered together with no kneading at all, which ensures it is extremely tender, but it will be very friable, and thus needs to settle well in the refrigerator.

4. Gather it into a ball, enclose in plastic wrap and refrigerate until firm. Most pastries require only 20 minutes to 1 hour, but with the richness and sweetness of the orange juice, Stephanie prefers to leave this one overnight.

The dough will come together in a food processor if you prefer to make your pastries this way. Proceed by combining all the ingredients, and process until the pastry comes into a ball. Gather the ball together, adding a little more flour if it feels too wet. This depends on the texture of the flour and the varying humidity content it picks up in more or less humid kitchens.

5. As the pastry is extremely fragile, it is best rolled out between 2 sheets of greaseproof (parchment) paper. The dough should be very firm, and the paper floured. Sprinkle the top of the dough with flour also, place a second sheet of greaseproof (parchment) paper on top, and ease the dough out into a circular shape by rolling your pin on top of the second sheet. Then carefully pull away the top sheet, using the flat of your hand against the pastry to prevent it coming with the top sheet.

To line the mould:
6. Pick the pastry up from the bottom sheet of greaseproof (parchment) paper by rolling it carefully onto your rolling pin.

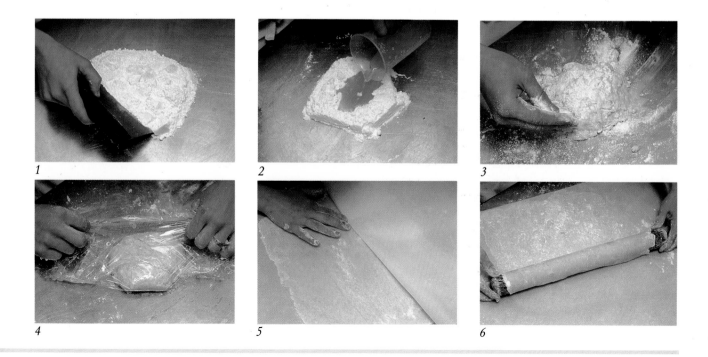

1　　*2*　　*3*

4　　*5*　　*6*

7

8

9

10

11

12

7. Transfer to the tart mould, and unravel over the mould from the side nearest you to the far side. Some prefer to take the pastry to the mould still sitting on the bottom sheet of paper, and then upend onto the mould and press it into shape. Do this only if you are used to handling pastry this way, for with the fragile ones, it is sometimes difficult to lift the paper free.

You may of course use your usual pastry which is probably less friable, but this one is a dream of crispness and finesse. I dare you to try to graduate to it when you can.

8. Press the pastry into the mould; roll the pin over the edges to lift off any excess pastry, thus leaving only a superbly fine layer. Prick with a fork to allow the passage of air. This prevents air entering from below and forming a blister, and also yields a much crisper tart.

9. Press foil over the pastry, making sure it is pushed well into the edges to help prevent shrinkage, and leave an overhang at the top. Leave it in the refrigerator for 1 hour so there is absolutely no chance of shrinkage, then bake the tart blind with this lining in a pre-heated 200ºC/400ºF oven. It needs only 8 minutes; it's very fine.

The filling:

10. Break the eggs and sugar into a bowl, whisk momentarily, then whisk all the filling ingredients together, except the macadamia nuts.

11. When the pastry is cooked, remove the foil lining and scatter the macadamia nuts over the pastry.

12. Pour in the filling mixture. Turn the oven down to 180ºC/350ºF and place the tart low in the oven for 30 minutes. After that time, move it to a higher rack and cook for a further 15 minutes. The result should look not just firm, but slightly toffee-like.

To serve:

The tart cuts well with a good heavy knife. It is easier to cut if the nuts have been lightly chopped, but Stephanie prefers the look of them whole. She serves the tart with honey and lavendar ice-cream (see recipe below).

Honey and Lavender Ice-cream

Makes about 2 litres/3½ pints (Br.)/scant 9 cups (U.S.)
1 litre/1¾ pints (Br.)/4¼ cups (U.S.) milk
500g/1 lb 2 oz (Br.)/1½ cups (U.S.) honey, your favourite variety
8 egg yolks
600ml/1 pint (Br.)/2½ cups (U.S.) cream, preferably with 45% milk fat (heavy cream)
1 cup lightly packed lavender flowers, washed

Boil the milk and pour over the lavender. Allow to infuse, covered, until the milk is cold.

Beat the egg yolks well. Beat the honey into the eggs. Strain the cold lavender milk onto the honey mixture, and beat gently to combine. Stir in the cream. Churn in an ice-cream machine according to the manufacturer's instructions.

Rockpool Revisited

Rockpool Revisited

Serves 6

Stephanie prepared her first version of this dish many years ago, when Janni Kyritsis (now head chef at Berowra Waters Inn) was working with her. Together they dreamed up a sea fantasy which was based on a clarified delicate fish jelly. By the time Stephanie decided to 'revisit' the rockpool, she found she wanted the pool to have a more definite taste. She designed this version with the flavours of a Sichuan hot and sour soup in mind.

350g/good 12 oz pork fillet, very thinly sliced
3 teaspoons light soy sauce
1½ teaspoons sesame oil
3 teaspoons cornflour (cornstarch)
2 tablespoons (Br.)/scant 3 tablespoons (U.S.) oil
3 teaspoons sugar
5 spring onions, chopped (this makes about ½ cup)
2 teaspoons chopped hot chilli
2 tablespoons (Br.)/scant 3 tablespoons (U.S.) chopped ginger
1 tablespoon Sichuan peppercorns, ground and roasted in a dry pan over heat
5 litres/8¾ pints (Br.)/22 cups (U.S.) water
¼ cup chopped coriander (cilantro) leaves and roots
180ml/6 fl oz (Br.)/good ¾ cup (U.S.) light soy sauce
180ml/6 fl oz (Br.)/good ¾ cup (U.S.) rice vinegar

The clarification:
250ml/8 fl oz (Br.)/1 good cup (U.S.) egg whites
½ cup coriander (cilantro) leaves
4 leaves/3 teaspoons granulated unflavoured gelatine for every litre/1¾ pints (Br.)/4¼ cups (U.S.) of finished base

The decoration:
Use your imagination with these ingredients. Stephanie uses freshly-opened oysters, 2 in a single shell, resting on the second (empty) upturned shell like a rock; shredded *hijiki* seaweed; gently braised *shitake* mushrooms, cut to resemble a starfish; Chinese shredded dried jellyfish (rehydrated); and some stems of watercress. On one of the biggest and flattest watercress leaves she places a small heap of the very best caviar.

To make the consommé base:
Mix the pork with the 3 teaspoons of soy, the sesame oil and the cornflour (cornstarch). Allow to stand for 1 hour. Heat the oil in a wok and stir-fry the pork briefly, just until it changes colour. Add the sugar, spring onion, chillis, ginger and roasted ground peppercorns. Stir together over a high heat for 1 minute and then add 1 litre/1¾ pints (Br.)/4¼ cups (U.S.) of the water. Scrape and stir and transfer the contents of the wok to a large pot. Add the rest of the water and the coriander (cilantro) roots and leaves. Add the light soy and vinegar. Bring to a simmering point. Simmer for 10 minutes. Allow to cool completely.

To clarify the consommé:
When the soup base is cold, strain it. Do not discard the debris in the strainer; whizz it in the food processor with the egg whites and ½ cup coriander (cilantro) leaves until it is well blended and frothy. Stir this very well into the strained stock in a very clean stockpot and bring gently back to simmering point, whisking well every few minutes. Stop whisking just as the liquid approaches simmering point. Adjust the heat to very low and allow to barely simmer for 1 hour. Turn off the heat and allow to settle for 10 minutes, then carefully remove the spoonfuls of the scummy 'raft' which has gathered on the top, and ladle the sparkling consommé into a clean container through a strainer lined with damp muslin.

Measure the volume of the comsommé. For each litre/1¾ pints (Br.)/4¼ cups (U.S.) measure out 4 leaves/3 teaspoons granulated gelatine. If using leaves soak the leaves in cold water for a few minutes. Heat a cup of the consommé to simmering point. Squeeze the moisture from the gelatine leaves and drop them into the hot stock. Stir to dissolve completely and then stir into the rest of the stock. If using powdered gelatine, soak it first in the cool consommé, then heat, stirring until dissolved. It is possible you will need to use two cups of consommé instead of one to have enought to soften the powdered gelatine.

The stock must be allowed to get quite cold and already slightly jellied before you assemble the rockpools, otherwise it will set as a solid block in the base of the bowls. Only the 'wavey' effect will get the play on light so necessary for a successful dish.

Place the oysters and other decoration in a shallow bowl and then allow a ladleful a jelly to slip and slide over and around. Do not serve too much jelly. It should tantalise with its subtle flavours, not be overpowering.

Stephanie's Mussels

Serves 6
72 small mussels, thoroughly scrubbed
3 to 4 parsley stalks, roughly chopped
2 onions, roughly chopped
1 bottle dry white wine

The sauce:
1 bulb fennel, finely diced
2 sticks celery, de-strung and finely diced
50g/scant 2 oz (Br.)/3 tablespoons (U.S.) unsalted butter
2 cloves garlic, finely chopped
200g/7 oz (Br.)/1½ cups (U.S.) walnut halves, blanched and peeled of their inner skin
1 bunch well-washed parsley, finely chopped
good pinch saffron threads
100ml/3 fl oz (Br.)/scant ½ cup (U.S.) cream with 35% milk fat (whipping cream)
300g/scant 11 oz (Br.)/1¼ cups (U.S.) unsalted butter, chopped into chunks

Place the diced vegetables with the 50g/scant 2 oz (Br.)/3 tablespoons (U.S.) butter in a wide pan and barely cover with water. Bring slowly to simmering

point then strain through a colander.

Film a non-stick pan with oil and briefly sauté the garlic. Add the peeled walnut halves and sauté for 2 to 3 minutes. Finely grind the walnut/garlic mixture in a food processor. Stir in the finely chopped parsley. Place in a bowl.

Place the mussels in a large baking dish, preferably in a single layer (or do this in 2 batches), then scatter the parsley stalks, onion and white wine over them. Cover the dish and place over a high heat for a few minutes until all the mussels have opened. Strain the juice into a large, enamelled cast-iron saucepan, add to it the saffron and cream and start to boil hard to reduce by two-thirds. Do not choose a small pan as the reduction needs to boil really hard and will rise up quite high as it is reducing.

While the sauce is reducing, remove the top shell from each mussel and place the halved, steamed mussels in a wide sauté pan which has a lid. Pour in about 1cm/½ in of water, which will provide the gush of steam needed to re-heat the mussels, and scatter the diced vegetables over them.

Place the lid on the mussels and place over a high heat. At the same time whisk the chunks of cold butter into the now simmering reduction. Taste for seasoning. The sauce should be a warm, golden colour and be pleasantly briny. Stir in the parsley/walnut mixture. It should now be quite green.

Ladle the mussels and vegetables into 6 warmed wide soup bowls and pour the sauce over them.

Jeremiah Tower

Stars Restaurant
San Francisco, U.S.A.

Not many chefs in the world began their lives with a silver spoon upbringing, but then, when you think about it, what better way to acquire a phenomenal palate than dining with the wealthy, at the best restaurants, and all over the world, from your early childhood.

Jeremiah Tower was an indulged child, with an industrialist grandfather and a wealthy, globetrotting father whose business life took him across the United States, to Sydney for a few years, and for many years to London, where Jeremiah did most of his schooling at King's College, before returning to Harvard to study architecture — reportedly with an open chequebook from his grandfather and instructions to enjoy his life and his youth.

As a boy of seven, Jeremiah vividly recalls treating the Hyde Park Hotel in London as his family dining room, eating on many occasions all by himself while his parents entertained or were entertained elsewhere. 'The waiters treated me royally; full-course silver service dinners were the rule, and I ate my way through all the changes of menu and knew intricately all the flavours and nuances of what I was eating and how it should be served, well before my tenth birthday. In the wake of the war, we were truly filthy-rich Americans, I suppose. To be living in England in the fifties on an American salary was just like being an Arab nowadays.'

As a student, Jeremiah often cooked for himself and his friends, memories of past meals guiding his palate, and experimentation rather than a knowledge of the rules getting him by on the small hotplates and bohemian equipment available to him to practise his skills. A favourite aunt, married to a Russian emigré and holding regular European-style 'salons' for their entourage of expatriate Europeans, furthered Jeremiah's valuable education and honed his palate both in practice and by endless philosophical arguments. In the smoke-filled environment of her 'soirées', political and philosophical arguments fuelled heated discussions, and always the excitement was enhanced by a table laden with Eastern European delicacies — caviar and buttery blinis washed down with ice-cold vodka; red cabbage salads, and guinea fowl braised in old red burgundies, served with the best French wines. His uncle steeped him in esoteric arguments as to whether excellence could be achieved through austerity or indulgence, purity or excess and, as Jeremiah tells in his book *New American Classics*, he went on to be a guiding hand in Jeremiah's development by opening only the best bottles in his cellar for his nephew, in order to teach him what he called 'the immense difference between excellent and the very best possible'.[1]

How it was then, that Jeremiah arrived in Berkeley, California en route for Hawaii with only seven dollars in his pocket and looking for a job, is somewhat of a mystery; but it was in this way that he struck up a partnership with the now legendary Alice Waters at Chez Panisse, and the two of them embarked on the careers that were to make them famous in the United States as the founders of the much-touted 'California Cuisine'.

That was in 1972. At Chez Panisse the menu was still largely French in origin, and Jeremiah searched books studiously for the inspiration to utilise the marketing he did daily and the growing amount of local produce Alice drew to her doors. Soon Jeremiah was head chef, promoted possibly for his natural talent, and possibly for his organisational abilities ('I'm a bit inclined to act like a monarch in the kitchen, and I don't tolerate fools very well,' he says in the restrained, well-mannered English voice.)

Bittersweet Chocolate Torte

By 1976, as Jeremiah tells it, something truly pivotal happened. He had been doing regional dinners of the French provinces 'for what seemed like years', and had really scratched the bottom of the barrel for something different to present time after time. After two Moroccan dinners and a Corsican one, he was at a loss for something else to do when he came across a book called *The Epicurean — A Franco-American Culinary Encyclopaedia*. In it were a series of recipes served at Delmonico's in New York from 1862 to 1894, among which was a green corn soup 'à la Mendocino' (Mendocino being a town up the coast from San Francisco). Realisation came like a flash. 'Why' — it came like a bolt out of the blue — 'Why am I scratching around in Corsica when I have fabulous produce all around me here in California?'

So the first Jeremiah Tower Californian menu was born and, as he says himself, it was American food using French cooking principles. The turning-point menu, for your historical knowledge, read:

Tomales Bay Bluepoint Oysters on Ice
Cream of Fresh Corn Soup Mendocino Style, with Crayfish Butter
Monterey Bay Prawns Sautéed with Garlic, Parsley and Butter
Preserved California-grown Geese from Sebastopol
Fresh Caramelised Figs from Sonoma
Walnuts, Almonds and Mountain Pears from the San Francisco Farmers' Market

'The restaurant — and I — were never the same again.'

A year later, Jeremiah was to leave Alice to her restaurant, as he looked for partners to create one of his own. With his architectural career behind him now, but closely dictating his feelings about the way this new restaurant should be, he started looking for a large warehouse of some sort to throw open into a large interior space with a bar, even a piano, and definitely an open kitchen. He envisaged a busy, bustling bistro or brasserie in the central district of busy, bustling San Francisco. Whilst waiting for this to happen for him, he gathered intellectual fodder by working on the Time Life series of cookbooks with Richard Olney, a period in which he lived in France again and recrystallised his love and understanding of its great cuisine. Back home, he worked in Big Sur, and then in the Santa Fe Bar and Grill, where he found his partners for his current venture, Stars.

Stars is a friendly, large, split-level room, just as Jeremiah pictured it. Painted a pale green and decorated with menus and stars of stage, screen and the culinary scene, the restaurant has a very cosmopolitan feel. An enthusiastic brigade of young dedicated staff serve at all hours of the day and night dishes with names like Jeremiah's Steak Tartare with a Spicy Cajun Remoulade, Spicy Lentil Soup with Mild Red Chilli Cream, Soft-shelled or Dungeness Crab with Tomato and Basil, Black Bean Soup, Gumbo, Chicken Breast Grilled over Mesquite with Béarnaise Sauce.

Jeremiah continues to be associated with the Santa Fe Bar and Grill, but the dizzy days when he used to spend his time running from it to Stars for an hour at a time are now over, and he concentrates only on Stars. He continues to cherish the aims he set himself, and specialises in a cuisine based on local produce (although he, like Alice, believes the term 'California Cuisine' was fabricated by the press so they could create an entity which they could then criticise and tear apart).

Jeremiah describes his cuisine as drawing on all sorts of influences from bar and grill to bistro, brasserie and classical restaurant food, and if he refuses to tout the term 'California Cuisine' in preference for the name he chose for his book, *New American Classics*, he is prepared to see himself, quite rightly, as a founding giant in its making.

1 Jeremiah Tower, *New American Classics*, Harper and Row, New York, 1986, p. 13

Bittersweet Chocolate Torte

Serves 8

The chocolate torte:
250g/9 oz dark (bittersweet) chocolate
185g/good 6 oz (Br.)/¾ cup (U.S.) butter
6 eggs, separated
60g/2 oz (Br.)/½ cup (U.S.) flour
200g/good 7oz (Br.)/1 cup (U.S.) sugar

The coffee *crème anglaise*:
550ml/18 fl oz (Br.)/2¼ cups (U.S.) milk
60g/2 oz (Br.)/¼ cup (U.S.) ground coffee beans (preferably espresso beans)
6 egg yolks
110g/4 oz (Br.)/good ½ cup (U.S.) sugar

The decoration:
300ml/½ pint (Br.)/1¼ cups (U.S.) cream with 35% milk fat (whipping cream), whipped with 1 teaspoon sugar
80g/3 oz dark (bittersweet) chocolate, melted with 80 ml/2½ fl oz (Br.)/⅓ cup (U.S.) cream with 35% milk fat (whipping cream), and cooled slightly chocolate, either grated or in flakes

Equipment:
8 small individual aluminium pudding moulds or, failing that, cup moulds or soufflé ramekins

1. Roughly chop the chocolate. Place it in a saucepan and heat over another saucepan of simmering water, stirring until the chocolate has melted. When fully melted, remove from over the water and stir in the butter. Blend until the butter has been absorbed, then set this mixture aside to cool slightly, but ensure it still remains liquid.

2. Cream the egg yolks with three quarters of the sugar until light and fluffy and white in colour. The mixture at this stage should have doubled in volume and the sugar should be completely dissolved. Sift the flour and gently fold it into the sugar-yolk mixture. Then add the cooled chocolate mixture and again fold in gently, making sure that all the mixtures are evenly combined.

3. Whip the egg whites until they form soft peaks, add the remaining sugar and whisk until the whites are fully firm. Then fold the whites gently into the chocolate mixture.

4. Cut a circle of baking (parchment) paper for the base of each of the baking pans which have been buttered and floured. Fill the prepared baking pans with the torte mixture. Bake the tortes in a 190ºC/375ºF oven for 18 to 20 minutes. Test the cake with a skewer:

the centre should be moist but not runny. The tortes will rise a little during the cooking process but will fall back down when cooled. Remove from the oven and cool them, still in their baking moulds, on a wire cake rack. The tortes will hold for a couple of days out of the refrigerator, individually wrapped in plastic. This extra time even helps them to set better. Unmould them only when you need them.

The coffee *crème anglaise*:
5. Scald the milk and the coffee grains to just under the boil. In a bowl mix the egg yolks well with the sugar and when the milk is hot, pour it over the egg yolks and sugar stirring as you do so. Blend all the ingredients well and put them back in the saucepan. Return the saucepan to a low heat and stir the contents of the saucepan continuously until the sauce thickens. Do not boil.

6. Once the sauce has thickened, remove it immediately from the heat and strain it into a bowl. If needed quickly, the custard can be rapidly cooled by sitting the bowl in ice and stirring the mixture occasionally to equalise the temperature. Otherwise cover the custard with plastic wrap, placed directly over the custard to prevent skinning, and allow it to cool. Then refrigerate it until needed.

1

2

3

4

5

6

7

8

9

To decorate:

7. Pour a little of the coffee *créme anglaise* on individual serving plates. Unmould the tortes onto the middle of the plates. Then top each torte with a little whipped cream to which you have added a small amount of sugar.

8. Melt a little chocolate to use for decorating, and mix in some cream, in the proportion of about 80g/3 oz chocolate to 80ml/2½ fl oz (Br.)/⅓ cup (U.S.) cream. When cool but still runny, spoon a little of this over the torte and cream, and drizzle a line of it through the coffee *créme anglaise*.

9. The final touch is to spoon a little coarsely grated chocolate or chocolate flakes over the torte.

Grilled Baby Octopus Salad

Serves 6
6 baby octopus or squid, cleaned
1 tablespoon mixed chopped fresh herbs, ideally thyme, marjoram and tarragon
250ml/8 fl oz (Br.)/1 good cup (U.S.) olive oil
4 red bell peppers (capsicums), roasted until charred, then peeled and seeded
3 bulbs fennel or sweet anise
1 to 2 small hot red chillis
½ teaspoon grated orange zest
½ teaspoon anchovy paste
1 tablespoon lemon juice
125ml/4 fl oz (Br.)/½ cup (U.S.) mayonnaise
1 small garlic clove, minced very finely
1 tablespoon finely chopped coriander (cilantro) or tarragon leaves
salt and freshly ground black pepper

Marinate the octopus in the mixed herbs and about 60ml/scant 2 fl oz (Br.)/3 tablespoons (U.S.) of the olive oil for a minimum of half an hour. When ready, season with salt and pepper and char-grill, barbecue or grill (broil) them, turning each once. They will take 3 to 4 minutes on each side. Allow to cool and cut each into 3 or 4 sections.

Segment the peeled bell peppers (capsicums) into the 3 or 4 natural sections of their lobes. Cut the tops off the fennel, cut in half and remove the core. Cut into thin slices. Blanch in a pot of boiling, salted water for 1 to 2 minutes; drain and refresh in iced water.

Seed and finely chop the chillies. Combine with the orange zest, anchovy paste and the lemon juice. Whisk in the remaining olive oil. Season with salt and pepper to taste.

Combine the coriander (cilantro) or tarragon and the garlic with the mayonnaise. If using tarragon, blanch the leaves for 10 seconds in boiling water, and drain and rinse in cold water before chopping. Arrange the bell peppers (capsicums) and

the octopus pieces around the plate. Drizzle with a little of the dressing over everything and then put a spoonful of garlic mayonnaise in the middle. Toss the fennel in the remaining dressing and place a mound in the centre of each plate. Garnish with chopped parsley if desired.

Peppered Beef Salad

Serves 6 to 8
2.25 kg/5 lb beef fillet (tenderloin), in 1 piece
¼ cup whole black peppercorns
1½ tablespoons (Br.)/2 tablespoons (U.S.) coarse salt
2 good tablespoons (Br.)/3 tablespoons (U.S.) mixed chopped fresh herbs, ideally thyme, marjoram, rosemary
250ml/8 fl oz (Br.)/1 good cup (U.S.) olive oil
8 small eggplants (aubergine), dwarf ones if possible
500ml/good ¾ pint (Br.)/2 good cups (U.S.) tomato *concassé* (peeled, seeded, chopped tomato)

6 handfuls mixed salad greens (*mesclun*), chosen from curly endive (*frisée*), watercress, lamb's tongue lettuce (*mâche*), rocket, baby cos, or other small greens
2 teaspoons lemon juice
salt and freshly ground black pepper
250ml/8 fl oz (Br.)/1 good cup (U.S.) mayonnaise
2 to 3 tablespoons red bell pepper (capsicum) purée
1 tablespoon blanched and finely chopped fresh tarragon leaves

Trim the beef fillet of fat and silver skin. With a mortar and pestle, or a well-cleaned coffee grinder, grind the peppercorns, coarse salt, mixed herbs and 2 to 3 tablespoons of olive oil into a paste. Rub the paste all over the beef and allow to stand for at least an hour.

Cut the eggplant (aubergine) into 4, lengthwise. If the dwarf ones, such as in our photo, are available, they may be halved only. Toss in the remaining chopped herbs and 50ml/1½ fl oz (Br.)/

¼ cup (U.S.) olive oil. Place the eggplant (aubergine) in a single layer, skin side down, on a baking sheet. Season lightly with salt and pepper and cover with aluminium foil. Bake in a preheated 180ºC/350ºF oven for 10 to 15 minutes or until cooked. Remove the foil and allow to cool.

Turn the oven up to 200ºC/400ºF and roast the fillet, turning once on each side, until rare — about 20 to 25 minutes, depending on thickness. Allow to cool.

Pick over, and wash and dry the greens. Make a vinaigrette with the lemon juice, remaining olive oil, salt and pepper. Mix half of the mayonnaise with the red bell pepper (capsicum) purée and the other half with the chopped tarragon.

Dress the greens on the bottom of the plates. Slice the beef and arrange on top. Arrange the eggplant (aubergine) around the plate decoratively. Drizzle the 2 sauces over the beef.

51

Alain Dutournier
Le Carré des Feuillants
Le Trou Gascon
Paris, France

I f you take a Parisian gourmet's word, never go to a three-star Michelin-rated restaurant when you can go to a two-star on the rise. Of course that means knowing the stars on the rise, not those on the decline or that have stayed stewing in the two-star slot for years. Aha, there's the game! Addresses are continually whispered knowingly to close friends, the latest dining experiences analysed and boasted about, and such is the sport of trying to spot a star on the ascent that it inspires as much gossip as do the latest football scores in other countries.

I came across chef Alain Dutournier by coincidence. His first restaurant, very much a bistro in unassuming quarters, was just around the corner from close friends. We often passed it, and somehow the name Le Trou Gascon seemed familiar. I had heard it was good, even if I couldn't place the origin of the recommendation, and above all I love food with the flavours of Gascony.

Coincidence followed coincidence. On the first visit, the taste of the food was so sublime — Gascon flavours in a modern interpretation applied with exceptional talent and skill — that I had to tell the chef how magnificent it was by calling him over and booking to return three days later with other friends. Conversation followed, my accent was spotted: 'Australienne?'. That was funny, he said. Another Australienne had been there only a week or so ago, and she had had one of the most amazing palates he had ever encountered. Her name was Stephanie Alexander, and she had liked the food too; and had astounded Dutournier by being able to analyse every one of the myriad of spices he had combined to give it its rare complexity. It looked like the Australians were on his wavelength, and before I knew it Alain was pouring Armagnac of the year of my birth —

his much-loved cellar boasts one of the best collections in the restaurant trade — and we were old friends.

Since then I haunt Le Trou Gascon as much as an irregular visitor from afar can be said to haunt a place. I can remember the days when Alain groaned that to mount high on the Michelin scale you had to be more political. He had actually gone once to this hallowed seat of gastronomy to demand why they ignored him when Gault and Millau (or one of the two) frequented his place regularly, seemed fond of it, and rated it better. There were days when he despaired of knowing how to earn more fame and days when he believed he'd never break through. Le Trou Gascon was too much of a bistro, it was too small, it was too regional, maybe he should have greased palms — he didn't know and in the end he shrugged it off as if he didn't care.

What a pleasure it was when I opened a Gault and Millau magazine a year or so later to find Alain named, along with Jacques Maximin and Bernard Loiseau, one of the three best young chefs in France. I'd known he was very good and I felt personally vindicated. Then Michelin awarded him his second star and with all the fame it became impossible to get a booking — although apologies from his wife Nicole, lamenting that they had to refuse 'regulars' in the name of people who'd booked weeks ahead, were consoling and beautifully made.

In 1985, Alain's dream of leaving behind his bistro for a truly elegant environment came true. A move to Paris's fashion quarter between the Place Vendôme and the Concorde, just one step from the Rue St.Honoré, gave Alain the best address he could have wanted; an enormous floor area where he could seat over a hundred, with space between the tables and room for roving trolleys; a centre-room fireplace caged in brass with glass walls; a courtyard entrance; a foyer

Escabèche de Rougets Barbés au Caviar d'Aubergines

for the Maitre d' to greet the guests; and a twenty square metre kitchen with room for twelve cooks. Le Carré des Feuillants, at 14 Rue de Castiglione, gives the former bistro cook a proud interior, and with it now, hoards of fashionable guests.

In the grandeur of this establishment, Alains's heart is still attuned to the wonderful Moorish flavours of the Arabic invasion that so influenced his region of France. He is still fired with enthusiasm to create, devise, stimulate his diners and never rest on his laurels. Although the ravioli of foie gras that delighted me on my first visit and is imbedded so strongly in my memory that I can still taste it, is no longer there; the foie gras so beloved of the Gascons is still there, impeccably pink and the lobes beautifully delineated; and as well the pickled carrots, the Moorish-influenced Gascon spicing, and the ubiquitous flavour of fresh coriander.

Three years on, Nicole is still running Le Trou Gascon, with chef Bernard Broux, a long-time member of Alain's team, at the helm. The menu is under Alain's supervision of course, but with a simpler, more regional approach to that of the grander restaurant. It remains a delight, with its painted ceiling and charming, personal atmosphere, and now claims one star in the Michelin and two hats and 16/20 from Gault et Millau. It is a pleasure to dine at Le Trou Gascon for less formal occasions than Le Carré des Feuillants, but for the grander times, Alain and his partner Gérard Garrigues will entertain you royally at the latter, which now boasts two stars and 18/20 in Gault et Millau with three red hats doffed to its innovative quality.

Much better value, the Parisians whisper, to visit a two-star chef with his eye on the future than the man who has 'made it'. It certainly seems that the talent of Alain Dutournier knows no bounds.

Escabèche de Rougets Barbés au Caviar d'Aubergines
Escabèche of Red Mullet

An appetising cold fish starter, prepared the day before it is needed.

Serves 6 as a starter
6 red mullet, also known as barbuna
30g/1 oz (Br.)/2 tablespoons (U.S.) sultanas (golden raisins)
200ml/scant 7 fl oz (Br.)/1 scant cup (U.S.) dry white wine
juice of 1 lemon, plus the grated zest
1 clove garlic, crushed
2 shallots, sliced
1 red bell pepper (capsicum), peeled and finely sliced
1 tomato, peeled, seeded and diced
8 pearl onions, or tiny summer pickling onions, peeled and quartered. If unobtainable, substitute with spring onions, peeled and sliced
6 small green chilli peppers (not the very hot ones), cut into julienne

2 eggplants (aubergines), wrapped in aluminium foil
1 teaspoon coriander seeds, crushed
200ml/scant 7 fl oz (Br.)/1 scant cup (U.S.) olive oil
a little cumin powder
salt and freshly ground black pepper
a little powdered dill seed
8 fresh mint leaves, shredded
10 stalks fresh coriander (cilantro)
sprigs of fresh dill for décor

1. The ingredients, showing the red mullet (barbuna) and the vegetables.

2. Soak the sultanas in the white wine. Place the eggplant (aubergine) wrapped in foil, in a 180°C/350°F oven to cook for 45 minutes. When cooked, slit them lengthwise and scrape out the flesh onto a plate. Heat a little olive oil and soften one of the shallots, then add the eggplant (aubergine); stir in. Transfer to a food processor or blender and blend to a purée. Salt and pepper this mixture, add the shredded mint and place in the refrigerator until serving.

3. Alain scales and empties the fish himself, thus retaining their livers. If this is not possible, ask for them when your fishmonger fillets the fish. Also, keep the bones and heads and cook them into a small amount of concentrated fish stock, using water and about half of the white wine in which you are soaking the sultanas. If you are able to retain the livers, pan fry them in a minimal amount of olive oil; drain them and crush them to a paste.

4. Salt and pepper the mullet (barbuna) fillets, add half the crushed coriander seeds and a pinch each of dill seed and cumin.

5. Heat a little more olive oil and soften the second shallot. Add the baby onions (or spring onion), the red bell pepper (capsicum), tomato, chillis, sultanas and grated lemon zest. Cook rapidly. Season with salt and pepper, ½ teaspoon crushed coriander seeds and a pinch each of dill seed and cumin. Wet this with the fish stock (very reduced), to which is added the pureé of the livers, if you have them, the remnants of white wine in which you soaked the sultanas, and the juice of the lemon. Set this aside in the refrigerator.

6. Lastly, sauté the fillets of fish in the remaining olive oil — skin side first. Turn for only 2 to 3 seconds and place them on a shallow dish. When the spiced vegetables and juice is cold, cover the fish with it. Cover the plate with greaseproof (parchment) paper or foil and leave it overnight in the refrigerator.

To serve:
Serve the cold fillets on a bed of eggplant (aubergine) caviar. Decorate with small sprigs of fresh coriander (cilantro) and dill, as in the large photograph.

3

6

'Gigotins' d'Agneau Gasconnade

Lamb 'Gigotins', Gascon Style

Serves 4

1 small leg of lamb (preferably milk-fed baby lamb) of 1.5 kg/use 3¼ lb
4 lamb cutlets
4 lamb kidneys
8 cloves glacéed garlic (It is in the style of the South West of France to preserve garlic by cooking it for a long time, maybe half an hour, very slowly in olive oil. If instead you use raw garlic, only 2 cloves, split into 4, are required as they are much more pungent.)
4 anchovy fillets
3 teaspoons fresh thyme leaves or wild thyme (*serpolet*)
strong French mustard
1 egg
100ml/3 fl oz (Br.)/scant ½ cup (U.S.) cream, preferably with 45% milk fat (heavy cream)
salt and freshly ground pepper
nutmeg
600g/1 lb 6 oz puff pastry
1 egg beaten with 1 tablespoon water (eggwash)

Split open the leg of lamb down the length of the bone and then remove the bones. Remove the meat from the skin and fat in the natural lobes (muscles) into which it falls. You should end up with 3 lobes of meat of unequal size: 1 elongated and 2 round muscles, of which the larger should be cut into 2. These 4 pieces now weigh approximately 200g/7 oz each. Set them aside. With the bones, make a well-reduced lamb stock. (As an example, see the recipes on pages 89, 110.)

The mousseline:

From the rest of the skin and fat you should be able to gather a further 170 to 200g/6 to 7 oz of meat, to which you add the meat from the eye of the cutlets (saving the bones). In all, the weight of this extra meat should now be about 250g /9 oz (Br.) /1 cup (U.S.) to blend correctly with the cream and egg.

In a food processor, purée this meat, and only when very well puréed, add first the egg, then the cream. Season with salt and pepper and about 1 teaspoon of the fresh thyme leaves. Set aside in the refrigerator. In default of a food processor, the meat can be passed through a mincer (meat grinder) fitted with a very fine disc, into a bowl, and then the egg and cream stirred in.

Split the kidneys in 2 lengthwise, and sauté them in a little butter, salt and pepper until just lightly seared but not cooked through.

To assemble the 'gigotins':

Take the 4 muscles of meat and cut a long slit into each to form a pocket. Break the hooked end from the cutlet bones, and keep the long slim bones only. Place one end of one of these bones into one of the pockets of meat, and insert also some of the forcemeat with 2 pieces of kidney and 1 fillet of anchovy in the centre. You should use about a quarter of the forcemeat, although, depending on the size of the lobes, you may end up with a little forcemeat over. Stick the meat with 2 cloves of glacéed garlic or 2 quarter pieces of garlic if raw. Make up the 4 'gigotins' in this way, patting them all to re-form the shape of an individual baby leg of lamb. With a pastry brush, paint each with mustard, and then sprinkle well with the remaining thyme leaves. Sprinkle with salt, freshly ground black pepper and nutmeg.

To encase in pastry:

Cut the puff pastry into 4 x 150g/use 6oz pieces and roll out each to the full. Place the 'gigotins' just a little above the base line of each, in the centre. Pleat the bulk of the sheet of the pastry forward over the lamb, leaving the bone of the cutlet protruding as would the bone on a large leg of lamb. So the pastry sticks together, use a little eggwash on the pastry protruding from under the lamb. Gather the edges together to shape the parcel into the desired form, and so that the juices from the cooking do not run out, it is best

to roll the accumulated pastry from the front and the sides of the parcel under the meat. Paint the whole with eggwash to give a good sheen, and cook in a 200ºC/400ºF oven for about 30 to 35 minutes to swell and become golden brown.

The 'gigotins' may be made a few hours before dinner and refrigerated. If this is done, glaze with eggwash before placing in the oven. Allow an extra 5 minutes if they have spent more than an hour in the refrigerator, as the centres will be quite cold.

To serve:

Serve the 'gigotins' 1 per person, garnished with the vegetables of the season, and a small light *jus*-style sauce made from reduced lamb stock seasoned well with thyme, salt and pepper.

Variation:

A simpler leg of lamb recipe may be made, with or without puff pastry, using a whole leg. Have the butcher bone the leg without cutting the piece through lengthwise, and preferably leaving the shank bone intact, so that the finished roast retains its shape. Stuff this pocket with the kidney and forcemeat you can make with extra lean meat bought separately. Paint with the mustard and thyme and roast in the usual way.

If you prefer to cover it with pastry, you must brown the meat first, or par-roast if for 1 hour, allowing it to cool before wrapping in pastry. If you intend to refrigerate it for much time before dinner, then the roast can even be fully cooked, because if very cold, it needs nearly the whole 40 minutes (the cooking time of the pastry) just to reheat, and very little further cooking will take place. Time the precooking to allow for these variables.

In partnership with Anton, Lyn is also Chairman of a second company, Cuisine Créative, which concentrates on food consultancy, providing information on numerous aspects of the food industry, from setting up restaurants to menu testing and development, restaurant design and professional equipment testing. Lyn also writes for *Taste* magazine, *Decanter* magazine and as well finds time to contribute to books and to cook for television and films. She helps Anton with the preparation of the food for his books, and has been part of his brigade on tour, including to the Munich and Stuttgart culinary competitions where she won gold medals as part of the winning Dorchester team. Lyn is currently engaged in writing a twelve-book cookery collection entitled *La Petite Cuisine Cookery Series.*

When you see Lyn in a kitchen, her precise, meticulous approach to presenting everything — from the typed-up recipes to the glamorously decorated finished dish — makes you realise why so many important chefs talk of her with such great respect. She's a perfectionist at all times.

1

2

3

4

5

6

7

8

9

Terrine of Fresh Fruit with Raspberry Coulis

Serves 10
600ml/1 pint (Br.)/2½ cups (U.S.)
apple juice
8 leaves or 6 teaspoons granulated
(unflavoured) gelatine
1 bunch fresh mint leaves, as perfect as
possible

The fruit:
1 punnet raspberries, about 200g /7 oz
(Br.)/1¼ cups (U.S.)
3 grapefruit and 6 to 7 oranges,
preferably navel, or alternatively 10
oranges
2 punnets strawberries, about 500g/use
1 lb (Br.)/4 cups (U.S.), hulled

The raspberry coulis:
2 punnets about 400g/14 oz (Br.)/2½
cups (U.S.) raspberries
60g/2 oz (Br.)/½ cup (U.S.) icing
(confectioner's) sugar
about 3 tablespoons plain yoghurt

The garnish:
2 segments orange per person
extra mint leaves

Equipment:
Loaf or pâté mould of 1.5 litres/2½
pints (Br.)/6 cups (U.S.) volume

Hull the strawberries; cut away the peel
and pith from the oranges (and
grapefruit, if using) and carefully remove
the orange/grapefruit segments. Remove
any pips. Stand in a bowl until needed.
Reserve any juice that falls; it may be
added to the apple juice if strained.

Heat about one-third of the apple juice.
If using leaf gelatine, soften in a little
water, squeeze dry and drop into the
heated apple juice. For granulated gelatine, soften in a little of the cold apple
juice then add to the heated juice. In
either case, stir until dissolved, then add
the remaining two-thirds of the juice.

Allow to stand at room temperature so
it remains liquid enough to pour.

Prepare the raspberry coulis by puréeing the raspberries in a blender or food
processor, adding the icing sugar and
lemon juice to sweeten and refine its
taste. Pass through a sieve. Refrigerate,
covered in plastic wrap, until needed.

1. Pour some of the apple juice into
the base of the mould to a depth of
about 6mm/¼ in and set the mould
in a large dish of ice cubes and water
to cool. Place in the refrigerator to help
speed the setting. Then place a line of
mint leaves all along the length of the
dish, pretty side (i.e. non-veined side)
downwards. Pour a tiny layer of apple
juice over this to help hold it in position.

2. Place a layer of raspberries over the
mint leaves, then place a layer of
grapefruit segments over the raspberries. If not using grapefruit, make this
first layer of orange segments.

3. Place a layer of strawberries over
the grapefruit layer, then a layer of orange
segments over the top of these. This
being the final layer, try to arrange the
segments prettily, and all facing the same
direction.

4. With the mould still sitting in the
dish of ice and water, pour in the remaining apple juice. It should just cover
the upper layer of fruit by about
4mm/3/16in. Place in the refrigerator
to set for at least 1½ hours. If you do
not intend to use it until the next day,
it is possible to use one less leaf of gelatine (about a scant teaspoon) lest it gets
a little too rubbery.

5. Before unmoulding the dessert, prepare the plates to receive the slices. Place
about 2 tablespoons of raspberry coulis
on the side of each dessert plate. Using
a small paper icing pocket or piping bag
with a very fine nozzle, pipe 4 vertical
lines of yoghurt across the coulis. Stir

the yoghurt to break up its texture before placing it in the piping bag.

6. Carefully pull a tooth pick through
these horizontal lines alternately toward
and away from you at equal intervals,
to make a herring-bone pattern through
the yoghurt. If this is difficult, the coulis is quite attractive enough on its own.

7. To unmould the fruit terrine, remove the mould from the refrigerator
and run a thin-bladed sharp knife around
the sides. Invert onto a smooth surface,
not something with a raised edge.

8. Slice carefully with a bread knife
or an electric knife and transfer the slices
quickly to each plate with an egg lift.
Move quickly as the juice is just nicely
held with gelatine and thus not too rubbery. It should not be left standing a
long time in a hot room.

9. Finish the decoration of the plate
with a couple of extra orange segments
and a mint leaf per person.

Leek Terrine with Hazelnut Vinaigrette

Serves 6
900 g/2 lb (about 14 medium) trimmed leeks, cut into 12cm/5in lengths
salt and freshly ground black pepper
½ bunch chervil
hazelnut vinaigrette (see recipe below)

Equipment:
Terrine mould 10 x 15 x 8cm/4 x 6 x 3in.

Slit the leeks lengthwise and wash them well under cold running water. Tie them in equal bundles and cook in boiling salted water until just tender. Refresh in a large bowl of iced water. Drain well, squeezing out any excess water.

Line the mould with foil, allowing an overhang, and pack the leeks in firmly, squeezing each to rid them of any water. Lay all the green ends together in the first layer, then arrange the white parts on this green, in the second layer. Repeat alternate layering until the mould is full. Season each layer. Fold the overlapping foil to cover the leeks. Place a board or a stiff piece of cardboard, the size of the mould, on top of the leeks. Invert the mould, with the board in place, onto a dish, and place a weight on top of the terrine.

Refrigerate for at least 6 hours — this will compress the leeks and extract the water.

To serve:
Place slices of the terrine on a serving plate, garnished with sprigs of chervil and served with some hazelnut vinaigrette.

The hazelnut vinaigrette:
1 egg yolk
30g/1 oz Dijon mustard
30ml/1 fl oz (Br.)/scant 2 tablespoons (U.S.) mild white wine vinegar
145ml/5 fl oz (Br.)/⅔ cup (U.S.) groundnut or corn (maize) oil
up to 30ml/1 fl oz (Br.)/scant 2 tablespoons (U.S.) hazelnut oil
salt and freshly ground black pepper

Hong Kong Steamed Prawns

Serves 4 as a starter
2 teaspoons fermented black beans, washed well
2 teaspoons salted yellow beans
large pinch sugar
½ teaspoon sesame oil
50 ml/1½ fl oz (Br.)/¼ cup (U.S.) groundnut or corn (maize) oil
1½ cloves garlic, peeled and finely chopped
1cm/½ in piece fresh root ginger, peeled and finely chopped
½ fresh green or red chilli, seeded and sliced into tiny rounds
3 teaspoons Shaosing wine or medium-dry sherry
12 large green prawns with shells on and heads of about 30g/1 oz each, called jumping prawns in Hong Kong
12 sprigs of coriander (cilantro)

Mash the black beans and the yellow beans together with the sugar and sesame oil into a paste.

Heat a wok over a high heat until very hot. Add the groundnut or corn (maize) oil and swirl it quickly around the wok. Add the garlic, and as soon as it begins to colour, add the ginger. Stir. Quickly add the bean paste mixture. Stir well, then add the chilli.

Splash the wine or sherry around the side of the wok. As soon as the sizzling dies down, lower the heat, stir well, then pour the sauce into a bowl and reserve.

Remove the prawn shells, split the prawns in two lengthwise but keep them intact at the tail, discarding the vein as you do so. Dry the prawns with paper towelling. Spoon the sauce onto the prawns and allow to marinade for about 15 minutes.

Bring a steamer to the boil, placing a serving plate over the top of the steamer to warm. Arrange the prawns in a single layer on the hot plate. Steam the prawns over a moderately high heat for 3 to 4 minutes. Remove when cooked. If serving cold, allow to rest in their juices.

Serve hot or cold, garnished with coriander (cilantro) sprigs.

Make sure all ingredients and equipment are warm. Beat the egg yolk, then add the mustard. Whisk well together. Add a few drops of vinegar and whisk. Slowly whisk in the oil and, when thick and creamy, add enough vinegar to taste. Add the hazelnut oil. If necessary, a little hot water may be added to thin the vinaigrette to the required consistency.

Damien Pignolet

Claude's
Sydney, Australia

I t took Damien Pignolet and his wife Josephine only two years before their tiny restaurant Claude's, in the Sydney suburb of Woollahra, was acclaimed as one of the best restaurants in Australia. Many — including the great Madeleine Kamman, whom I once caught telling a group of American cooks that Damien cooked better than Fredy Girardet — say the best.

When asked to pin down the reason why, the word that comes immediately to mind is passion — meaning dedication, taste and an absolute sleep-eat-think-dream-of-it approach to their art. They use a less emotive word, but in fact it's really the translation of this passion in actions. They pin their success on a good, solid determination to master all the technical aspects of their work. As such, they define theirs as a classical restaurant, for all their techniques are classical French techniques, tried and true. Sound technique, the best and most varied ingredients, simple dishes well executed, are truly the basis upon which all great restaurants earn their reputations.

'We don't really do anything that's different...we just set out to cook to the best of our ability in the best classical manner, armed with the best produce we can possibly find. We practise, and we study the great chefs, we argue with one another with *Larousse Gastronomic* in our hands, and we go to bed above the shop.' 'It's a passion,' explains Damien. 'No, it's a madness,' laughs Josephine. And their eyes light up as they say it.

Their paths just had to cross. Damien grew up in Melbourne, completed the Hotel Management course at William Angliss College, and ended up bonded to a hospital (which had paid his fees) for a few years. Real cooking was a hobby, until he was invited to start the cookery school for a local cookshop. Teaching, buying equipment, running a national food society and organising guest demonstrators ran him across the path of noted chef Mogens Bay Esbensen. Mogens was then running Pavilion on the Park and, recognising Damien's talent, he invited him to join him there and gave him the training he needed in the professional side of the industry. Before long Damien was in partnership with Mogens, and together they opened Butler's in Potts Point.

Mogen's most promising apprentice, just entering her final year, was a girl called Josephine Carrol. The same Josephine...

Co-chefs shortly became husband and wife, and in turn branched out on their own, and Claude's has been functioning under their baton since 1982. It was a little restaurant, rather claustrophobic, and Damien spent a lot of money making it more simple, more elegant. A beautiful hand-lacquered mirror by artist Donald Green helps make it look more spacious; white linen, flowered Villeroy and Boch china sets off the food; and there is a simple but thoughtful spacing of the tables which allows only thirty-five to partake of the evening meal.

Because the tiny kitchen makes work for more than three at a time impossible, the restaurant serves a *prix fixe* menu from Tuesday to Saturday, dinners only. This is usually four courses and is possibly the best value for money in Australia, particularly as the restaurant is licensed for patrons to bring their own wine. But it's the couple's special nights that *'vaut le détour'*, as the Michelin Guide says, for this is their real challenge and they give it all their love and attention. *Fine bouche* (or *fin bec*, depending on your sense of French slang) is the colloquial term the French use for an epicurean. On the first Saturday of every month Damien and Josephine design a *fine bouche* menu. 'It's like sitting for an exam', says Jo. 'The

Boudin Blanc of Chicken, Sweetbreads and Cèpe Mushrooms

clients are all sitting out there analysing you. They want something great, and it's a real thrill to try and live up to their expectations. You don't even know what they're expecting!'

The couple plan the menu together, arguing constantly yet always respecting each other's opinion. They're very good for each other, because they compete, and it's evident. Damien feels they have now developed a style uniquely their own as a result of each other's disciplines and philosophies. The *fine bouche* menus are undoubtedly the culmination. They comprise up to seven courses, but are designed with weight and balance in mind, and there is no hard rule. The thirty or so places are booked mostly by regulars and many places are booked for the year. There is not a food buff in the country who does not regard it as a pilgrimage.

In this tiny little restaurant with its impossible kitchen and all the limitations the little shop-front poses, sheer talent has outweighed everything and given to the couple their due.

Always gregarious and willing to talk about his work, Damien has given many classes over the years, and people always leave them with a deep appreciation of the intricacies of cuisine as an art form. You might think sausages are simple things, but if you have noticed how some restaurants have given them a new lease of life lately, with beautifully complicated flavourings and textures, you will understand how a restaurateur's sausage is simply so. Damien's beautiful sausages below are of chicken and sweetbread, the fine-flavoured, fine-textured flesh complimented by the pungent flavour of the greatest mushroom of them all, the *cèpe*. The result is marvellous, and the technique easier than you think. You need patience and an understanding of what you are doing, rather than any inherent skill.

In Australia they say, 'Have a go mate'!

In tribute to Josephine Pignolet (1956–1987)

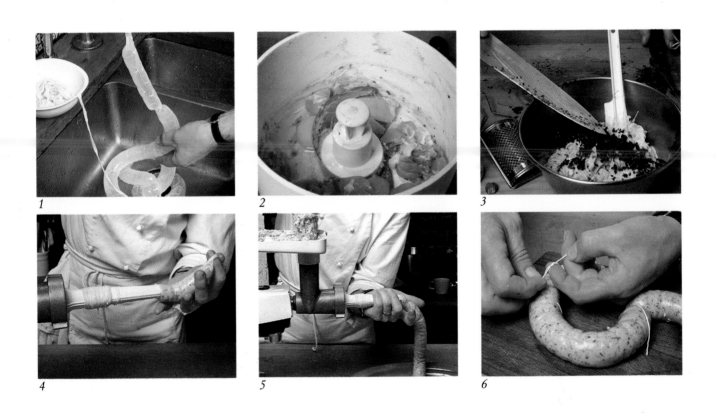

1

2

3

4

5

6

Boudin Blanc of Chicken, Sweetbreads and Cèpe Mushrooms

Serves 8 to 10
500g/use 1 lb chicken breast meat, diced and well chilled
1 whole egg
2 egg whites
500ml/good ¾ pt (Br.)/2 good cups (U.S.) cream, preferably with 45% milk fat (heavy cream)
10g/⅓ oz (Br.)/½ tablespoon (U.S.) salt
¼ teaspoon freshly ground white pepper
¼ nutmeg, ground (less if very large)
100g/3½ oz onions, finely diced (a good ½ cup [U.S.] diced onions)
4 tablespoons (Br.)/5 tablespoons (U.S.) finely chopped parsley
30g/1 oz (Br.)/½ cup (U.S.) dried *cèpe* (*porcini*) or boletus mushrooms or 15g/½ oz (Br.)/¼ cup (U.S.) Chinese mushrooms
250g/use ½ lb calves' sweetbreads

2 metres/6 ft 6 in thick sausage skins from your butcher or chinese foodstore. (Called 'hog casings', pork skins are used for a thick sausage. They are dry and salted when you buy them, but soften in water before you use them. They can be stored dry or, in the home situation, it is easier to rinse them off then place them in a plastic container and freeze until needed.)

180g/6 oz (Br.)/2 good cups (U.S.) fresh white breadcrumbs
200ml/scant 7 fl oz (Br.)/1 scant cup (U.S.) clarified butter

Equipment:
You will need a mincer (meat grinder), which may be either a hand mincer or a mincer attachment on a large, free-standing electric mixer. You need also a sausage attachment for the mincer. For this sausage stuffing a food processor is the best tool, as the stuffing is fine; for other stuffings a mincer will do.

The day before, or at least 6 hours ahead:
Soak the sweetbreads in cold water and a tablespoon of salt for an hour.

Prepare a *court-bouillon* of 200ml/scant 7 fl oz (Br.)/1 scant cup (U.S.) white wine, 300 ml/½ pt (Br.)/1¼ cups (U.S.) water, a small onion chopped, a small carrot sliced, a stalk of celery sliced, and a bay leaf, a few sprigs of parsley, 8 peppercorns and 1 teaspoon of salt. Cook for 10 minutes, add the sweetbreads and simmer for 5 to 8 minutes or until they feel firm. Drain them, and while they are warm, peel them and cut them into small pieces ready for use. Retain in the refrigerator.

Soak the mushrooms for a minimum of 1 hour in hot water; drain and dry them, and chop them finely. Set them aside together with the chopped parsley.

Sauté the diced onion in a tablespoon of butter until golden. Set it aside.

1.   To prepare the skins: The dried, salted hog casings are lightly rinsed in water until they soften, then laid out in a bowl. As you fill the skins, you will later make them into sausage lengths. For now, pass water from the tap through the skins to open them up and check for holes or leaks. If you find a leak, consider this a starting point and break the casing there, so the hole will not be in the middle of a filled sausage.

To make the sausage stuffing:
**2.   Make a purée of the chicken flesh in the food processor, adding the salt, egg, egg whites, seasonings and onion as the chicken reduces to a purée.

**3.   Add the cream last, emulsifying only a little more, as the speed will cause the cream to curdle. Transfer the mixture to a bowl and add the chopped sweetbreads, mushrooms and parsley. Chill while preparing the skins on the sausage attachment.

**4.   The sausage attachment consists of a plastic nozzle over which you slide the skins, and a further ring and disc you attach to the mincer (meat grinder) which has large holes so that the stuffing can pass through it readily without being further pulverised. Attach this nozzle firmly into position and then, using a little water on the nozzle to help the skins slip over it easily, place a length of skin over the nozzle and accordion all its length onto the end of the nozzle closest to the mincer. Then pull about 15cm/ 6 in towards you and tie a knot in the end. Using the mincer (meat grinder) in the usual way, feed some of the stuffing into the funnel until it works through the nozzle and out into the skins.

**5.   The skins are now filled as the sausage meat feeds through the tube. Do not attempt to twist them into sausage lengths as the mixture comes into the skins. Concentrate only on gently pulling the skins from the nozzle at an even rate to coincide with the amount of stuffing you need to lightly fill the skins. Do not force too much stuffing in; but at the same time, be aware that they are filling evenly and without air holes.

**6.   Twisting sausages is a complicated procedure. Butchers lay their sausages on a large round platter in a spiral, pat them to thoroughly even out the 'fill', then twist them by turning each sausage in the opposite way to the next one so as to avoid them spiralling and turning on the platter. In the home, the most convenient way is to tie the sausages with string lengths of approximately 15cm/6 in.

7

8

9

7. These sausages have a large amount of cream in them so must be poached while fresh, and then they may be stored, though a maximum of only 3 days is recommended. To poach the sausages, place them in a pot of salted warm water and poach them gently until firm, never allowing the heat to go over 85°C/160°F.(At around 90°C/190°F the skins will burst. It is better to leave them for 10 minutes at around 85°C/160°F than to risk this.) The water should simmer only, not bubble. Allow the sausages to cool so they can be handled and then store them in the refrigerator door until needed, when they can be either grilled, fried, or oven baked.

8. Damien's choice is to peel the skins off when they are cooled and easily handled and toss them in fresh bread-crumbs. If you prefer, the skins may be left on and this step omitted.

9. For Damien, the final choice is to pan-fry the sausages in a little clarified butter until they have a light golden colour. He often serves them beside a purée of spinach — a lovely colour contrast and a beautifully tasty sauce-like accompaniment.

Grilled Guinea Fowl Breast with a Ragoût of Wild Mushrooms

Serves 6
3 guinea fowls (if not available use pheasant or chicken but less cooking time is then required)

The stock:
bones and drumsticks of the fowl
1 small carrot, finely diced
1 small onion, finely diced
½ stick celery, finely diced
bouquet garni
1 teaspoon tomato paste

The stuffing:
6 rashers belly bacon, rind removed
1 teaspoon fresh sage, chopped
(or ½ teaspoon dried)
1 small clove garlic
pepper

The ragoût of mushrooms:
1 tablespoon dried mushrooms per person soaked in boiling water for about 30 minutes. (Ideally a mixture of *bolets jaunes*, morels, *chanterelles, mousserons* and *cornes d'abondance*; if a blend of interesting mushrooms eludes you, try a ragoût of tinned morels.)
6 cloves garlic
1 shallot
½ small carrot, cut in fine julienne
butter to fry
250ml/8 fl oz (Br.)/1 good cup (U.S.) guinea fowl stock (see above)
100ml/3 fl oz(Br.)/scant ½ cup (U.S.) cream, preferably with 45% milk fat (heavy cream)

salt and pepper
dash lemon juice

The day before:
Bone the guinea fowl breasts by removing the thighs and drumsticks in 1 piece. Sever the drumsticks from the thighs; the thigh meat will go into the *crépinette* that is served with the dish; the drumstick flesh is too sinewy, and will be added to the stock. Remove the wingtips by severing the wing at the second joint in, so that only the fleshier joint (the wing butt) is attached to the breast. Now bone out the breasts from the carcass with the wing butt attached. You will have 2 pieces, known as the *suprèmes*, as you would for Chicken Kiev. Leave as much skin on the breasts as possible. Refrigerate, well covered, till the next day.

To make the stock:
Brown all bones and drumsticks well in a little butter. Add the diced vegetables, brown them a little then add the bouquet garni, tomato paste and water to cover. Bring to the boil and reduce to a gentle simmer for 4 to 6 hours, skimming from time to time and replenishing with water if required. Strain, and allow to cool overnight so that the fat can be easily removed. Reduce the next day to a gelatinous glaze, about a fifth of its original volume (about 1 cup).

To prepare the guinea fowl breasts:
Using a food processor, chop the bacon almost to a paste with the garlic and sage. Season with pepper. Gently holding the skin in place at the top of the breast, slide your fingers under the skin from the belly side to create a pocket. Distribute the stuffing between the 6 breasts and stuff it lightly under the skin. Pat the breasts into shape, spreading the stuffing evenly into a thin layer. Pressing with the fingers will help the skin adhere to the flesh at the edges.

The guinea fowl can be char-grilled or cooked on a cast iron griddle (hot plate) or in a frying pan. Brush the breasts with oil. Place them skin side down and cook for about 5 minutes. Then turn and seal them on the underside for

a further 4 minutes. Don't have the heat too high or they may go leathery. When cooked, the breasts should feel just firm to the touch (not hard). Remove them to a board, cover and leave in a warm place for 10 minutes.

To prepare the ragoût of mushrooms:

Drain the soaking mushrooms. In a pan, heat a little butter and sweat the finely chopped shallot, carrot and garlic. Add the mushrooms, cook a moment, then add the guinea fowl stock and the cream. Reduce to sauce consistency, and season with salt, pepper and lemon juice.

To serve:

Carve the breasts diagonally into 3 or 4. Plate 1 breast per person, with a little pile of mushrooms alongside the guinea fowl in its sauce. For added finesse, serve the breast on a purée of celeriac with a *crépinette* of guinea fowl alongside.

The *crépinette* is made by mincing the thigh meat with a little pork, seasoning with herbs, salt, pepper, lemon zest and brandy, and adding an egg. Pat the mixture into rissoles, wrap with caulfat and fry slowly for 10 minutes. (See recipe page 151 for assistance.)

Tartare of Scallops

Serves 6
600g/1 lb 6 oz scallops
150g/good 5 oz salmon roe
2 avocados

The vinaigrette:
3 tablespoons (Br.)/3½ tablespoons (U.S.) olive oil
1 tablespoon lime (or lemon) juice
salt and pepper

The garnish:
chervil or chopped chives

Clean the scallops, removing the coral and any sinew. Chop to a medium dice and dry on paper towelling for 20 minutes. Pat dry, and season well. Dress with sufficient vinaigrette to moisten and bind, but not enough to run. Arrange on individual small plates in a neat mound.

Slice the avocados in 2 and remove the seeds carefully. Peel them, and with the cut sides facing down, slice them thinly enough so that they have sufficient flexibility to curve to form a border around the scallop mound.

Top each mound with a teaspoonful of salmon roe, and garnish with sprigs of chervil or chopped chives.

Grilled Scallops with Cider Vinegar Butter Sauce

Serves 6
1 kg/use 2 lb large scallops
olive oil to grill (broil)
salt and pepper
250g/use ½ lb lamb's tongue lettuce (*mâche*), washed and spin-dried

The cider vinegar butter sauce:
90ml/scant 3 fl oz (Br.)/good ⅓ cup (U.S.) cider vinegar
2 tablespoons (Br.)/scant 3 tablespoons (U.S.) water
30g/1 oz (Br.)/2 tablespoons (U.S.) very finely chopped shallots or onions
200g/7 oz (Br.)/1 scant cup (U.S.) unsalted butter, cut in small pieces
salt and pepper
extra cider vinegar if necessary
finely chopped chives (optional)

Equipment:
cast iron griddle (hot plate)

To prepare the scallops:
Clean the scallops of the little digestive tract on the edge but leave the coral attached. Prick the coral once; it helps stop it from spitting when char-grilled.

To make the sauce:
Reduce the onion, water and vinegar to a moist purée. Over a moderate heat add the butter, whisking all the time to produce a thick creamy sauce. Season and add more vinegar to balance the sauce.

To cook the scallops:
Heat the griddle (hot plate) and brush it with olive oil. Cook the scallops very quickly; they need only be sealed on both sides for about 1 minute. To check, touch each one with your finger; it will be very slightly 'springy'. As they are cooked transfer them to a warmed plate and cover with another plate.

To serve:
Arrange the lettuce on the plates, place the scallops on top and dress them with the sauce. Serve immediately.

Roger Vergé

Moulin de Mougins
Côte d'Azur, France

If there's a strong feeling of Ernest Hemingway in the air in the presence of the bulky frame of white-haired, florid-faced, mustachioed Roger Vergé, let me assure you the resemblance is more than physical. For Vergé, famed chef from the town of Mougins in the South of France, flies his own planes, has in his turn tramped and hunted in Africa, and is to this day a lover of fast cars, which he is seen from time to time racing along the narrow, cliff-hanging streets of his beloved Riviera. He still lives life in the fast lane, running two establishments in France and jetting (with his food) for ten days each month to America where, with his friends Paul Bocuse and Gaston Lenôtre, he runs the French restaurant in Florida's Disney World. He is responsible for an hotel in Rio de Janeiro, has developed a fabulous range of spices with arguably the most interesting and personal combination of flavours ever bottled, has had his first book *The Cuisine of the Sun* translated into four languages, and has won several awards with his second, *Roger Vergé's Entertaining in the French Style*.

And yet this forerunner of modern, innovative French cuisine is quietly spoken, almost shy, and with his gentle smile and warm gaze, Vergé is the true gentleman of the small band of French chefs who have gained international 'star' reputations.

Roger has run the beautiful Moulin de Mougins since 1969. Under previous owners the restaurant had three times gone bankrupt and observers were none too sure Roger Vergé could make it work. With his classical training under the great chef Lucien Diat at the Plaza-Athénée (extraordinarily grand for the tiny village), his years in Africa where he had got used to excitement and adventure working in exotic hotels in Casablanca and Algiers, catering in Zimbabwe, even

giving grand banquets in the jungle, few believed he could settle. Instead, within four years, Roger, with his wife Denise as stylist, front of house and admirable hostess, turned the Moulin into one of the greatest restaurants in France. The Moulin boasts three Michelin stars, and Roger's talents have earned him the coveted Meilleur Ouvrier de France (1972) and a score of 19/20 and four red chef's hats in the Gault et Millau Guide.

A converted 16th-century olive oil mill, the restaurant is situated in the town of Mougins, in the foothills behind the French Riviera. The old mill has been extended, but with a modern, low slung, white stucco charm in keeping with the *mas* design of the Provence area. The many rooms are airy and roomy, with wide-spaced tables covered in white damask, surrounded by high-backed Louis XIII tapestry-covered chairs. The monogrammed glassware and silverware are of only the best quality. The surrounding gardens are wondrously manicured, and you can dine outside on the lawns and terraces. There are flowers everywhere — in the garden beds, on the tables, and in the magnificent free-flowing huge decorations that Denise prepares daily in every nook and cranny of the restaurant.

As for the cooking, Roger has embraced the cuisine of the south as much as he loves its sun and the open air, and the dishes of the Moulin abound with the flavours of the local herbs, olives and tomatoes; updated versions of *estouffades, ratatouilles* and *tapenades*; and the fresh vegetables and fish of this jewel of an area. As one of the leading chefs of the decade of nouvelle cuisine, he has kept his cooking light, flavoursome (more flavoursome in fact that many of his peers) and very much in tune with the daily produce in the markets.

Somewhere along the line (in his spare time?), Roger has managed to spread his charm and share his recipes

Le Blanc de Loup Belle Mouginoise

with others by furbishing the upstairs of his second restaurant, l'Amandier, as a cooking school. Like its big brother, the Moulin, l'Amandier is situated in an old olive oil mill, and the tiny, three storey building with its steep, white stone staircases and old oak doors is quite as beautiful as the grander one and perhaps more romantic. Roger bought the building thinking of making it the family home, but couldn't tear himself away from his modern, more expansive Mediterranean hillside home to move into the cramped streets of the miniscule perched township in the heart of Mougins.

In 1975 he opened l'Amandier, intending it to be a simple, inexpensive restaurant with country charm. Within very little time it gained two stars in the Michelin guide, and startlingly strong recommendations as value for money, and l'Amandier has now assumed its own importance. Roger oversees

it with his craftsman's skill, and there is a very strong presence of Denise's stylish taste. In charge of the cooking school is Roger's second chef, the multi-lingual Alain Pastre, who has spent ten years in the Moulin's kitchen, and manages to do day shifts in the school between his nightly shifts at the Moulin. The programmes vary and include recently instigated professional classes; but most people go for a week at a time, do daytime classes, spend time in the kitchen of the two restaurants, take their midday meals in the school, and their evening meals in the restaurants. All this in some of the most beautiful scenery in the world.

It was at l'Amandier, overlooking the terracotta roofs and the hillsides of Provence, that we filmed the making of one of the summer season's specialities from the Moulin de Mougin's menu, *Le Blanc de Loup Belle Mouginoise*.

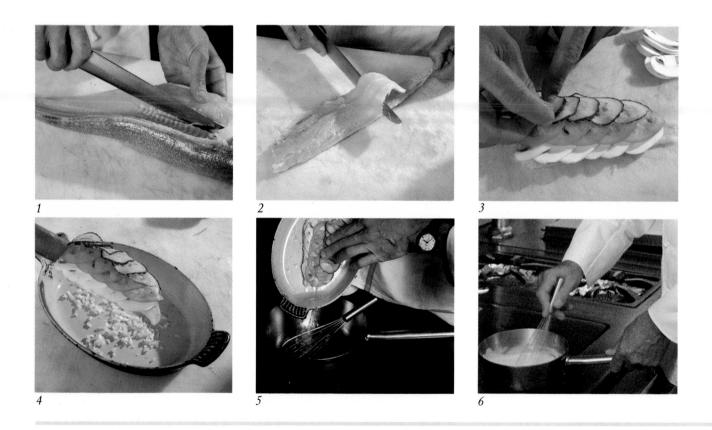

1

2

3

4

5

6

Le Blanc de Loup Belle Mouginoise
Fillet of Sea Bass Belle Mouginoise

Serves 6

6 slices of fish about 1cm / ½ in thick and weighing about 120g/good 4 oz each. Roger most often uses sea bass, the famous *loup* of the Provence area. He also uses *palandre*, known as 'the whiting of the Mediterranean', John Dory (*St. Pierre*), ling, orange roughie or turbot, and in fact most thick-lobed, large, white-fleshed fish are possible substitutes.

3 firm red tomatoes, 325g/¾ lb in all
6 very large champignons (baby mushrooms), as white as possible
2 medium cucumbers, unpeeled
salt and freshly ground pepper
3 tablespoons (Br.)/3½ tablespoons (U.S.) finely chopped shallot or pickling onion
3 tablespoons (Br.)/3½ tablespoons (U.S.) vermouth
5 tablespoons (Br.)/7 tablespoons (U.S.) white wine
chopped chives
3 tablespoons (Br.)/3½ tablespoons (U.S.) strong, jellied fish stock
150ml/good 5 fl oz (Br.)/scant ¾ cup (U.S.) cream, preferably with 45% milk fat (heavy cream)
75g/2½ oz (Br.)/5 tablespoons (U.S.) butter for the sauce, plus a little to grease the baking dish

1. With a very sharp knife, remove the fillets from the fish. If you prefer, the fishmonger can do this for you.

2. Skin the fish. To do this, use the flexible blade of a filleting knife. Hold the very tip of the skin at the tail end with your fingers, slip the knife under the flesh at the tip, and run the knife between the flesh and the skin keeping the blade as flat as possible against the wooden cutting board. When skinned, cut the fillet into individual slices. Each fillet should give you 2 or 3 pieces, depending on its length. If you choose to use rectangular pre-cut fillets pared from larger fish by your fishmonger, request them skinned and start at this point.

3. Plunge the tomatoes into boiling water for 1 minute, refresh momentarily under cold water, then peel and slice them thinly. Finely slice the cucumber and champignons (baby mushrooms) to match. Arrange the 3 vegetables in 3 neat rows along the length of the fish, slices overlapping decoratively. Lightly salt and pepper each preparation.

4. Butter an oven dish large enough to hold the fish. Scatter the chopped shallots in the base of the dish, then place the fish fillets on top. Add the vermouth and wine to the base of the dish, salt and pepper the fish lightly and place in an oven pre-heated to 200°C/400°F for about 4 minutes or until the fish turns a milky white.

Remove immediately lest the vegetables overcook and wither.

5. Remove the fish fillets and keep them warm. Pour the cooking juices into a saucepan and add the fish stock and cream.

6. Reduce the liquids to sauce consistency, whisking vigorously. Boil for approximately 1 minute in all.

7. Incorporate the butter into the sauce to bind and enrich it. Whisk well then add the chopped chives. Check the seasoning and remove from the heat.

8. Sauce the base of the dinner plate. With a small pastry brush paint a little melted butter or cooking juice on the vegetables to give them a sheen.

9. With the aid of an egg-lift, gently place the fish onto the plates in the centre of the sauce.

7

8

9

La Crème de Pois Frais au Curry

Curried Cream of Green Pea Soup

Serves 4

1 onion
1 bunch parsley, preferably Italian parsely rather than the curly leafed variety
1 small head mignonette (soft-leafed, continental-style) lettuce, or half an iceberg (crisp-leafed) lettuce
1 tablespoon curry powder
300g/scant 11 oz (Br.)/2 cups (U.S.) green peas, weighed shelled (may be fresh or frozen)
60g/good 2 oz (Br.)/¼ cup (U.S.) butter
1.5 litres/2½ pints (Br.)/6 cups (U.S.) water, hot from the tap
1 chicken stock cube
4 slices bread
5 tablespoons (Br.)/6 tablespoons (U.S.) cream, preferably with 45% milk fat (heavy cream)
salt and pepper

Chop the onion finely and cook it in half the butter in a saucepan until the onion is transparent, about 7 to 8 minutes. Wash the lettuce, chop it coarsely, and add it to the onion. Let it wilt for 2 or 3 minutes. Add the curry, mixing it in well with a wooden spatula. Add the hot water and pop in the stock cube. Salt lightly (the cube is already salty). Bring to the boil and simmer for 5 minutes. Then add the washed and stemmed parsley and the peas. Do not cover the saucepan, and the peas will stay green.

Meanwhile, cut the crusts off the bread and cut the bread into small cubes. Heat the remaining half of the butter in a frying pan and toss the bread cubes in to fry, shaking the pan so that they brown evenly. Let them drain in a sieve, then put them in a small serving bowl. Keep them warm.

When the peas are cooked, purée the soup to a fine smooth cream in a blender or food processor. Put this back into the saucepan and let it boil once, adding the cream. Check the seasoning and serve in a soup tureen. Serve the croûtons in a separate bowl so they can be added at the table and thus remain crisp.

Les Fleurs de Courgettes aux Truffes

Zucchini (Courgette) Flowers Stuffed with Truffles

An expensive dish to make, but not really difficult with this detailed descriptive recipe.

Serves 6 as a starter

6 small zucchinis (courgettes) with their flowers intact
500g/use 1 lb champignons (baby mushrooms)
1 lemon
6 truffles of 15g/½ oz each (may be canned)
1 tablespoon finely chopped shallots
300g/scant 11 oz (Br.)/1¼ cups (U.S.) butter
5 tablespoons (Br.)/6 tablespoons (U.S.) cream with 35% milk fat (whipping cream)
2 egg yolks
450g/1 lb fresh, tender spinach (English spinach), de-veined; or lamb's tongue lettuce leaves (*mâche*)
a few stalks chervil (optional)
salt and pepper

Several hours in advance, wash the de-veined spinach, or alternatively clip back the stalks of the lamb's tongue lettuce (*mâche*) and wash and dry that.

Trim the tails off the champignons (baby mushrooms). Wash the champignons quickly so they avoid taking in too much water. Chop them finely and sprinkle instantly with lemon juice so they don't blacken. Using a deep frying pan, or *sauteuse*, heat 1 tablespoon butter with the chopped shallot. As soon as it is well heated, add the champignons (baby mushrooms) and stir for 3 or 4 minutes. Salt and then drain immediately through a stainless steel colander. Set any liquid aside for later use. Transfer the champignons to a larger saucepan and on a hot flame stir until any remaining liquid has evaporated. Mix the cream and egg yolks together, add to the champignons and incorporate well. Cook for a further 2 minutes on a high flame, check the seasoning and then remove to a large plate to spread out for cooling.

Drain the truffles, and add any juice to the champignon (baby mushroom) juice.

The zucchinis (courgettes):
Do not wash the flowers unless it is really necessary, but pat them over with tissues to remove any grit. Open up the petals of the flowers and place a scant tablespoon of champignon (baby mushroom) purée inside. Place a truffle in the middle of each and re-form the flower. Arrange the zucchinis (courgettes) carefully onto the rack of a steamer and cover them with a sheet of aluminium foil. 15 minutes before serving, steam them over hot water. Test the cooking to see that the point of a knife or skewer will penetrate; how long it takes will depend on the size of the vegetables.

The sauce:
Reduce the liquid from the truffle juice and champignons (baby mushrooms) until you have only about 3 tablespoons (Br.)/3½ tablespoons (U.S.). Whisk in the butter (it should take about all the remaining 250g/½ lb [Br.]/1 good cup [U.S.]) in the manner of a *beurre blanc*, that is incorporating it bit by bit, whisking all the time, so that it melts and forms an unctuous sauce, rather than allowing it to reach too high a temperature where it would go to the consistency of melted butter. Now salt and pepper the sauce to taste.

To serve:
Spread the raw spinach or lamb's tongue lettuce leaves (*mâche*) over the individual serving dishes. Carefully cut the zucchinis (courgettes) lengthwise with a small knife, without going quite to the flower end, in order to be able to fan out the vegetables for attractive serving. Then pose the zucchinis (courgettes) on the plates, and give each a turn of the peppermill. Coat with the sauce and decorate with a few leaves of chervil as you wish.

Les Fleurs de Courgettes aux Truffes

Cabillaud au Beurre de Champignons

Fresh Cod with Mushroom Butter

Serves 4

4 slices fresh cod weighing approximately 300g/¾ lb each. (You may use, instead of cod, any large, white-fleshed fish, such as John Dory (*St. Pierre*), ling, trevally, barramundi or snapper.)
200g/7 oz (Br.)/1 scant cup (U.S.) unsalted butter
200g/7 oz champignons (baby mushrooms)
juice of ½ lemon
1 bunch of chervil (if unavailable use parsley)
1 sprig of thyme
1 bay leaf
1 pinch cayenne pepper
½ cup dry sherry
salt and pepper
1 tablespoon jellied veal stock or ½ chicken cube
1 sheet of aluminium foil
1 handful rock salt

Pre-heat the oven to 240°C/475°F.

Clean the champignons (baby mushrooms), wash them in cold water containing the juice of ½ lemon, and drain. Set aside 20 round champignon caps without stems. Chop the rest of the champignons and put them aside in an enamelled or stainless steel saucepan.

Separate the leafy parts from the chervil or parsley stems. Salt and pepper the fish and lay it in the middle of the foil on a bed of thyme, bay leaf, and chervil stems. Wrap it well in the foil.

In a roasting pan just big enough to contain the foil package, spread a heavy layer of rock salt, and place the package on top of this. Put the pan in the pre-heated oven for 25 minutes.

While the fish is cooking, pour the sherry over the chopped champignons (baby mushrooms) in the saucepan. Add the

cayenne pepper and boil slowly for 10 minutes. Put the result through a sieve,

pressing the champignons to extract all the juice. Put the juice on to boil again and plunge the 20 reserved champignon caps in it for 2 minutes. Remove them with a skimming spoon and keep them warm in a bowl.

Leave the juice over medium heat, adding veal stock or, if unavailable, ½ chicken cube. Add the butter, cut into small pieces, a little at a time, all the while beating with a wire whisk until the sauce is smooth and creamy. Verify the seasoning and keep warm but do not let it boil.

Remove the fish from the foil and herbs. Spoon some sauce into the bottom of 4 dinner plates. Place the fish on top and add the champignon (baby mushroom) caps as a garnish.

Albert Roux

Le Gavroche
London, England

As far as is known, nobody in France actually died of apoplexy, but when the 1982 Michelin Guide for Great Britain arrived on the bookstands, the presence of three tiny asterisks sitting to the left of the entry for London's fashionable restaurant Le Gavroche must have caused a few cases of heartburn back across the Channel.

Such, of course, is the enormous significance of those asterisks — their potency out of all proportion to their hopelessly understated size — in the world of international gastronomy. And here they were, in their most potent form of all, a cluster of **three**, alongside the name of an English restaurant! A closer look would have reassured the uninitiated: the ultimate accolade of the famous guide, rarely given outside France and certainly never before in Britain, had been awarded to two expatriate French boys. Much better!

From then on press articles all over the world — including an entire page in *Time* magazine — made Le Gavroche and the marvellous Roux brothers responsible for its direction, a name on the lips of everyone even remotely interested in good food.

Michel and Albert Roux were born in the Burgundy area of France, but their contact with England began at a young age. After they both did apprenticeships in pâtisserie, Michel worked at the British Embassy in Paris and Albert at the French Embassy in London. Both then went to work in big aristocratic households where private brigades of chefs were still employed. Albert began at the top — with Lady Astor — and, like Michel, attributes his dedication to perfection to having begun his career where it was not just a cliché to say that 'only the best will do'.

There was always plenty of money for 'the best'. In both the embassies and in the households they had largely a free rein as they entertained top politicians,

bankers, Heads of State — or even just the family and the numerous houseguests who formed part of the habitual lifestyle of the English aristocracy of the period. With enormous budgets and nothing but their own imaginations placing limits on their work their skills were finely honed, and with little of the repetition that would have curbed them in a more restricted restaurant environment. It was truly a unique training. Neither chef had ever worked in a restaurant before they opened their own.

Today the brothers own six restaurants. The most quoted of the four they actually run themselves are Le Gavroche where Albert is responsible for the day-to-day direction, and the beautiful Waterside Inn, where Michel is in charge. The brothers take all major business decisions together, and now run an extremely large empire. Meetings take place in beautiful offices in their grand but highly personal private hotel which adjoins Le Gavroche in the heart of London. Known simply as Forty Seven Park Street, in Mayfair, the 1920s building has an understated wooden and brass entrance; but deceptively this leads into a marble reception hall, and a gracefully curving staircase leads upstairs to fifty-four magnificent, Edwardian-style high-ceilinged suites. These are luxurious, with marble bathrooms, private loungerooms with marble fireplaces, bedrooms with down-filled quilts and remote-control televisions, Joseph Perrier champagne in silver ice buckets by the beds and vases of orchids, courtesy of the management, on the tables.

The hotel is only one element of the Roux brothers' extensive business empire, which ranges through many aspects of the food and service industry — including the pre-cooked, vacuum-packed food division which produces boil-in-the-bag dinners for the domestic gourmet under the absolutely magnificent name of Roux'l Brittania! After a whirl of flak from the media

Souffle Suissesse

at the famous couple selling products in supermarkets, the controversy seems to have settled down, and now food buffs are delighted to have at their command dishes such as Trout Stuffed with Lobster Mousse, Scallop of Salmon with Julienne of Vegetables, Lamb Cutlets with Sorrel Sauce, Navarin of Lamb, Summer Pudding — all of which are current or former favourites of the restaurants themselves.

With all this talk of empire, both men are none-the-less hard-working restaurant chefs, highly visible in their establishments. Albert is pretty well acknowledged as the greater cook of the two, and much more of a classicist than Michel, and there is clearly a difference in their cuisine. Albert is a great *saucier*, and the intensity and flavour of his dishes is legendary. There is always a classic *velouté*, a classic *consommé*, on his menu, a perfectly executed *Mousseline de Homard*, a sauce with cream and morels, or a classic meat dish roasted in its own *jus* with herbs. Michel on the other hand likes to add a touch of the exotic, and it is his dishes that leap from the plate with colour, that bear threads of ginger in the sauce, that are garnished with green hazelnuts or fruits; he who invented the *Feuilletés* of Oysters with Raspberry Vinegar. Albert concentrates on texture, viscosity and flavour. His chefs bring each dish under his eye with the sauce apart, and Albert sauces each plate from the silver saucepots that he checks for seasoning and balances individually. With the finishing touches made by Albert the meals are then taken to the guests.

Lest one feels that the empire has no heir to the throne, Michel's son Alain is following in his father's footsteps with a great love of pâtisserie, and Albert's son Michel, now in his thirties, has already earned great respect and is said to be able to take over either kitchen at any time. Mainly based at Le Gavroche, Michel has had the same painstaking training as the brothers themselves, undertaking a series of 'stages' with confrères in many of the three-star restaurants of France. There will be a dynasty.

The atmosphere of Le Gavroche's famous dining room must not be left undiscussed. With a staircase leading down to walls lined with bottle-green velour, there is an extreme elegance in the dining room. The feeling is warm and highly English. The sitting room up one end, which doubles as a bar or an excellent area to drink an after-dinner cognac, has a fireplace, large club chairs and the sort of couch one sinks into. There is polished woodwork everywhere, including a trolley laden with the best liqueurs, and a huge cigar humidor. A printed cloth hangs to the floor from a table bearing a homely lamp and family album photographs of the brothers personalise the room. It is a wonderfully restful place to wind up the evening in this, the best and most elegant restaurant in London, and one of the great restaurants of the world.

1

2

3

Soufflé Suissesse
Swiss Cheese Soufflé

Serves 4
140g/5oz (Br.)/⅔ cup (U.S.) butter
65g/good 2oz (Br.)/good ½ cup (U.S.) plain (all-purpose) flour
700ml/scant 1¼ pints (Br.)/scant 3 cups (U.S.) milk (Sometimes Albert enrichens the milk by replacing some of its volume with cream)
4 egg yolks
6 egg whites
200g/7oz (Br.)/4 cups (U.S.) grated gruyère and cheddar cheeses, preferably 50% of each
500ml/good ¾ pint (Br.)/2 good cups (U.S.) cream with 35% milk fat (whipping cream)
salt and freshly ground white pepper

Equipment:
4 shallow tartlet moulds greased very well with softened butter

1. Over a low heat melt the butter, add the flour and make a roux, stirring well with a whisk to prevent any lumps. Cook the mixture, stirring continuously, for 2 to 3 minutes. This helps rid it of a flour taste. Remove it from the heat and allow the roux to cool slightly. Bring the milk to the boil, then whisk it into the cooled roux. Return the pan to a high heat, bring it to the boil, stirring all the time, and allow the mixture to cook for 3 minutes. Beat in the egg yolks. Season to taste with salt and freshly ground white pepper. Set aside in the fridge, covered with well-buttered paper to prevent a skin from forming. This way, the soufflé base may be made in advance.

When ready to cook the soufflés, place the cream into an ovenproof pan or large skillet, one that will be presentable at the table (Albert uses copper). Place in the oven to warm but do not boil.

2. Meantime, whisk the egg whites with a pinch of salt till very firm.

3. Fold the egg whites into the soufflé base, incorporating one-third quickly at first then taking care to fold the remaining two-thirds in more gently.

4. Arrange the buttered tartlet moulds on a baking tray. Divide the mixture into 4, and heap it into the moulds, piling them decoratively. Bake in a 200ºC/400ºF oven for 3 minutes until the tops begin to turn golden.

5. Remove from the oven and upend each soufflé in turn into the pan of warmed cream. They will float.

6. Sprinkle with the cheese. There is enough for quite a thick crust. They now look like savoury floating islands. Return to the oven and cook for a further 5 minutes.

To serve:
Serve the soufflés immediately, taking care not to crush them as you serve. Take an ample portion of the creamy sauce. Provide your guests with a spoon and fork.

4

5

6

stock over the chicken. Place the casserole dish over a moderate heat. Bring to a gentle boil. Cover and transfer to cook slowly in a moderate oven(180ºC/350ºF).

To serve:
Arrange the chicken breasts, sliced, and a piece of the leg onto each plate. Spoon the lentils, vegetables and cockscombs (if using) over them and serve.

Tarte des Demoiselles Tatin

Tart Tatin

Serves 4
6 medium dessert apples
juice of ½ lemon
120g/4½ oz (Br.)/⅔ cup (U.S.) butter
200g/good 7 oz (Br.)/1 cup (U.S.) sugar
250g/use ½ lb puff pastry (see recipe page 171)

Equipment:
Deep-frying pan or round heat-proof dish, 26cm/10 in diameter, 7cm/2¾ in deep

To prepare the apples:
Peel, core and halve the apples. Sprinkle with lemon juice and place in the refrigerator.

Evenly grease the base of the frying pan or dish with butter. Cover the bottom of the pan with the sugar, then arrange the apples, rounded side down, on the bottom of the pan.

To prepare the pastry:
On a lightly floured board, roll out the pastry to a circle 3mm/1/8 in thick. Lay the pastry over the apples, allowing an overlap of about 2cm/1 in all around. Trim off the excess with a sharp knife. Leave to rest in a cool place for at least 20 minutes.

To cook:
Set the pan over a high heat for 15 to 20 minutes, until the butter and sugar are bubbling and have become a deep amber colour. With a small palette knife,

Poulet Fermier en Cocotte aux Lentilles

Braised Chicken with Lentils

Serves 6 to 8
2 chickens, farm bred if possible
12 baby carrots
12 baby leeks
18 *lardons* (bite-sized pieces of continental bacon)
50g/scant 2 oz (Br.)/3 tablespoons (U.S.) butter
100g/3½ oz (Br.)/½ cup (U.S.) clarified butter
1 litre/1¾ pints (Br.)/4¼ cups (U.S.) cooked green lentils
6 cockscombs (optional)
thyme flowers
200ml/scant 7 fl oz (Br.)/1 scant cup (U.S.) white wine
450ml/¾ pint (Br.)/2 scant cups (U.S.) veal stock
salt and pepper

The chicken:
With a sharp knife dissect the chicken into breast and leg portions. Divide the drumstick and thigh.

The vegetables:
Clean, wash, trim and cut the carrots and leeks. Cook in boiling salted water. Refresh and set aside for later use. Blanch the *lardons* by placing in cold water and bringing to the boil, then drain them and fry them quickly until they become golden in colour. Set them aside.

To cook the dish:
Season and sauté the chicken pieces in the butter and clarified butter until golden brown but still very uncooked in the middle. Place the chicken in a flameproof casserole dish with the lentils, carrots, leeks,*lardons*, cockscombs (if using), and thyme flowers. De-glaze the pan with the white wine, reduce, add the veal stock, and bring this to the boil. Correct the seasoning and strain the

lift a little of the pastry away from the edges to ensure even cooking. Cook in a 220°C/425°F oven for 20 minutes, until the pastry has risen and is golden.

To serve:
As soon as the tart is cooked, remove it from the oven and invert it onto a plate, taking care not to burn yourself. The pastry will now be on the bottom of the plate, with the apples on top. If any have slipped, push them back into place with a small knife. Albert prefers to serve the tart piping hot.

Jacques Maximin

Le Chantecler, Hôtel Negresco
Nice, France

In the past seven years, Jacques Maximin has turned the Hôtel Negresco into an unlikely Mecca for gastronomy. Unlikely? Definitely — and on many counts. Firstly the grand old Negresco Hotel is a crazy, pompous, mad monument to another era. Sitting along the Promenade des Anglais facing the beachfront, its opulent pre-World War 1 style was designed to cater for the idle rich who wintered in France. Its glittering season was in the winter months when princes, lords, crowned Heads of State and Russian exiles sipped tea in the plush surrounds of the grand salons. The Negresco was, and still is, the archetypal palace hotel, but it fell into decline as war and the Depression marched through Europe, money changed hands, and history rewrote society's codes.

The hotel picked up a second wind in 1952 when its present owners, Paul Augier and his wife, came to the Negresco determined to restore it to its former grandeur. Madame Augier set out to renovate all the rooms with extravagant antiques only and in the most flamboyant style. The exquisite six hundred square metre Savonneries carpet, nowadays valued at three million francs, still sits in the oval grand salon, and antique commodes, canopied beds, gilt mirrors, tapestries, red velvet chairs and plush *toile de joie* wallpapers are the rule. The hotel was declared a national monument in 1976.

Beautiful, but yes, unlikely. Ask any gastronomes and they will assure you a palace is the most unlikely place to find fabulous food.

Manager Michel Palmer set out to change this and in 1977 he spied the twenty-seven-year-old Jacques Maximin, who had recently studied with Roger Vergé and was beginning to make a name for himself at a glitzy restaurant in Marina-Baies-des-Anges. Michel asked Jacques to take over the kitchens of the hotel. As Executive Chef he would be in charge of five dining rooms, the banquet halls, the pâtisseries in all the bars, and even room service of this giant hotel. It was an enormous job, and most doubted it would allow Jacques the time and personal attention to bring Le Chantecler, the main dining room, onto a par with France's top restaurants.

But Jacques's genius had the gastronomes eat their words. Within two years, in a competition run by Gault et Millau magazine, his peers voted him the best chef in France under the age of thirty-five. In his spare time, Jacques sat the gruelling series of technical exams which make up the accreditation Meilleur Ouvrier de France, and in 1979 he attained this title, an honour which he sees as the highlight of his career. The Michelin Guide gave Le Chantecler, the small, select dining room where Jacques concentrates his creativity and genius, first one and then two stars, stopping there, many say, only because in all its history, the Michelin has balked at giving large hotels a third star. In the Gault et Millau Guide however, no one outranks Jacques Maximin. In 1982, they gave him 19½ out of a possible 20, the highest score it had ever given, and four red chefs hats, the red indicating that his cuisine is original and innovative rather than traditional.

If a palace is an unlikely setting for one of France's top restaurants, there's another 'unlikely' for us to consider, and that is the story of Jacques himself. Born in the tiny town of Rang-de-Fliers, hardly more than a railway siding in the north of France and in one of France's most bleak and unimaginative culinary areas, the chances of Jacques becoming France's top innovative chef were most unlikely. Moreover, Jacques has made his name for remodelled and innovative creations based on the cookery of Provence in the south of France.

Le Tian d'Agneau Niçois

He himself says it took him a long while to understand and even like the foods of the south, so different were they from the foods he had grown up with in the north. His was a classical training, mostly in the wealthy beach resort of Le Touquet, where cream and wine reigned high, and cooking hearty dishes with heavily thickened sauces and a heavy fat content was the rule of the region where the cold sat heavily and people ate to keep warm.

When Jacques first escaped the north he went to Paris, where his well-executed classic cuisine won him places in good restaurants, thus allowing him to broaden his horizons. But the turning point in his career came when he went south to work with Roger Vergé. After fifteen years in classical cuisine, Jacques found he had suddenly been liberated and had seen another world. Here was a cuisine without a rule book, a cuisine of a spontaneity that he had never imagined, where the brigade was inventive and every day experimented with new combinations of flavours based on ingredients from the market and combined according to the whims and palates of the young chefs rather than the book of Escoffier from which he had always worked. 'I loved the world of the innovative, the decade of the nouvelle cuisine, where we went to market and exercised our imaginations and let the produce lead us to new and intriguing tastes.'

Jacques found the produce foreign to him however, and he loved the countryside and the way of life before he really took to the tomato, olive oil, and anchovies that were so contrary to his northern upbringing.

Soon, however, he began to research old Provençal texts, looking for the 'true feel' of the area, and from there set out to refine the old dishes for modern, mostly lighter versions with updated presentations. His *tian*, for example was inspired by an old bourgeois recipe which comprised several layers of vegetables weighted down with rice and several kinds of local fish, most prominently sardines and anchovies. This was traditionally cooked for large family gatherings, mounted in large terracotta dishes, each serving at least ten people, topped with breadcrumbs and baked in the oven. Jacques first made a version with scallops, and still presents it this way sometimes, but lately his preferred version is with lamb, which he cooks for us here. Nowadays, Jacques is stirred by Provençal ingredients and works almost entirely with the produce of his new-found region.

1   *2*   *3*   *4*

5   *6*   *7*   *8*

Le Tian d'Agneau Niçois

Tian of Lamb Niçois

Serves 4

3 lamb fillets boned from the larger side (eye) of loin, and trimmed scrupulously to leave no trace of fat or sinew

4 large ripe tomatoes, skinned and seeded

about 125ml/4 fl oz (Br.)/½ cup (U.S.) olive oil

1 small onion, finely chopped

salt, pepper and basil

450g/1 lb fresh spinach (English spinach)

225g/use ½ lb champignons (baby mushrooms)

6 to 8 tablespoons (Br.)/7 to 10 tablespoons (U.S.) butter, including 3 tablespoons (Br.)/4 tablespoons (U.S.) diced, cold butter to finish the sauce

6 to 8 cloves garlic

175ml/6 fl oz (Br.)/scant ¾ cup (U.S.) dry white wine

300ml/10 fl oz (Br.)/1¼ cups (U.S.) lamb stock*

1 tablespoon truffle juice (available canned) (optional)

salt and pepper

*For the lamb stock Jacques places the bones and trimmings in a hot oven until very brown, then transfers them to a pot, covers them with water (1.2 litres/2 pints [Br.]/5 cups [U.S.] is enough for 4), and adds chopped shallots, ½ carrot, 2 tomatoes, garlic, thyme and a bay leaf. He simmers this slowly for 2 hours, reducing the stock by three quarters of its original volume, then strains it. The fat should be skimmed off well before using.

Equipment:

4 metal rings 10 x 1.5cm/4 x 5/8 in deep, like those used in hamburger shops to fry eggs. If unobtainable, it is possible to fabricate these rings using heavy cardboard strips stapled together and covered with foil or, as Jacques advises, heavy plastic 'plumber's' tubing, which can be easily cut with a saw to desired height.

To prepare the vegetables:

Prepare the vegetables in advance. They can be briefly reheated in small saucepans before assembly. The quantity you see in the photo is only for 1 person; the amounts above are for 4 people.

1. Peel and seed the tomatoes. Chop them coarsley and sweat them with a little chopped onion in 2 tablespoons (Br.)/scant 3 tablespoons (U.S.) oil. When the moisture has evaporated and the tomatoes are mashable, salt and pepper them and add some freshly chopped basil for flavour. De-vein the spinach, wash, blanch momentarily, then refesh it and squeeze all the moisture out by pressing between your hands. Chop and sauté in a little butter ready for use. Chop the champignons (baby mushrooms) finely and sauté in a little olive oil until they release their water. Remove with a slotted spoon, season with salt and pepper, and set aside.

To cook the lamb:

2. Season the lamb fillets with salt and pepper just as you go to cook them, then heat 4 tablespoons (Br.)/5 tablespoons (U.S.) butter (not clarified) until hot and sauté the lamb for 4 to 5 minutes, rolling it to brown well, until it is cooked but pink inside. For taste, Jacques adds 6 to 8 cloves of garlic to his cooking pan. When cooked, remove the lamb fillets to a plate and keep warm, covered, in the oven. Save the garlic for later.

3. De-grease the pan and add the white wine. Reduce the wine to a teaspoon or 2 only, stirring up all the sediment, then add 250ml/8 fl oz (Br.)/1 good cup (U.S.) of lamb stock. Add the truffle juice, if using it, then salt and pepper the sauce, giving it one good boil while you stir. Strain over a bowl and return to the pan to keep warm.

4. Reheat the little vegetables in small, separate saucepans. The strained lamb sauce is seen in the background.

To assemble the *tian*:

5. Rub a little of the fried garlic on the base of each plate and place the rings in the centre of each. Put the spinach in the bottom of the rings, in a fine layer, pressing down with a fork to spread and pack them well.

6. Next make a layer of champignons (baby mushrooms) on top of the spinach.

7. Place a layer of tomato purée on top of the champignons (baby mushrooms). Slice the fillets of lamb on the vertical **extremely finely** with a very sharp knife. You should be able to get 2 *tians* out of 1 fillet, but we've included an extra fillet to be sure. You need 12 to 14 slices, which are now spread evenly around the inside of the ring on top of the tomato in a spoke shape.

8. Lift the rings carefully from each plate to reveal the layered *tian*. Jacques says that, as the dish is difficult to serve hot during home-plating, he often puts the lamb into a hot oven for about 30 seconds (no longer, or it greys) before removing the ring. Quickly stir 2 tablespoons (Br.)/scant 3 tablespoons (U.S.) of cold, diced butter into the sauce and spoon around each of the *tians*.

To decorate:

The centre of the *tian* may be decorated with either a slice of truffle, or some diced, skinned tomato and a scattering of chopped chives.

Note for the home cook: For the *tian*, metal rings may be better than plastic or cardboard if you need to place them in the oven while preparing enough for 4. For more than 4 people, you will find cutting and assembling the lamb dish difficult in domestic circumstances. To serve this dish for larger numbers, it may be easier to use a simple, layered effect without the circle. You can do this by spooning each vegetable ingredient one over the other onto the individual plates in a long line and then fanning the finely sliced meat over them in a loose, linear presentation. This may not have as great an effect as Jacques's presentation but I'm sure, unlike Jacques, you don't have a brigade of twenty-seven, many of whom are the finest cooks in the world! Neither do I!

The sauce:

Dice the peeled and seeded tomato into small, neat shapes. Place in a sauceboat and season with salt and pepper. Cover with the olive oil, sprinkle with the shredded basil and allow to sit before serving, preferably in a warm place near the stove, as it is to be served tepid.

To serve:

Cook the fish by bringing the water in the steamer to the boil, covered with the lid. Cook for about 5 to 6 minutes, or until the fish becomes opaque, and test to see that it is cooked to its core. Arrange the vegetables on the plate and place the fish on top. Serve accompanied by a bowl of coarse salt and the tomato and olive oil sauce. The guests help themselves to the salt at the last moment so that it remains crunchy and does not melt into the fish and oversalt it.

Salade Surprise
Surprise Salad

Serves 4 as a starter
1 kg/use 2 lb (about 32) yabbies or freshwater crays, cooked, carcasses peeled away and their intestines removed. You may substitute Moreton Bay bugs, sea cicadas, marrons or large prawns.
1 long carrot of medium thickness
4 large tomatoes, as red and ripe as possible, peeled, seeded and diced
100g/3½ oz beans

The vinaigrette:

6 tablespoons (Br.)/7 tablespoons (U.S.) walnut oil
2 tablespoons (Br.)/scant 3 tablespoons (U.S.) red wine vinegar
1 teaspoon French mustard
salt and pepper

The garnish:

150ml/¼ pint (Br.)/scant ¾ cup (U.S.) cream, preferably with 45% milk fat (heavy cream)
juice of 2 lemons
salt and freshly ground black pepper
sprig chervil or basil

Truîte de Mer au Gros Sel
Ocean Trout with Flaked Sea Salt

Developed as a variant of the famed classic Beef in Coarse Salt, Jacques first invented this dish using Atlantic salmon, which may be substituted for the ocean trout.

Serves 4
The vegetables:

1 carrot
1 cucumber
1 turnip
1 zucchini (courgette)
100g/4 oz (Br.)/½ cup (U.S.) green beans, topped and tailed
4 slices ocean trout or salmon of about 150g/6 oz each, cut from the fillets of large fish
salt and freshly ground black pepper

The sauce:

2 tomatoes, peeled and seeded
250ml/8 fl oz (Br.)/1 good cup (U.S.) olive oil
1½ to 2 tablespoons shredded basil leaves

The garnish:

Flaked sea salt: serve in a small bowl with a teaspoon. Rock salt is coarser and, if you use it, would benefit from a few pulse actions of the food processor.

To prepare the vegetables:

Peel the carrot, cucumber and turnip and leave the zucchini (courgette) unpeeled. Cut these vegetables into 2cm/1 in strips and boil each in turn until tender, refreshing them quickly under cold water. Drain them, combine them, and strew over the rack of a steamer.

The fish:

Season the fish and arrange on the steamer rack over the vegetables.

fresh green salad leaves, of whichever type is seasonal: lamb's tongue lettuce (*mâche*), curly endive (inner, yellow leaves only), Belgian endive (witloof), etc., washed and well dried

Equipment:
4 metal or plastic rings 10 x 1.5cm deep/4 x 5/8 in (see equipment note for *Le Tian d'Agneau Niçois* above)

To prepare the vegetables:
Peel the carrot and with a potato peeler or professional mandolin, cut long fine strips the length of the carrot. You will need about 8 slices. Plunge into boiling salt water for about 1 minute to soften them, then refresh under cold water and set aside on paper towelling to drain well.

Chop the diced tomato very finely, then place into a fine strainer and set over a bowl to allow the juices to run off.

Trim the beans, string them and cook in boiling salted water until tender but still a little crunchy. Refresh in cold water, halve them, then set aside.

Make a vinaigrette with the oil, vinegar and mustard. Season to taste with salt and pepper.

To assemble the salad:
Place a ring mould in the centres of the 4 serving plates. Using 2 lengths of carrot per person, dip them momentarily into the vinaigrette, then wind them around the internal wall of the rings, trimming anything overhanging.

Mix the yabbies (freshwater crays) or chosen seafood with the beans in a bowl, and moisten with vinaigrette. Season with salt and pepper, then lift carefully with a slotted spoon so as not to take excess moisture with them, and pack the mixture firmly into the ring mould. Pressing down, make sure there is just a very fine distance remaining between the top of the salad and the rim of the mould, to top with tomato.

Spread a fine layer of tomato over the top of the salad, using a metal palette knife to smooth the top. Leave the moulds for about 10 minutes to allow any juices to run off; mop these up carefully, then, just before going to the table, carefully lift off the ring moulds.

To serve:
Season the cream with the salt, pepper and lemon juice and spoon a couple of tablespoons around the edge of each salad. Decorate with a few leaves of your chosen greens, and perhaps a sprig of chervil or basil on top.

Jean-Pierre Lemanissier

Ma Maison
Los Angeles, U.S.A.

Some great names are automatically associated with restaurants, and the name 'Terrail' is now so famous on two continents, one has to say, 'Which Terrail?' On one side of the world there is Claude Terrail, whose spectacular three-star restaurant La Tour d'Argent in Paris has celebrated its 400th birthday. At the same time, Claude's nephew Patrick is an even more recognisable name to the American population, where his famous Ma Maison has, since 1973, been **the** dining place of Hollywood stars, food lovers, name droppers and socialites alike.

Patrick is perhaps the consummate restaurateur. Having grown up in the business with his family in France, he was sent to Cornell University's Hotel and Restaurant School in the United States, the family having had always believed the English language to be an imperative in the trade. But Patrick decided to make his career then and there and since the early sixties, he has worked his way through some of the most prestigious restaurants in the States, including The Four Seasons and El Morocco in New York. For a while he taught his trade at the New York Community College, where he was Assistant Professor to the Hotel Division, and then started a business in New York. When this was bought out by a larger company, he became Assistant to the President and later worked his way through the system in a large hotel chain that saw him do duty in Tahiti and Africa. Returning to the west coast of America, he finally felt ready to go out on his own, and successfully built Ma Maison up to become a restaurant to the stars, counting among his clients Orson Wells, George Segal, Ryan O'Neil, Burt Reynolds, Jack Lemmon and a host of other celebrities.

Decorated by the French Government in recognition of his ambassadorial work for French cuisine, Patrick also became a provincial celebrity in Los Angeles when he invented, way back in 1974 in honour of Bastille Day, the annual Waiters Race on Melrose Avenue. The race has taken on such an identity in the community that the Mayor has declared July 15th the official Waiters and Waitresses Day, and the race now donates its proceeds to charity every year.

Probably the dressiest restaurant in a town where people are out to flaunt their fame and wealth, Ma Maison has a glittering reputation and a glamour that is hard to find elsewhere. The cuisine is French imported, the chef French imported, and the remarkable Patrick — more extroverted and more visible than his uncle Claude — oozes Gallic charm in his pin-striped suit, waistcoat and red-carnationed lapel as he pulls back a chair, seats his guests, lifts his hand in the air for a waiter and generally commands all eyes as host-proprietor of his establishment.

Patrick has no doubt that French cuisine is the great cuisine of the world. However, he is something of an innovator. He has always favoured the use of local products and so encouraged his former chef, the famed Wolfgang Puck to expand his repertoire. Since 1984, French-born Jean-Pierre Lamanissier has been Patrick's Executive Chef, and together they have continued to break from the classic cuisine. Born in the north of France, Jean-Pierre did much of his training in Paris before he joined the celebrated Connaught Hotel in London as *Chef de Partie*. After a couple of years there, and a couple more with Paul Bocuse gaining experience at the highest level, he was given the opportunity to migrate to the United States, as Chef for L'Ermitage in Los Angeles.

Since joining Ma Maison, both Jean-Pierre and Patrick have together concentrated on perfecting lighter, *cuisine du marché* style recipes, for which Ma Maison

Duck and Artichoke Salad

is now known. 'The restaurant is open lunch and dinner,' explains Patrick. 'We get a lot of women for lunch, and they very much appreciate eating light dishes. Light salads with local produce are ideal luncheon dishes; and everything must be very visual, for people do so love to talk about food.' 'We don't change every day,' adds Jean-Pierre, 'but we recycle, and use our style to create effects from the marketing that comes in.'

In November 1985, Patrick decided to close the familiar Melrose Avenue premises, and recycle something even more impressive — the whole restaurant. Having felt for a long time that his first premises were becoming a little *passé*, he embarked on a project which he thought would bring Ma Maison into the 1990s. Dispatching Jean-Pierre to Tokyo on sabbatical as Executive Chef for Uncle Claude's Tokyo branch of La Tour d'Argent, Patrick started negotiating with the developers of the new Sofitel, the famous international French hotel group, in Los Angeles. As a result the whole complex is now known as Ma Maison Sofitel (the first time Sofitel has extended its name to capitalise on an entity outside their own company) and Ma Maison, the restaurant, is housed in an annexe alongside the hotel as its foremost dining room.

The former restaurant had not been built as a restaurant, and it was with great excitement that Patrick set out to design his ideal premises. He settled on an elegant version of a French inn. There is a spacious bar with a plastered ceiling with wooden beams, and French country décor which is warm and friendly; and from the bar, two steps lead down into the restaurant, a large room with a series of French windows overlooking two tiers of flowers. High-backed chairs, a green carpet and potted trees bring the garden setting indoors, and a sliding roof, touched off at the push of a button, highlights this even further when the weather is on their side.

Jean-Pierre, back from Tokyo, has returned to lead the brigade and Patrick is set to recapture and enrapture his old audience. Ma Maison is well and truly back in business.

The dishes that we feature for you here are perfect for summer dining and at the same time reminiscent of the lighter, innovative style both Patrick and Jean-Pierre love. From the hand of Jean-Pierre Lemanissier — four summer salads with a difference.

To Prepare Artichoke Bases:

  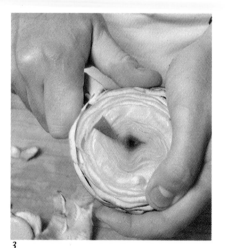

1　　　　　　　*2*　　　　　　　*3*

Duck and Artichoke Salad

Serves 4
2 whole ducks, large breasted
(about 2kg/4½ lb each)
salt and pepper
light soy sauce
4 artichokes
2 ripe avocados, peeled, cored and
sliced
4 large white mushrooms, sliced
2 romaine lettuces, trimmed and
washed, cut into bite-sized pieces

The dressing:
2 tablespoons (Br.)/scant 3 tablespoons
(U.S.) Dijon mustard
4 tablespoons (Br.)/5 tablespoons
(U.S.) sherry wine vinegar
2 shallots, minced
8 tablespoons (Br.)/⅔ cup (U.S.) salad
oil
salt and pepper

To prepare the ducks:
Season the ducks with salt and pepper.
Roast them in a preheated 220ºC/425ºF
oven for 20 minutes or until medium
done, then transfer them to a bowl and
marinate them in light soy sauce for 3
to 4 hours. Set aside.

To make the dressing:
In a bowl, combine the mustard, vinegar and shallots. Slowly whisk in the
oil. Season with salt and pepper to taste.
Set aside until needed.

To prepare the artichoke bases:
1. Snap or cut the stalk back to the
base. Trim or tear off the outer leaves.
Cut the leaves off just above where the
base will be, i.e. discard nearly two-thirds
of their height.

2. With a small knife, pare back any
tougher (outer) parts of the leaves until
the tender flesh area of the base is completely exposed.

3. Turn the base over in your hand
and pare down the left side until the
choke (hairy section) is just visible. Do
not attempt to remove the choke now.

4. Place each artichoke base in a pot
of acidulated water while peeling the
others, otherwise the artichokes will
tend to discolour quickly.

5. To further protect the colour, the
artichoke bases are cooked in a *'blanc'*
(water into which has been whisked 1
tablespoon plain [all-purpose] flour).
Cook until tender then drain.

6. The choke (hairy part) has now
softened and is easily removed by either
pulling with the fingers or scooping
with a melon baller or knife.

Note: Artichoke bases are ideal for salads,
garnishes or as vegetable 'containers' for
cooked dishes, particularly seafood.

To make the salad:
Cook the prepared artichoke bases in
boiling water with a little bit of flour
whisked in. This is called a *'blanc'* and
is used as a technique for preserving the
colour. Cook until tender. Allow to cool
and slice.

Fan out slices of artichoke, avocado and
mushroom on the border of the serving plates. Toss the lettuce with dressing. Place a mound of salad decoratively in the centre of each plate as in the
photograph.

Cook the breasts and legs (optional) over
a griddle (hot plate) skin side down,
until crisp. Slice and arrange them
decoratively over the salad. Coat with
the remaining dressing.

4

5

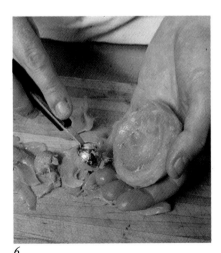
6

Chicken Breast Salad Stuffed with Foie Gras

Serves 4
4 chicken breasts
4 x 30g/1 oz strips foie gras
salt and pepper
use 1 litre/2 pints (Br.)/5 cups (U.S.)
chicken stock
2 Belgian endives, cut into 5mm/¼ in
slices
1 radicchio or salad greens, washed,
trimmed and cut into bite-sized pieces

The dressing:
2 tablespoons (Br.)/scant 3 tablespoons
(U.S.) Dijon mustard
4 tablespoons (Br.)/5 tablespoons
(U.S.) sherry wine vinegar
2 shallots, finely chopped
8 tablespoons (Br.)/⅔ cup (U.S.) salad
oil
salt and pepper

Butterfly the breasts of chickens. Season with salt and pepper. Place a piece of foie gras in the centre and roll the chicken to enclose the stuffing. Wrap each breast with plastic wrap and form it into a tube shape. Be sure to roll tightly to secure the stuffing. Poach the wrapped chicken in chicken stock for about 10 minutes. Transfer to a plate and cool. Set aside.

To make the dressing:
In a bowl, combine the mustard, vinegar and shallots. Slowly whisk in the oil. Season with salt and pepper to taste. Set aside.

In a bowl, combine the prepared endives and radicchio or salad greens. Toss with dressing.

Arrange the salad attractively on serving plates. Carefully unroll the poached stuffed chicken, slice it into *rondelles* (round slices) and arrange on top of the salad.

Asparagus in Red Wine Dressing

Serves 4
1kg/use 2 lb asparagus
4 thick chives, or alternatively a slice of
the green part of a spring onion or leek

The red wine dressing:
½ bottle red wine, preferably
burgundy
500ml/good ¾ pint (Br.)/2 good cups
(U.S.) mayonnaise (about ¾ quantity
of the recipe below)

The mayonnaise:
2 egg yolks
1 good tablespoon Dijon mustard
4 tablespoons (Br.)/5 tablespoons
(U.S.) red wine vinegar
500ml/good ¾ pint (Br.)/2 good cups
(U.S.) salad oil
salt and pepper

Peel the stem part of the asparagus. Cut it to even lengths, then blanch it in boiling water until tender, about 5 to 7 minutes. Allow it to cool. Divide the asparagus into 4 batches and tie it with a blanched chive or a slice of spring onion or leek, to form bundles. Reserve.

To make the mayonnaise:
In a bowl, combine the egg yolks, mustard and vinegar. Stir until well blended. In a slow steady stream, whisk in the oil until the mixture emulsifies and thickens. Season.

To make the red wine dressing:
In a saucepan, reduce the red wine until it becomes very syrupy and reduced. Whisk into the prepared mayonnaise.

Coat the serving plates with red wine dressing. Arrange an asparagus bundle on each, over the dressing. Garnish with tomato wedges and carrot flowers.

Snails in Tomatoes

Serves 4

32 snails, drained of brine from the can
32 cherry tomatoes
60g/2 oz (Br.)/¼ cup (U.S.) unsalted butter
1 clove garlic, crushed
salt and pepper
4 bunches spinach (English spinach)

The curry sauce:
1 chicken carcass, cut into pieces
1 onion, thinly sliced
1 clove garlic, crushed
2 shallots, finely chopped
1 branch lemon grass, chopped
1½ tablespoons (Br.)/2 tablespoons (U.S.) roasted coriander seeds, pulverised
pinch of pepper
1 to 2 dried red chillies
pinch of cumin
pinch of nutmeg
pinch of cinnamon
250ml/8 fl oz (Br.)/1 good cup (U.S.) beef stock
250ml/8 fl oz (Br.)/1 good cup (U.S.) cream, preferably with 45% milk fat (heavy cream)

To make the curry sauce:
In a saucepan, sauté the pieces of chicken carcass. Add the onion, garlic, shallots, lemon grass and spices. De-glaze with brown stock and reduce until it begins to thicken. Then add the cream and continue to reduce until the desired consistency. Strain and keep warm.

The cherry tomatoes:
Cut off the top quarter of the tomatoes and scoop out the insides (core and seeds). Reserve the tops and bases. In a sauté pan, melt the butter over a high heat. Sauté the snails and garlic for 1 to 2 minutes. Season with salt and pepper.

Place a snail inside each cherry tomato and garnish with the reserved tomato tops. Trim and wash the spinach. Steam and drain off the excess liquid.

Spoon the spinach onto serving plates and arrange the stuffed tomatoes on top. Coat them with warm curry sauce.

Jane Grigson

Author
Wiltshire, England

I s it from *Food with the Famous* that we learn most about renowned English cookbook author Jane Grigson, or is it her highly acclaimed *Vegetable Book*, *Fruit Book*, or the first cookery book she ever wrote, *Charcuterie and French Pork Cookery*?

Perhaps the greatest thing about Jane Grigson's books, is that every time you read **anything** she writes, you learn a little more about her. This may seem an obvious statement but, to anyone who has reviewed as many cookbooks as I have, the deploringly sad thing is that very few of them reveal anything at all about the author.

Jane Grigson, on the other hand, imparts in her writing not only her personality but a little as well of her poet's soul. I can think of only about six modern-day cookbook authors working in English who might have been literary figures even if they had not chosen to write about food. M.F.K. Fischer, Joseph Wechsberg, Richard Olney and Madeleine Kamman are among them, but Elizabeth David and Jane transcend them all, and have surely influenced more chefs and food buffs than any others. Undoubtedly, many readers would hotly dispute other personal favourites. Fortunately, I'm not available for argument.

Jane Grigson is above all a writer, and almost incidentally — as she describes it, almost accidentally — a food writer. Having taken out a degree in English at Cambridge University in 1949, Jane then worked in art galleries, publishers' offices and as a translator. In fact she earned her first literary prize as a translator: in 1966, she shared the John Florio Prize (with Father Kenelm Foster) for her translation of Beccaria's *Of Crime and Punishment*. Married to poet Geoffrey Grigson, Jane would undoubtedly have continued to share his more literary environment had it not been, as she recounts, for two things.

One, the Grigsons found themselves proud owners of a charming, rural, thatched-roof, farmhouse with a 17th-century kitchen of overpowering presence. Picture it — it is just as one would imagine Jane Grigson's kitchen. It has thick-stoned walls (one with the date 1642 blithely etched near the window) and a polished flagstone floor, warm and brown, and of course slightly uneven. A small window carved into the wall leaves just enough depth for a wooden bench which is aptly placed for gazing into the delightful English cottage garden. The adjoining pantry has a low-slung roof and wooden beams and once served to make Wiltshire cheese. Jane now hangs her hams there to cure; beneath them garlic hangs drying and a basket of shallots, piled high to last to the next season, rests nearby in the cool, airy environment. The walls of the kitchen are lined with bookshelves, full of Jane's works and their endless editions in countless languages.

But the kitchen is not the only room in which you'll find books. From the front entrance throughout the house, books are stacked high. In the office, where the typewriter is at the ready, books and magazines are piled on the floor, on stools, on sideboards and along the walls. There are more books on the table in the hall — today's haul — and in amongst the collection of plates that lines the walls and cupboards of one of the three annexes to the kitchen. One senses a path between the typewriter and kitchen, and that this path is the driving force in Jane's house.

But we are never far from the main kitchen and, indeed, the kitchen that dictates Jane's life is the gravitational centre of the house. An iron stove, converted to oil, and with three ovens, is the predominant method of cooking and for Jane will always be the chosen one; although a tiny old-model

Take One Duck . . . Confit of Duck Legs, Duck Neck Sausage

gas stove now sits alongside. A huge oak table dominates the centre of the room — with stools ready to be pulled up by those involved in the daily activities that spring so vitally from this area. One imagines that most of what goes on in this house takes place in the kitchen, that no one lasts in the loungeroom very long, and that only the garden may come in second as Jane's favourite place for harbouring her friends.

The second thing that Jane says influenced her strongly in her chosen profession is her overwhelming love of France. She and Geoffrey bought a little house in the Touraine area along the Loire many years ago, and have annually spent the summer months there; longer when Jane is researching or writing about France. Always instilled with a love and respect for good food, a fact she attributes to her North-East England upbringing, France broadened her interest and her curiosity.

It was due to the frequency of her trips to France that a publisher asked Jane if she could gather information for a book on French *charcuterie*, and although she says she was most dubious at being able to succeed — even to understand the procedures — she thus wrote her first book on food. She still attributes much of its success to the fact that she was a learner herself and therefore able to guide and lead the home cook to master the art of pâtés, sausage-making etc, instead of being blinded by its technical details.

And so Jane followed her *charcuterie* book with the many others that have made her famous — *Good Things*, the *Vegetable Book, Food With the Famous,* the *Fruit Book, English Food, European Cookery* — and the myriad of articles, most often for the London newspaper, the *Observer,* to which she has penned her name.

Like so few writers, Jane talks to you, cajoles you, amuses you, enlightens you, even scolds you. She walks you through orchards, French market places, the ports of Portugal, or she sits you at the table of famous writers of another era. Her research is formidable, but the facts she slips into her writing are never heavy and academic, rather snippets of insight, anecdotal and dropped lovingly to help her readers uncover with her the thrill of even quite familiar sights and sounds and smells. I remember instantly her introduction to the lemon in the *Fruit Book.* 'A pleasure Northerners never forget is a first proof that lemons (and oranges) actually grow on trees — a first sight, somewhere around the Mediterranean, of actual lemons hanging from actual lemon trees, in a lemon orchard...¡ As an Australian who takes for granted the lemon tree in every backyard — try to convince an Australian to part with real money to buy a lemon — I suddenly saw lemons afresh. Instantly, they became a precious object.

With simple phrasing, Jane can astound you. Her books are a goldmine of information, warmth, wit, love, and commonsense. Just like her.

1 Jane Grigson, *Jane Grigson's Fruit Book*, Michael Joseph, London, 1982, p. 205.

TAKE ONE DUCK...

In the interests of good cooking and lest the commonsense law of good housekeeping, 'thou shalt not waste', be forgotten, Jane takes you step by step through the skilful sectioning and preparation of duck, giving recipes for using every section of the beautiful bird. From making duck breast ham, to stuffing the boned neck into a sausage, preserving the legs under duck fat (a French classic process known as *confit*), and rendering the fat for preserving the remaining parts of the body if you choose to *confit* the whole duck, Jane shows you why she is one of the most read, most revered and most remarkable cooks in the world.

Tricks and 'trucs'. An introductory note by Jane:

Buy large ducks if you can, about 1.8 to 2 kg/4 to 4½ lb in size and, if you're to go to the trouble of putting these preserved dishes down, spend the day at it relaxedly and work with three ducks at a time to make it worthwhile.

The *confit* keeps for six months in the fridge, providing it is well sealed from the air. Once cured, the hams can theoretically be kept also, but the fridge dries them more and more with time, and they are more tender if consumed within two to three weeks. The sausage can be kept in the fat with the *confit* and confined from the air to make it last, but is probably better eaten in the week that follows.

In a way, like all curing these days, what we are doing here is cosmetic, and for pleasure rather than for its former purpose, storage. When I go to the South-West of France, from whence these dishes come, I find them all rather overcooked, and a little stringy and salty. I prefer a light cure. Nowadays, when it's no longer a question of preservation, we can afford to cure more lightly for a better technique. Our result will give a sort of Bayonne ham texture to the flesh.

The ducks:
1 or, for preference, 3 fleshy, well-fed ducks of about 1.8 to 2kg/4 to 4½ lb.

The ducks that Jane used are the British Aylesbury ducks. You may use the Pekin, the Muscovy, or the Canard de Barbarie, Rouennaise or de Challans, depending on availability in your area. The Muscovy is evidently going to yield a more fullsome product, since the species is a larger, more fleshy variety. The ducks must be bought as intact as possible, and thus from a poultry merchant rather than the supermarket. Make sure the full length of the neck is left on the bird.

For the breast hams:
For each duck:
1 tablespoon coarse sea salt
¼ teaspoon thyme
½ small bay leaf
½ teaspoon coriander seeds
½ teaspoon black peppercorns

For the *confit* of duck legs:
For each duck:
2 large cloves garlic

½ tablespoon sea salt
1 teaspoon pepper
1/8 teaspoon grated nutmeg
1 sprig thyme
½ bay leaf, crumbled
about 500g to 1kg/1 to 2 lb goose fat, duck fat, or lard. The goose or duck fat may be bought canned.
extra bay leaf, extra sprig thyme

For the duck neck sausage:
For each duck:
150g/6 oz high quality sausage mince (sausage filling)
the duck's liver
salt and pepper
perhaps a few grains fennel

To bone and apportion the duck:
1. First take off the legs for the *confit*. Cut through the flesh with a small pointed knife to release the legs. Snip the tendons around the hip joints with scissors to free them, then remove the legs.

2. With the breast side up, and using the scissors, starting at the fleshy part of the neck, make a V-shaped cut, snipping through the fatty flesh until you can see the neck bone. (You may need to snip the oesophagus if it is still in there, although mostly it has already been removed by the merchant.) Remove the neck of the duck at its longest possible length by cutting it off right down near the breastplate.

3. Pull the neck bone out lengthwise from its skin without piercing the skin any further. Save the head (if it's on) and the neck for the stockpot.

1

2

3

4

5

6

7

8

9

10

11

12

13

14

15

4. Removing the breasts for the ham comes next. Using a pointed knife, cut down the length of the breastplate. Scrape the meat from the carcass to release the breast from the bone. Most people find it easier to turn the bird around to repeat the action for the second breast on the other side. Remove the wishbone from the breasts.

5. If you're a respectful cook like Jane, you will remove the 2 little breast fillets that fall loose from the larger breast fillets. Together with the little 'oysters' that nestle in the hip joints, these can be roasted with the wings, or pan fried as dinner for one, if you choose to put the wings into the stockpot. For Jane they are a delicacy with a small salad of lamb's tongue lettuce (*mâche*).

6. All bits, including as much of the fat (for the *confit*) as possible, are saved. The line-up of the end result is in this photo — and to make your efforts worthwhile, should be multiplied by 3 ducks. The remaining bared carcass is in the background, with the wings and offcuts, ready for the stockpot — a no less important result of our work here. Back row left stands the fat, later to be rendered for the *confit*.

To make the breast ham:
7. First make a curing salt, which is a combination of 1 tablespoon coarse salt; ¼ teaspoon fresh thyme, crumbled; ½ small bay leaf, crumbled; ½ teaspoon coriander seeds, crushed; ½ teaspoon black peppercorns, crushed. For 3 ducks, make up a little bowl of this by tripling the quantities. Combine all these ingredients, and rub them into the breasts — approximately 1 flat teaspoon in all per side of breast. Rub the mixture into the skin side as well as the flesh side, place the breasts in a dish and leave in the refrigerator overnight — from 12 to 18 hours.

8. The next day, brush off the excess, mop off any brine that has wet them, and lay in a doubled muslin cloth. Fold the cloth over the breast lengthwise, tuck up the end and fix it with a toothpick.

9. Knot some string or rope around it, and hang in a cool, dry place that allows the air to circulate. The refrigerator is fine in hotter climates, but tends to dry it. Beware of humidity and great heat; find a cool, airy place, and hang for 5 to 8 days.

10. After the period of hanging, carefully unwrap the duck ham and cut finely. It may be cut either lengthwise or widthwise, depending on which way suits your plate. In our picture Jane has served it with a salad of curly endive, lamb's tongue lettuce (*mâche*) and mango. The fat may be retained or pared off as you will. The longer the curing time, the fat loses its whiteness and becomes less appealing.

The confit of duck legs:
11. You may add the first (fatter) of the wing joints, the *gésier* (the opened-out stomach, grains removed), and even the breasts if you choose to *confit* a whole duck. First rub the parts to be preserved with garlic, and then in salt and spice. These are stronger spices than those used for the hams, as they will have less time to give up their flavour. Combine in the ratio of ½ tablespoon sea salt, 1 teaspoon pepper, 1/8 teaspoon grated nutmeg, 1 sprig thyme, ½ bay leaf, and mix them all together. Rub in well and leave to stand for about 8 hours.

12. Render all the bits of fat and lard you've saved by putting them in a saucepan on slow heat. If you have saved a little duck fat from the prior roastings of duck (it keeps in the refrigerator for months), then you can add some of this in order to have extra depth to help cover the meat to be preserved. Or you may top up with goose fat, which can be bought canned. (You'll need nearly a kilo in all.) It does not matter if there are some bits of fat not perfectly rendered when you commence, as everything will be strained later.

After the 8-hour maceration, lower the duck legs into the fat. Bring back to a simmering point, add an extra bayleaf and a sprig of thyme, and the remains of the garlic with which you rubbed the legs. Leave to simmer very slowly for an hour. Check they are cooked by piercing with a skewer.

13. Strain a layer of fat into sterilised jars or earthenware crocks. Put 2 or 3 bits of wooden skewer in the base so that the meat does not touch the bottom. Put the legs in 2 by 2 and strain the fat over them to cover. Let the whole thing cool until set, then pour an extra layer of fat over the top. Store the jars in the refrigerator.

To serve:
Stand the jars in basins of hot water until the pieces can be extracted with tongs. Brown and serve hot with fried apple slices, and fried potatoes (see photograph). Or drain them and serve them cold with a salad and spiced apple or orange.

The duck neck sausage:
14. Make up a filling by combining 150g/6 oz high quality sausage mince with the duck's liver, chopped. Any loose bits of meat that have come up during the boning may also be chopped into the mixture. Season with salt and pepper, and if you like it, a few grains of fennel. Stuff the necks without making the mixture too firm.

15. Close the ends with toothpicks, or stitch them with a needle and cotton. Don't bother to plump it up; leave a natural neck shape. You have a choice now to cook the necks with the duck's legs, which makes them much more fatty, or to bake them with a little goose or duck fat or lard in a moderate oven for 30 to 45 minutes, until browned slightly. Drain, cool, and slice on the bias. They can be served with other *charcuterie*, or as part of a mixed hors d'oeuvre. They can also be served hot.

Take One Duck . . . Breast Ham

Michael Smith's Buttered Oranges

Michael Smith, from Yorkshire, has studied the appearance as well as the flavour of food from the past. He did the food for *Upstairs, Downstairs*, a very popular British television series of life in an Edwardian family. He is a popular writer and restaurateur, and a great friend of Jane's. Jane often makes this dish, which is based upon a recipe which can be found in Michael's book *Fine English Cookery*.

Serves 6

8 sweet oranges, preferably seedless
5 egg yolks, lightly beaten
60g/2 oz (Br.)/scant ⅓ cup (U.S.) sugar
1 teaspoon triple-distilled rosewater
110g/4 oz (Br.)/8 tablespoons (U.S.) unsalted or lightly salted butter, chopped into small chunks
150ml/¼ pint (Br.)/scant ¾ cup (U.S.) cream with 35% milk fat (whipping cream), whipped
large piece glacéed (candied) orange peel, chopped

Cut 1 end off 6 oranges and keep aside to be used as lids in the presentation. If desired you can cut a decorative pattern into the orange rind of the lid, starting about 2cm/1 in from the edge.

Remove the pulp from the orange carefully so as not to break through the skin; a teaspoon does the job quite well. Grate the zest of the remaining two oranges and squeeze their juice. In a saucepan place the juice of the oranges, and grated zest. Beat in the egg yolks and add the sugar. Place the saucepan

over a pan of simmering water. Stir continuously until the mixture has become very thick.

Rapidly cool the custard to tepid. Placing the pan in a bowl of ice cubes and a little water will help. Stir occasionally to equalise the temperature.

When cool, stir in the rosewater and the softened butter pieces. It is important that the custard is not too hot as it will melt the butter rather than allow it to blend into the custard. Beat the custard mixture until it is smooth and cold. Fold in the whipped cream which has been beaten to soft peaks.

Chill, add the chopped glacéed (candied) orange peel. Place the chilled custard into a pastry bag fitted with a large star nozzle. Pipe the custard into the prepared orange shells and replace the lid at a jaunty angle on top. Store in the refrigerator for 2 or 3 hours before serving.

Mogens Bay Esbensen
Nautilus Restaurant, Port Douglas
Butler's, Sydney
Australia

Meet Mogens Bay Esbensen. A Danish chef of broad international experience, Mogens is arguably the chef with the richest background in Australia. He has worked for large hotel groups all over the world, including Sweden, Hollywood, Rio de Janeiro and Bangkok. As Executive Chef he opened in turn the Bali, Manila, Singapore and Bangkok Hyatt Hotels.

As well Mogens has run his own restaurants in Bangkok and Manila, for many years ran diplomatic functions at the Danish Embassy in Thailand, and was often invited to the Palace of the Thai Royal Family, to cook for the guests of King Bhumpiphon and Queen Sirikit. With this background he is also a consultant to Thai Airways on their routes to and from Australia.

Mogens has worked in kitchens with a brigade of forty and in small restaurants, and is grateful to have done his apprenticeship in one of the former — the famous Wivex restaurant in the Tivoli Gardens in Copenhagen — for such a disciplined and hard-going apprenticeship has given him a technical mastery of his craft that few nowadays have the chance to acquire.

He is a member (by invitation, for there are only one hundred and fifty seats, and one waits for a death to vacate a place) of the Académie de Gastronomie Brillat Savarin, and was invested years ago into the French-based international food society La Chaine des Rôtisseurs, for which he has subsequently set up branches in Thailand, the Philippines and Australia.

Mogens went to Australia to open the Sydney Hyatt, fell in love with the life-style, and has now made it his home. In Sydney, first at the Pavilion on the Park, then his current restaurant Butler's, he made a tremendous name for himself with his personal, very inventive cuisine, strongly influenced by the many Asian countries in which he has lived.

Essentially a very private and a very quiet man, Mogens has still managed to impart his techniques and his impassioned love of food to his apprentices, many of whom are fast becoming the best young up-and-coming restaurateurs in Australia. His need to do this, he feels, dates back to his own past.

Mogens was born a farmer's son just outside of Copenhagen. With what he recalls now as the interminable eggs, milk and pork that were the products of the farm, he says, 'No wonder I got out. Eating was so boring there, there just had to be a better way!' At fifteen he got his apprenticeship at Wivex. 'I shed tears for it,' he says. 'In those days, apprenticeships were tough and only the devoted got through. We started at seven a.m. and after the evening service, a bag of onions was placed before all the young apprentices. We were not allowed to go until we'd peeled our bagful. All the apprentices literally left the place crying every night!'

He laments, however, that nowadays the system is no longer the same. 'By the time we'd finished, we knew every classic sauce backwards: how to make them for four or forty, how to save them if they broke, how to vary them, enrich them, lengthen them, garnish them. We knew the bones of every carcass, and how to cut each piece of meat perfectly, whether it was from chicken, lamb, venison or reindeer. We knew every trick of buffet decoration — how to blow sugar, how to carve ice — and every skill in the pastry larder. The technical colleges of today teach convenience foods and call them 'the foods of tomorrow', use short cuts and pre-prepared merchandise, and mechanical methods are taught in preference to a real understanding of the food.' No wonder people vie for positions in Mogen's kitchen, and count it as one of the most important credentials in their careers.

Mogens is a great believer in simplicity, and led

Lamb with Tamarind

the Australian move to bring out the natural value of produce, presenting beautifully plated food at its best. At a time when its Anglo-Saxon background had many still serving large, overcooked meat dishes with three, most often boiled, vegetables, Mogens served perfectly cooked red meat with sauces that were reduced rather than thickened — commonplace now, but in their time a revolution. Mogens says his vegetable bill is the largest bill of the restaurant's week. Herbs too, he uses unsparingly, even to decorate the restaurant's counters.

Mogens has simply never put food on a plate that didn't look beautiful — it is not within his capabilities. The first time I ever went to his house privately, it was a Monday night. 'Don't go to too much trouble, it's your night off,' I protested. 'Never mind,' said Mogens 'we'll just have eggs!' And there they were, scrambled eggs, spilling out of two beautifully placed cracked shells on a rectangular plate with tiny triangles of toast, and red salmon eggs topping them off generously. That was followed by quail and salad, cheese, a nectarine with chestnut purée in it and redcurrants spilling decoratively out of the top, and goodness knows what else. Mogens loves to cook...

No one who knew him well was surprised when the call of the tropics saw Mogens build a second restaurant on the northernmost coast of Australia at Port Douglas. The tiny-framed, bespeckled blonde, who speaks a fluent, gutteral Thai at the drop of a hat, and whose personal entertaining is most often done in the Thai manner, found himself totally at home in the north, where he could gather mangoes from the trees, find avocados in abundance, and pick pawpaws while still green for his curries and his favourite salads. A born gardener — as he is a painter, sculptor and even a surprising hand at Swedish needlepoint — Mogens treasures the lushness of the north, where he now grows his own vines of fresh green peppercorns, every type of pepper and chilli, fresh avocados, mangoes, jackfruit and tamarind.

Neither was anyone who knew him well surprised when he took a look at the people currently reshaping Port Douglas as a resort paradise, and strategically retreated. Mogens has left his Nautilus restaurant in the charge of one of his able pupils, John Forrest, — as he had left Butler's in the charge of Grant Lawrence and his extraordinarily capable front-of-house, Joyce Johnson — and now runs the restaurants from afar. He is in Cardwell, just south of the Tropic of Capricorn, building his current dream — a group of tropical cabins in the rain forest, which he intends to run as a weekend hotel. It's a new project for Mogens, who feels he can fit it in and still have time to run the restaurants, write articles and books — his first book *Thai Cuisine*, is soon to be followed with another on tropical fruit — take the classes he loves to teach all over the country and the professional seminars he is constantly asked to run at hotel training schools.

Mogens loves inspired concepts, and the excitement of seeing them to fruition. On the opening night of his restaurant Pavilion on the Park in 1978, I recall him telling me that Pavilion was his seventeenth restaurant. I'm now up to the count of twenty-one. There is no indication that that will be all.

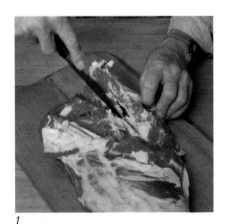

3

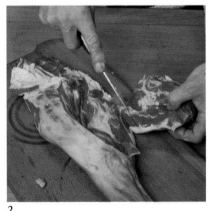

2

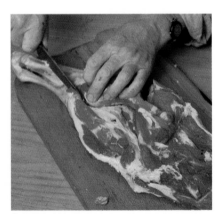

1

LAMB IN THREE DIMENSIONS

When is a leg not a leg? When it's divided into its muscles and served pan fried like large, thick carvable steaks. Mogens believes the one criticism of lamb is its rather acrid 'woolly' taste and the strange furry flavour which is left in the mouth when the fat is allowed to stay on the meat. Animal fat is bad for us — it is much more healthy to remove all the fatty sections of meat and render it lean. Modern chefs delight in the new-found cut known as the fillet, which is really the eye of the loin, boned out, and served as a pan fry. What few cooks seem to have realised is the manner in which we can arrive at the same lean cuts — four of them to be precise — from the boned-out leg.

To begin with you need the 'long' leg, that is the whole leg which comes up to a triangular point. The butcher may cut the lamb for you. Just ask for it to be boned the way one does a leg of veal or beef — into the topside, the silverside, buttock and the shin (which is the lesser muscle and the fourth piece you can obtain from the leg). The pieces must then be individually and totally cleaned of all fat, sinews and skin. If the butcher doesn't cut it for you, here's how you do it:

To bone the lamb:
1. With a pointed, well-sharpened knife, take off the shank at the point it has been slit by the butcher. Start now at the hip (large) end of the leg and cut it along the length of the cross bone until you reach the knuckle. Staying as close to the bone as you can so as not to leave any flesh on it, gouge out this bone as you progress down the lamb. When you reach the knuckle, free the tendons from the joint, release the cross bone and cut it free from the leg. The longer leg bone is removed later.

2. Turn the small (shank) end toward you, bone pointing straight ahead of you. Where the natural muscle divides the flesh into 2 obvious parts, free the flesh so as to remove this block of meat completely. Note: You are working on the side of the bone with the smaller, fatter piece of meat on it (the topside).

3. Release the tendons that are holding the meat to the long bone. Gouge out the bone and cut it free from the flesh. (Sometimes the whole shank can be on, as here, but this is rare since most butchers slit and fold it back. Hence you cut it off at the start.)

4. The large piece of meat with which you are now confronted is easily separated down the natural division of the muscles into 2 pieces. The pointed, long piece is known as the silverside.

5. The other piece must now be divided into 2 (the buttock and the shin). The shin will be less pretty than the other, but if you clean off its fat, it can be used to form the fourth piece.

6. Working on the 4 pieces of boned leg, remove the fat, take out the large sinews, and remove the skin. Save the scraps and bones for stock, except for the very fattiest pieces, since too much fat gives an acrid taste when it renders.

The various possibilities:
Now that you have large pieces of muscle that are suitable for frying, they can be served with an amazing number of sauces, all based on de-glazing the pan with a variety of different liquids and spices. Using the tamarind recipe as a base, you have only to change the ingredients of the marinade to accentuate the one you prefer, and to finish the sauce with the lamb glaze, marinade liquor and the chosen garnish to change the effect. The following are just a few Mogens suggests — there must be thousands more that you can explore:

The marinades:
Mogens always marinates the nobs of lamb with olive oil and herbs or the special flavouring he uses for the sauce. In his recipe with sweet walnuts, he

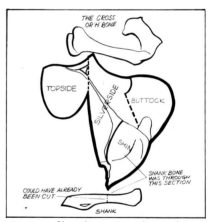

Diagram of boned meat opened up to show the four pieces you or your butcher must end up with.

4

5

6

uses canned Russian sweet walnuts in syrup (available in continental delicatessens). Marinate the lamb in both the olive oil and the sweet syrup from the walnuts for 2 days. (Mogens has also done the recipe with pickled walnuts. The resultant flavour is, of course, very different, as this traditional British speciality is spicy rather than sweet.) After finishing the sauce, into which you incorporate a little of the liquid from the walnuts, it has the same butter finish as the lamb with tamarind, and the heated halved walnuts go alonside as a garnish.

Alternatively to make a sauce of green peppercorns Mogens crushes some of the peppercorns, adds this to the oil marinade, and allows the lamb to absorb the taste of the peppercorns along with the marinade. The sauce is finished with the green peppercorns, a touch of brandy, and the usual butter addition.

Sometimes he accentuates the sauce with loads of chopped mint, a typically British flavour combination. Simply put a few good mint sprigs alongside the meat in the marinade, and add chopped mint to the final pan sauce, as you mount it with the butter.

For lamb with fresh tamarind (pictured here), Mogens breaks a couple of the seedpods and leaves the beans in the marinade. If fresh tamarind is unavailable, a few of the sticky pieces of tamarind paste sold by Asian food shops can be added instead.

For lamb with a sauce of red bell peppers (capsicums), Mogens likes to use some of the grilled, skinned peppers (capsicums) in the marinade — it makes the lamb quite sweet. A garnish of large pieces of roasted peppers (capsicums), skinned and lightly pan fried with sliced onion on the side, is more typical of the garnish of barbecued beef, and with the lamb it is a refreshing change. A simple sauce can also be made by blending the skinned roasted peppers (capsicums) with cream in a blender or food processor until puréed. In this case, the lamb is fried, no de-glazing is needed,

and the reheated creamy purée provides the only sauce.

The stock:
For these recipes it is essential that you keep the bones from the lamb leg, as you will need them for a strong jellied stock for your sauce. To make the stock, discard all the fat and skin, which can leave an acrid taste as well as leaving the stock unclear and greasy. Brown all the bones, meat bits, and scraps with 2 carrots and 2 onions cut into halves in a baking tray in a 230ºC/450ºF oven for about 20 minutes. Remove from your roasting pan to a stock pot, scrape up the sediment from the pan with a generous amount of white wine and transfer this to the stock pot. Bring to a simmer wih 4 ripe tomatoes, a sprig of thyme and parsley and about 2 litres/3½ pints (Br.)/scant 9 cups (U.S.) water. It is important that it never boils, but only simmers slowly for about 2 hours.

Strain, return to the heat and reduce it to one-third of its original volume. Cool and refrigerate. It can also be frozen and taken out when you need it. It will keep for 2 to 3 months in a sealed container in the freezer.

Lamb with Tamarind

The tamarind tree is one of the most attractive trees of the tropics and its fruit has many uses in Asian cooking. It gives a very refreshing, lemony taste to a sauce or a soup, it has a complex richness of exotic flavours, and it lends itself well to a lamb sauce, where the slight acidity of the tamarind cuts the richness of the lamb. Fresh, the tamarind will keep for weeks in the vegetable compartment of your refrigerator.

Serves 4 to 6
1 leg of lamb, boned and marinated as described above
4 seedpods of fresh tamarind or a tablespooon of compresssed tamarind from Asian food shops

500ml/good ¾ pint (Br.)/2 good cups (U.S.) lamb stock (reduced, well-jellied stock prepared beforehand as above, or from the freezer)
salt and pepper
50g/scant 2 oz (Br.)/3 tablespoons (U.S.) butter

On the day you cook the dish, reheat the lamb glaze and reduce it with the seeds of the tamarind to a very rich jelly.

The meat should be cooked shortly before eating.

Heat a cast-iron pan with no grease, remembering the meat has been marinating in olive oil. Brown the meat well on all sides. When well browned, place the pan in a 230ºC/450ºF oven for 10 minutes. Remove the meat, place it on a platter, and let it stand to equalise the heat. De-glaze the roasting pan with your lamb stock and tamarind and oil marinade.

The meat should be quite rare and pink. The sauce should be quite strong and acid. Thicken the sauce at the last moment with a few lumps of cold butter stirred into the sauce, and serve on the individual plates under the slices of pink lamb. Do not smother with sauce. The sauce is to enhance the flavour of the meat. Garnish with a few tamarind seeds (peppercorns, too, if you like) and sprigs of fresh coriander (cilantro).

Baby Chicken with New Season's Garlic

Serves 6 to 8
6 spatchcocks, baby chicks or Cornish game hens
12 whole baby garlic heads (on the roots and in their skins)*
12 whole white baby (pickling) onions or shallots
100g/3½ oz (Br.)/½ cup (U.S.) butter
6 sprigs thyme
500ml/good ¾ pint (Br.)/2 good cups (U.S.) chicken stock
salt and freshly ground pepper

To serve:
Serve on hot plates garnished with 2 whole garlics and 2 baby (pickling) onions or shallots. Coat the birds with the sauce. On the side, Mogens has served a salad of cos lettuce and grilled, skinned, red bell peppers (capsicums), dressed with olive oil and red wine vinegar.

Janson's Temptation

This is the potato dish photographed alongside the chicken.

Serves 6 to 8
7 to 8 medium potatoes, peeled and cut as described below
40g/½ oz (Br.)/3 tablespoons (U.S.) butter
3 to 4 onions, thinly sliced
16 anchovy fillets
100ml/3 fl oz (Br.)/scant ½ cup (U.S.) milk
150ml/¼ pint (Br.)/ scant ¾ cup (U.S.) cream with 35% milk fat (whipping cream)
2 tablespoons (Br.)/scant 3 tablespoons (U.S.) breadcrumbs

Butter a porcelain flan dish or a rectangular ovenproof dish. Sauté the finely sliced onions in the butter without browning. Cut the potatoes into slices 5mm/¼ in thick and then again into long strips.

Using half of the potatoes, make a layer with the potato strips in the dish, then add half the cooked onion. Spread the 16 anchovy fillets evenly over the onion layer then, using the remaining onions, make another layer. Finally top with another layer of potato. Season with salt and pepper, but watch the salt, remembering that anchovies can be salty. Mix the milk and cream and pour the mixture over everything. Sprinkle the breadcrumbs over the top and dot with a few cubes of butter.

Cook in a 180°C/350°F oven for 45 minutes or until the potatoes are cooked.

*If you can't get the baby garlic, add 4 cloves of unpeeled garlic per person. For a different but novel taste, try also the whole heads of picked garlic sold in jars in Chinese grocers.

Rub the cavities of the birds with salt and pepper and place 1 sprig of thyme in each. Truss into shape with string.

Heat a little butter in a cast-iron casserole large enough to take all the birds. Brown the birds well on all sides. Add the whole garlic and baby (pickling) onions or shallots. Cover tightly with a lid and cook over a slow heat for 10 to 12 minutes. Remove the birds, garlic and onions and keep warm.

The sauce:
Add the chicken stock to the roasting juices in the casserole. Reduce over vigorous heat to about one-third of its original volume. Check for seasoning and thicken the sauce with the remaining butter, adding any juices from the birds.

Coconut Custard in a Pumpkin

Serves 8
1 whole pumpkin approx 1½kg/3lb
5 oz or 8 baby ones, the latter
sometimes known as golden nugget
pumpkins

The custard:
4 large eggs
100g/scant 4 oz (Br.)/½ cup (U.S.) sugar
200ml/scant 7 fl oz (Br.)/1 scant cup
(U.S.) coconut cream (bought canned)

Wash the pumpkin and wipe it clean.
With a small knife cut the stem out
like a lid, with the actual stem as a
handle. Do not make the opening too
large as this will affect the amount of
custard filling and also the final slicing
of the chilled custard. Spoon out the
fibre and seed and discard the fibre. (You
may choose to keep the seeds — they
are delicious used in mayonnaise sauces).

Place the pumpkin upside down in a
steam basket and steam for 15 minutes
to partly cook the meat. (The little ones
need only 6 to 8 minutes here.)

Crack the eggs into a bowl with sugar
and beat together, then add the coconut cream and stir over a pot of boiling
water to warm it. This will shorten the
steaming time of the pumpkin. If you
are careful, this can be done directly over
a low flame.

Pour the warmed custard into the partly cooked pumpkin, place it in the steamer and steam for about 45 minutes until
the custard is set and the pumpkin
tender. (The individual ones need about
25 minutes.) It is wise to test with a
skewer or baking tester by piercing the
side of the pumpkin. If any juice oozes
out it needs to steam a little bit longer.

When cooked, remove the steam basket
from the heat and leave to cool. When
cold, remove the pumpkin to a platter
and refrigerate overnight. In fact, in the
refrigerator, it will keep for days.

This dish may be served with whipped
cream or a coconut or cinnamon
ice-cream.

Banana Prawns and Crab in Coconut Sauce

1 cooked crab, about 800g/1 lb 12 oz
1kg/use 2 lb fresh green banana or tiger
prawns
2 cloves garlic, chopped
2 stalks fresh lemon grass, bruised and
cut in pieces
3 small chillis, chopped
300ml/½ pint (Br.)/1¼ cups (U.S.)
coconut milk (bought canned)

Sauté the garlic in a little vegetable oil,
add the lemon grass and chillis, then
pour in the coconut milk and bring to
the boil. Reduce the heat and simmer
for 4 minutes.

Wash the prawns and toss them in the
coconut sauce. Crack the crab and clean
it, break it into pieces, and add it to
the prawns in the coconut sauce. Toss
and cover to warm through. Check the
seasoning, it may need a little salt.

Serve sprinkled with fresh coriander
(cilantro) leaves and shredded coconut.

Joël Bellouet

Pâtissier
Paris, France

When Joël Bellouet gave in to the pesterings of a nagging student, and in 1982 agreed to give up his annual holidays from the Lenôtre Ecole de Perfectionnement outside Paris to cross the world and teach in Australia, he embarked on a journey that was to change his whole future.

Joël had spent the last twelve years teaching pâtisserie, chocolate, ice-cream and sugar work in the renowned school of Gaston Lenôtre, where he was involved also in developing new cakes, pastries and confections to extend the range of Lenôtre's shops. His role, along with the other teachers of the school, was to teach young apprentices the highly skilled work they were to do on the factory floor — the time-and-motioned, exceptionally well-mechanised factory that furnishes seven Parisian Lenôtre shops and a flourishing catering business that springs from them.

Joël was happy there. Born into the pastry and bread-making business as the son of a *boulanger* from Orléans in France's Loire Valley, he did his apprenticeship in the Loire, but joined Lenôtre early in his career and, with his broad smile and extraordinary enthusiasm for his work, he had become a favourite on Lenôtre's floor. To this day his whole life is his work, and not only is he the perfect craftsman, he is also the over-enthusiastic one who turns out twice as much as everyone else, stays later than everyone else, asks if he can use the lab after hours to develop recipes, keeps the light burning until four to painstakingly make sugar figures for Christmas decorations, and then comes in first in the morning to prepare a demonstration.

A bachelor (probably until his dying days — he always means to date, but he's always working and always late), there was nothing to keep him from travelling with Lenôtre when he worked overseas; and

so Joël travelled, demonstrating at international exhibitions and, when Lenôtre took over the pastry section of an hotel in Rio, he flew there regularly.

With that sort of enthusiasm, the largest smile in the business and hooting laughter, Joël was a natural to teach in the school when Lenôtre decided to open its doors to the public, including other French professionals and even competitors in his own trade. As the proposal took shape, Lenôtre engaged a Meilleur Ouvrier de France Pâtissier, Gérard Ponée, and he in turn gave Joël and another of the senior Lenôtre pastrymen the necessary instruction, laboratories at their disposal, and time to study and prepare for the country's top award themselves. Becoming a Maître Pâtissier, Confiseur and Glacier Diplômé was nothing to becoming Meilleur Ouvrier de France and Joël took the gold medal in 1979. During the seven years he taught in the Lenôtre school, Joel also became a Member of the Académie Culinaire de France, gained the Médaille des Cordons Bleus, the Médaille d'Argent de la Confédération des Glaciers de France and numerous medals in regional competitions. (Later in 1987, he also won the Grand Cordon d'Or de la Cuisine Française.)

And then came Australia. What happened to Joël was that he discovered that teaching, which he loved, was also a passport to the world. Even when he didn't speak the language, his warm and seductive manner made his classes a success. And then he thought, if he had been asked to Australia and it had worked, others might ask him elsewhere, and that could work too . . .

Within the year, Joël had dropped his secure job with Lenôtre and since 1984 has demonstrated his skills all over the world. For the most part he works with major confectionery companies, small factories or chains of pâtisseries. He does consultant work for a large

La Bagatelle

chocolate corporation with international distribution, demonstrating with their chocolate at exhibitions and to their major clients. He works also for Cointreau, developing cakes and chocolates that feature their liqueur, the recipes for which are then distributed to working pâtissiers around the globe; and he works with interested pâtissiers who want to update or upgrade their recipes or who need to revamp their working procedures.

Washington, Monte Carlo, Canada, Belgium, Italy, Japan, England, Brazil, Germany, Spain. You name it, Joël's new life has taken him there. Occasionally, just occasionally, he also stops over at a Club Méditerranée — but I get the feeling they're just quick stopovers, and to this day, Joël is still the most eligible bachelor I know, and a fabulous catch for any girl with a sweet tooth.

Meantime, Joël writes books — wonderful, glossy books with the most delicious cakes photographed and explained in detail, and drawings to show the various layers and how to put them together. His third, and latest, written in 1987 and called *La Pâtisserie: Tradition et Evolution* makes me wonder why I didn't get him to demonstrate for you something in rich chocolate, something with layers of different creams in it and dripping with wickedness. But most of those are strictly for the pros, and Joël is also in his element teaching the home cook to do something more realistic. So I asked him for some professional advice in bringing into the home some of the secrets of the wonderful work of French croissants and cake-making.

Up my sleeve I have photos of him making chocolates, a few Bavarian creams, step-by-steps to making brioche and two chocolate cakes. We'll just have to get together to write a sequel some other time.

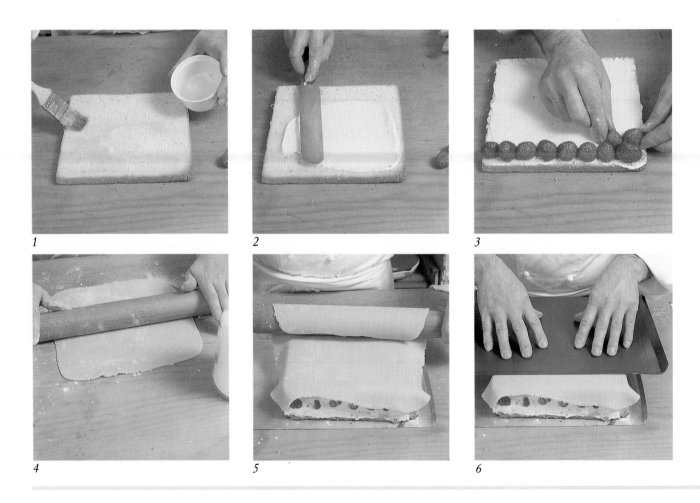

1

2

3

4

5

6

La Bagatelle

The Bagatelle Strawberry Cake

This famous French strawberry cake is one that fascinates people, for they see the beautifully aligned seam of halved strawberries and are never quite sure how this is done.

The cake itself is a *genoise* sponge-cake (sometimes known as a whisked sponge) and the filling, a vanilla-flavoured butter cream — both common enough entities to good cake makers. It can be lightened with eggwhites, depending on how rich you like your cakes. Once these are made, Joël takes you by the hand for the assembly.

The *genoise* spongecake:

4 eggs
100g/scant 4oz (Br.)/½ cup (U.S.) sugar
90g/3 oz (Br.)/¾ cup (U.S.) plain (all-purpose) flour, sifted
4 tablespoons (Br.)/5 tablespoons (U.S.) butter, melted and cooled

Equipment:

23cm/9in square cake tin

The butter cream:

300ml/½ pint (Br.)/1¼ cups (U.S.) milk
150g/5½ oz (Br.)/¾ cup (U.S.) sugar
½ vanilla bean, or vanilla essence to taste
125g/4½ oz egg yolks (approximately 6 eggs, but pastrymen weigh them, as sizes differ)
500g/use 1 lb (Br.)/2 good cups (U.S.) unsalted butter

The syrup:

2 tablespoons (Br.)/scant 3 tablespoons (U.S.) sugar and 6 tablespoons (Br.)/7 tablespoons (U.S.) water, boiled and cooled, then mixed with kirsch to taste. You will need about 200ml/8 fl oz (Br.)/1 scant cup (U.S.) in all.

The strawberries:

3 punnets strawberries, about 750g/1¾ lb (Br.)/7 cups (U.S.) large but not giant-size strawberries, preferably all of even shape. They should all be hulled except the 2 or 3 prettiest ones which should be used for decoration.

The marzipan:

140g/5 oz marzipan
2 to 3 drops green colouring
arrowroot or cornflour (cornstarch)
small amount red-currant jelly

To make the *genoise* spongecake:

Combine the eggs and sugar in a bowl and whisk over steam until lukewarm. Remove from the steam and continue beating at high speed until cool, and until it has tripled in volume. Fold in the sifted flour gently, then the butter. Pour into a buttered and floured cake tin and bake at 190°C/375°F for 25 to 30 minutes. Cool on a cake rack until ready to use, when it will be cut in half horizontally.

The butter cream:

Bring the milk, half of the sugar and the split vanilla bean (if using) to the boil. Place the egg yolks in a bowl with the remaining sugar and cream them well. Whisk them into the boiling milk, return the milk to the saucepan, and stir well with a whisk until the mixture forms a thickened custard.

Note: It must not boil as the egg will scramble (curdle), but it should thicken until it coats the back of a spoon. (If using a thermometer, check that it doesn't cook higher than to 85°C/160°F.)

Pass through a strainer back into the original bowl and beat with an electric mixer until cool. If using vanilla essence instead of the bean, flavour the custard now. Soften the butter to a creamy consistency, soft and fluffy, but not melted. Then beat in the cooled custard mixture, blending the two together well with the electric mixer.

Note: If you find this too rich, the mixture may be lightened by adding 3 egg-whites beaten to a firm snow with 3 tablespoons (Br.)/3½ tablespoons (U.S.) sugar or 150g meringue Italienne (see page 175).

Butter cream may be kept in the refrigerator but if the butter resets, it is difficult to work it back to a spreading consistency without separating the butter from the more liquid custard. However, it can be done successfully with the low wave element of a microwave. If the mixture is too liquid when you have finished making it, it should be refrigerated just enough to firm to spreading consistency.

To assemble the cake:

1. With a pastry brush, douse the cake well with half the quantity of the syrup.

2. Spread the cake with a layer of butter cream. It may be up to 1cm/½in thick, so the strawberries can be set well into it.

3. Arrange the strawberries across the cake, in as straight and linear a sequence as possible, then spread butter cream on top, saving about 4 tablespoons (Br.)/5 tablespoons (U.S.) for later. Carefully make sure that some of the butter cream falls between the strawberries as well as on top. Now souse the underside of the second layer of cake with the other half of the syrup and place the top of the cake over the strawberry and butter cream filling. With a metal spatula, make sure the edge of the cake is well covered with butter cream too, and then spread a **very fine** layer on top of the cake to help the marzipan covering stay in place.

4. Flour the workbench with a little arrowroot or cornflour (cornstarch)and work the ball of marzipan until it softens a little, kneading into it a couple of drops of green colouring to obtain the desired colour. Continue to knead until the colour is well blended and the texture of the marzipan becomes pliable enough to roll. Roll the marzipan out to about 2cm/1 in larger than the top of the cake, using the arrowroot or cornflour (cornstarch) to stop it sticking to both the benchtop and the roller.

5. Wind the marzipan up onto the rolling pin in order to transfer it easily to the cake. Unwind carefully into position, allowing a little overlap.

6. Smooth it with your hands, from the centre outward, place a baking tray on top and press firmly but not too hard, to amalgamate the butter cream and strawberries with the top layer.

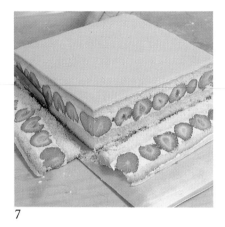

7

8

9

7. Take a long, serrated knife and cut the edge back about 6mm/¼ in to expose the centre of a row of strawberries sitting in the butter cream. It is this trick that makes the edge of the cake so attractive.

8. Take a little of the offcut of marzipan, roll it out and cut out 3 marzipan leaves. Mark out the veins in the leaf with the back of a knife.

9. Dip the 3 unhulled strawberries in a little red-currant jelly that has been warmed and stirred to smooth it, and place with the leaves on one corner of the cake to garnish the top. Refrigerate the cake until served.

Croissants

Makes about 25

For the leaven:
20g/½ oz (Br.)/1 tablespoon fresh (compressed) yeast
100g/3½ oz (Br.)/scant ½ cup (U.S.) tepid water
75g/2½ oz (Br.)/good ½ cup (U.S.) baker's (strong) flour

For the dough:
500g/1 lb 2 oz (Br.)/3¾ cups (U.S.) baker's (strong) flour, which has a gluten content of around 12 to 13%
30g/1 oz (Br.)/1 tablespoon (U.S.) gluten powder (sometimes known as gluten flour), (available from health shops)
50g/scant 2 oz (Br.)/3 tablespoons (U.S.) unsalted butter, melted

45g/1½ oz (Br.)/scant ¼ cup (U.S.) sugar
1 teaspoon table salt
175g/6 oz (Br.)/¾ cup (U.S.) milk
flour for rolling the dough
180g/6 oz (Br.)/¾ cup (U.S.) unsalted butter

Note: If baker's (strong) flour is unobtainable, results will be much improved by increasing the gluten powder to 50g or even 60g/scant 2 to 2 oz (Br.)/⅓ to ½ cup (U.S.) (i.e. 10 to 12% of the flour weight).

Equipment:
Although croissants may be kneaded manually, Joël's method has been devised for an electric mixer fitted with a dough hook.

1

2

3

The leaven:

1. The leaven is to be the raising agent for the croissants. It can be made in a small bowl and transferred for later incorporation into the flour, or made directly in the base of the mixer bowl where the dough will be made. Using a wooden spoon, blend the crumbled yeast, water and flour together. Then take 2 to 3 tablespoons of the flour set aside for the dough and scatter over the top of the yeast mixture.

2. Place the bowl in a warm spot in your kitchen until the growth of the yeast has cracked the flour open and the frothy leaven starts to break through from below. This should take half an hour depending on room temperature.

3. Sift together the flour set aside for the dough and the gluten powder. Melt the sugar and salt in the milk by stirring them to lukewarm on the stove. (Note: lukewarm temperatures help activate yeast, but a high temperature will kill it.) Place the flour on top of the leaven in the mixer bowl, add 50g/scant 2 oz (Br.)/3 tablespoons (U.S.) butter and then pour in the milk mixture. Blend these ingredients together lightly with the dough hook attachment of your machine. Stop mixing when just blended (excessive blending will bring out too much elasticity in the flour by overworking the gluten). The result should be able to be removed in one piece from the bowl, but has not yet the even texture of finished pastry.

4

5

6

7

8

9

10

11

12

4.   Using your hands, knead the pastry lightly into a ball on a floured benchtop, then shape it into a flattened rectangle and let it rest at room temperature for 10 to 15 minutes (to allow the yeast to start working). Refrigerate for 2 hours, covered with plastic film to prevent dehydration.

5.   After the rest period, flour the benchtop from time to time to prevent sticking and roll the pastry into a rectangle about 3 times the length of its width i.e. about 18 x 54cm/7 x 21in. The technique for croissants resembles the method for puff pastry, but instead of placing a large brick of butter in the centre of this rectangle, half the stipulated quantity of butter (that is 90g/good 3 oz [Br.]/6 tablespoons [U.S.]) is now worked to a creamy paste and then spread with the fingers over two-thirds of the rolled-out area.

6.   Now fold the rectangle into 3 upon itself. Start by folding the unbuttered end in first so that the butter is now sandwiched evenly between the 3 folded layers.

7.   Turn the dough so the fold seam is to your left, and roll the dough again into the large rectangle 3 times the length of its width, as you did before. You are now stretching the dough in the opposite direction from the first rolling. The purpose of this is to spread the layer of butter evenly between the flour layers, and also to develop the gluten evenly, rather than only along one axis of the pastry, so ensuring regular rising in the finished product.

Roll as evenly as you can, so that the flour and butter layers remain separate; try also to keep the ends and sides as straight and squared off as possible so that when the dough is folded, the layers are evenly formed. As with puff pastry, it is the steam from the melting butter that gets trapped between the flour layers which causes the pastry to rise in flaky, buttery layers. In the case of croissants, the effect is heightened by the added raising ability of the yeast.

Each time the pastry is rolled in one direction it is called a 'turn'. You have now completed 2 'turns'. Again the pastry must be rested for a minimum of 2 hours, but if it is more convenient, it may now wait, covered and refrigerated, overnight.

8.   After the rest period, steps 5, 6 and 7 must be repeated. The dough is again rolled out, the remaining 90g/good 3 oz (Br.)/6 tablespoons (U.S.) of softened butter is incorporated in the same manner as before, the dough is folded into 3 again, the folded seam turned toward your left, and then the dough is rolled into the long rectangle yet another time, and again folded into 3.

You have now completed 4 'turns' and with the successive pleating and rolling you have layered the butter 162 times through the flour. The dough must again be rested for a minimum of 2 hours, or overnight. Resting overnight at one point may be convenient, but remember only one rest period should be overnight for, although the croissants can still rise if the procedure is elongated, more than once will inhibit their ability to rise. Find a schedule that suits you, but always allow at least the 2-hour period stated so that even the butter in the central core of the pastry is well firmed and will not risk blending in with the flour layer.

9.   After this final resting, the dough is ready to be formed into croissants. Roll the dough to a large square about 3mm/1/8in thick. From this square you should be able to cut 3 strips of dough about 18cm/7in wide, across the width of the pastry. Cut the dough into the typical croissant triangles, noting from our picture just how pointed the triangle should be — the length nearly 2½ times the width.

10.   For a further touch of finesse — and so there is not too much dough in the centre, which risks not cooking through and thus making the croissants heavier — Joël makes a tiny slit in the base of the triangle and opens it out a little. Now the croissant is rolled, starting at the tips of the fingers and up to the palm of the hand, so that it forms a closed roll. You may hold the tip of the triangle while rolling to ensure that it doesn't roll too loosely, but strive only to keep the rolling firm and even, not to stretch the dough, or it will unfurl later. The Lenôtre method is **not** to turn the edges of the croissant into a crescent shape, for their belief is that these squeezed edges become dry and overcrisp on baking. Joël leaves the ends straight, as they come, but use your preferred method.

11.   Unless you have a teflon baking tray, line the tray with baking (parchment) paper. Place the croissants on the tray, with the point of the triangle tucked underneath to prevent the tip springing up. Leave to rise for 1½ to 2 hours, depending on the temperature of the room. Ideal rising temperature is 22ºC/74ºF.

When swollen, glaze with a little beaten egg, using a pastry brush and tapping only very gently so as not to disturb the texture of the risen croissant. Bake in an oven preheated to 240ºC/475ºF, turning the heat down to 200ºC/400ºF as soon as you put the croissants in the oven. Baking time is exactly 15 minutes.

12.   Cool on a wire cake rack with legs, so no condensation forms.

visit, I repeated the experience with a lamb cutlet.

Gualtiero is inclined to do that to you, to make you look again at food and redefine your understanding of it. Nothing looked extraordinary on that plate. In fact the plate may well have been the most undergarnished large white plate I have ever seen — one double lamb cutlet, pink, thick and delicious; two or three tablespoons of perfect, creamed, oven-baked sliced potatoes; and a spoonful or two of flavoursome demiglace underneath the cutlet. That was all, and for me, this plate of food redefined the lamb cutlet.

Marchesi's defied all records by immediately getting one Michelin star in the Italian version of its guidebook and, by the second year, it got a second. In 1986 Marchesi's became the first restaurant in Italy to gain three Michelin stars. It has also been awarded 18/20 and three red hats in the Gault et Millau Guide. The Italian guidebooks still look upon Gualtiero as *troppo Francese* (too French) and, fiercely proud of their origins and their traditional *cucina nazionale*, are wary of giving him their highest awards. At the same time they constantly interview him on television, make a fuss of him, and revere him as a hero of the international press.

There is, however, no question that the man derives from and has his heart in Lombardy. Having asserted early in his career that pasta had no place in a refined meal, Marchesi's maturation, and perhaps the certainty of the development of his own style, combined eventually to make him interested in adding a pasta course to his menu — but in his own inimitable way.

All that had to be done, he found, was to refine the pasta recipes, and he finally devised highly stylised pasta dishes that first appeared on his menu *after* the main course. First there was pasta with foie gras, then stylised shapes simply served with reduced cooking juices rather than sauces. Later came the *trenette* (fine vermicelli) with minute baby squid and black ink sauce, then seven or eight perfectly placed *penne* (quill-shaped pasta) with fresh garden vegetables like asparagus spears and broccoli.

Italian cuisine thus turned upside down, pasta has returned to its rightful place and the creative visionary to his. The cuisine of 'il Francese' has become the cuisine of 'il divin Marchesi'—truly his own cuisine, rich in the traditions of Italy with the blessings of a modern, inventive creator-chef interested in enhancing the flavours of the wonderful produce of his country. 'I am simply a purist,' he says. 'It is not necessary to have ideas, only to know how to develop them.'

1

2

3

4

5

6

FRESH PASTA

Gualtiero's Classic Recipe

Makes 1.5kg/about 3 lb pasta
500g/1 lb 2 oz (Br.)/3¾ cups (U.S.)
white (all-purpose) flour
8 egg yolks
100ml/3 fl oz (Br.)/scant ½ cup (U.S.)
water
25g/1 oz (Br.)/1 tablespoon (U.S.) salt
1 tablespoon oil

Spinach pasta:
The same ingredients as above, plus
100g/4 oz (Br.)/scant ½ cup (U.S.) well-drained, cooked spinach (English spinach), puréed and incorporated with the eggs before kneading the pasta.

Gualtiero's Milk-based Recipe

This unusual recipe has milk, whole eggs, but only half the egg content of Gualtiero's classic pasta recipe.

Makes 1.5kg/about 3 lb pasta
500g/1 lb 2 oz (Br.)/3¾ cups (U.S.)
white (all-purpose) flour
4 eggs
40ml/1¼ fl oz (Br.)/2 tablespoons
(U.S.) peanut oil
40ml/1¼ fl oz (Br.)/2 tablespoons
(U.S.) milk
pinch salt

To make the pasta:
The method for all Gualtiero's pastas is the same: On a pastry board, made

7

of wood or preferably of marble, arrange the flour in a mound with a well (hole) in the centre. In this well place the eggs, oil and salt (and, if used, milk and/or spinach purée).

Mix together all that is in the centre and then gradually knead in the flour until everything is incorporated and you have a well-kneaded and homogeneous ball of dough. Rest the dough, covered with a teatowel, for 2 hours before using the hand-driven pasta machine to roll it out to the lengths of the required thickness.

Note: For a more detailed step-by-step coverage of making home-made pasta, see page 21.

Raviolo Aperto
Open Ravioli

Serves 4
½ recipe fresh white pasta dough, per recipe above
½ recipe fresh spinach pasta dough, per recipe above
For the plain white pasta dough, large leaves of Italian parsley, washed and well dried
450g/1 lb large scallops, preferably dry shucked
200ml/scant 7 fl oz (Br.)/1 scant cup (U.S.) dry white wine
100g/3½ oz (Br.)/½ cup (U.S.) butter
2 to 3 tablespoons cream, preferably with 45% milk fat (heavy cream)
1 teaspoon shredded fresh ginger root

The spinach pasta:
Make up the spinach pasta following your chosen recipe. Draw through the pasta machine to the finest notch. You will have more than is necessary and can cut the rest into tagliatelle and freeze it for later use. Meantime, for this recipe, cut out four rectangles of 10 x 8cm /4 x 3½in. Set them aside until needed.

The white pasta:
Make up the white pasta following your chosen recipe. Again you will have more than you need. For this recipe you will

need 4 rectangles of 10 x 8cm/4 x 3½in, with a leaf of Italian parsley embossed into each. To accomplish this:

1. Use a hand-driven pasta machine to roll the length of pasta out to the second finest notch. Lay this length onto the workbench, place a line of Italian parsley leaves along the centre through half the length of the pasta at intervals of about 7cm/4in, then fold the other half of the length back over the first half.

2. Pass the pasta again through the second finest notch of the pasta machine.

3. Cut the length of pasta into rectangles, each rectangle to centre a leaf of the now elongated parsley as an emblem. Now pass these rectangles through the finest notch of the pasta machine, in the opposite direction to the last time. This allows the parsley leaf to stretch widthwise as it has already stretched lengthwise. Then trim the rectangles back to about 10 x 8cm/ 4 x 3½in.

You will need one green and one white rectangle (with parsley emblem) per person. The pasta may be made in advance and kept until needed. It may also be par-cooked in advance, drained and quickly brought up to temperature in boiling water whilst making the scallop garnish.

The scallop garnish:
4. Clean and pick over any blood clots on the scallops. Dry on paper towelling. Heat 30g/1 good oz (Br.)/2 tablespoons (U.S.) of the butter in a pan and sauté the scallops for a few moments, turning them. Add the white wine, and bring to the boil.

5. With a slotted spoon, remove the scallops to a strainer over a bowl or pot, then add the ginger to the pan, squeezing it to extract all the juice.

6. Add any scallop juice to the wine, then reduce to 2 or 3 tablespoons.

7. Add the remaining butter in small quantities, whisking it in well, then add the cream. Season with salt and pepper, then return the scallops to the pan.

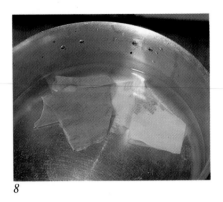

8

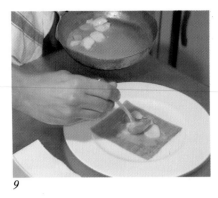

9

10

8. Meanwhile, heat or cook the pasta rectangles.

9. Take the spinach rectangles first, drain off any excess moisture by placing them on a teatowel momentarily, then onto the plates. Onto each rectangle, spoon a little of the scallop garnish and its sauce.

10. Now drain off the white pasta rectangles, and place one on a 45° angle over the scallop garnish and the bottom spinach rectangle.

Remove any remnants of skin from the liver and cut the meat into fine slices of about 15g/½ oz a piece. In a wide frying pan or skillet, heat the other 50g/scant 2 oz (Br.)/3 tablespoons (U.S.) butter to pale brown and sizzling and sauté the liver slices on a high flame for a couple of minutes, taking care to

brown them on either side but keeping them pink in the centre. Salt and pepper.

Divide the onion compôte onto the serving plates and arrange the liver piccatas in the centre. Decorate with leaves of chervil placed between the slices of liver.

Piccata di Fegato con Cipolle

Piccata of Calves' Liver with Onions

Serves 4
300g/¾ lb calves' liver
400g/good 14 oz onions, chopped (good 2¼ cups (U.S.) chopped onions)
100g/3½ oz (Br.)/½ cup (U.S.) butter
100ml/3 fl oz (Br.)/scant ½ cup (U.S.) dry white wine
chervil leaves
salt and pepper

In a frying pan, place 50g/scant 2 oz (Br.)/3 tablespoons (U.S.) butter, the white wine and the onions. Salt and pepper, cover the pan, and cook slowly on a medium heat for about 30 minutes without allowing it to colour. Check from time to time and, if the wine has evaporated, add a little water and lower the flame. Remove from the heat and keep warm until serving. Don't allow it to dry out; the onion should be a creamy texture.

Aragosta Fredda alla Crema di Peperoni

Cold Lobster with Red Pepper Coulis

Serves 4

2 green lobsters or crays of 300g/about ¾ lb each. They should be bought and cooked live, but may be drowned in fresh water before use.*

400g/good 14 oz (Br.)/about 5 large red bell peppers (capsicums)

125g/4½ oz (Br.)/¾ cup (U.S.) finely sliced onion

1 clove garlic, finely chopped

50ml/1½ fl oz (Br.)/¼ cup (U.S.) extra virgin olive oil

150g/6 oz (Br.)/¾ cup (U.S.) peeled fresh tomato, weighed after having been skinned, seeded and diced

250ml/8 fl oz (Br.)/1 good cup (U.S.) water

130ml/4½ fl oz (Br.)/good ½ cup (U.S.) cream with 35% milk fat (whipping cream)

salt and freshly ground white pepper

*Gualtiero loves to do this dish with the true lobster (*homard*) claw, as it is very picturesque. However, you may substitute crayfish meat, marron, bugs or the lobster-style meat of your area.

Trim the central seed and ribs from the red bell peppers (capsicums) and cut them into small pieces. Set aside with the onion and garlic.

Cook the lobsters in boiling water. This takes about 7 to 8 minutes for a live lobster of this weight. Remove and cool the lobster, remove the head and detach the tail meat and, in the case of a lobster, the meat from the large front claws.

(Claw meat is not needed in the case of a crayfish).

Heat the olive oil in an ovenproof saucepan, add the garlic and onion and cook for about 2 minutes, turning it all the time with a wooden spoon to prevent it colouring. Add the red bell pepper (capsicum) and the tomato, salt and pepper, and water, cover, and let it cook in a 170ºC/325ºF oven for 30 minutes. Allow it to cool and process it to a purée in a blender or food processor. Transfer to a bowl and incorporate the cream well. Check the seasoning, for it will be eaten cold.

To serve, cut the lobster tail meat lengthwise into 2. Ladle a round of coulis into the centre of each plate and place a half tail on each, accompanied by the claw meat if you have it.

Paul Bocuse

Bocuse Restaurant
Lyon, France

L arger than life-size international super-cook Paul Bocuse is undoubtedly the stuff legends are made of. Never has a French chef been so well known outside his country, and after his recent television series went to air around the world, his down-to-earth, 'eat as your French grandmother would have taught you' approach held people glued to their television sets and extended his international recognition even further.

You only have to look at Paul Bocuse to understand why he's a phenomenon. Blessed with an extraordinary width across the shoulders, and a frame and height reminiscent of a gridiron player, his person is enormously commanding. Many tall people find they have to look down; Bocuse looks out. He is not loudly spoken, but has a well-formed opinion on all aspects of his profession, he has an aggressive taste in art and décor, loves jokes and practical joking and, sure enough, has an enourmous ego. But when you look around at the huge photos and paintings of him full blown around the restaurant, at its strident peach-coloured walls, gilt light fittings and decorative silverware and crockery, you can't help wondering whether this is him, or whether success has imposed it on him and caught him just a little out of his depth.

Bocuse's friends among the other great chefs, like Vergé and the Troisgros brothers, say his generosity is legendary and not only to his friends. His practical joking is even more legendary and there is hardly a conference or party at which the gang of great chefs gets together, where Bocuse is not leading them on some antic or another, dressing up, cooking for them all, or in other ways, springing surprises. There's an absolutely wonderful photograph on the dining room wall of Bocuse's restaurant that shows thirteen of the major chefs of France sitting around a dining table

in perfect imitation of Leonardo da Vinci's last supper. And who is the central figure on whom all eyes are focused? The photographer was right — there was no other choice.

Bocuse's name is not only on the menu, the plates, the serviette rings, but on wines, saucepans, and even a French postage stamp. He is the only chef ever to be declared a member of the Légion d'Honneur — by Giscard d'Estaing in 1975 — whereupon all his friends came together to create the most marvellous celebratory banquet. Guérard, Vergé and Troisgros created dishes in his honour for the night; yet one chef's dish hit the headlines and went on to be so memorable that it is quoted in every modern text on French cuisine — and of course it was Bocuse's own, the extraordinarily flamboyant *Soupe aux Truffes Elysées,* the pastry-topped soup that is nothing but a simple broth of truffles, the most luxurious and heaven-sent fungus on the French food market, dug from the ground under oak trees by pigs in the south of France. The pastry is the most wonderful foil for their pungent aroma, for the soup goes to the table enclosed in pastry and only when you crack the crust with a spoon is the aroma released directly to the diner's nose.

Obviously it is too expensive a soup for most of us to reproduce, but it is still found on the Bocuse menu, a classic amongst others like his *Loup en Croûte* (the beautiful sea bass of the Mediterranean wrapped and cooked in pastry and served with *sauce choron*). Hardly a first-time diner goes to the Bocuse Restaurant without tasting one of these two dishes, or a third equally noted one, the *Poularde en Vessie*, the classic dish of the surrounding Bresse area, a grain-fed chicken, the natural pungency and flavour of which is maintained by being cooked in a tightly sewn pig's bladder. The secret of these three dishes is probably the same — that to keep the essential flavours of perfect

Rougets en Ecailles

produce, there is nothing like enclosing them and allowing them to steam in their own juices so that all the goodness is maintained.

Such is the fairly simple philosophy in all Bocuse's cooking, and essentially the dishes that have made his name famous are not extremely complicated, but rather the expression of a belief that natural flavours should not be smothered, that a cook's duty is to deliver to the table the best produce of the marketplace, in whichever way its flavour can be brought out most.

Bocuse's philosophy was already very much in line with the build-up of feelings in the late 1960s and 1970s that eventually cast aside much of the culinary heritage of Escoffier.

In the 1950s Bocuse had been apprenticed to one of the foremost chefs of the century, Fernand Point of La Pyramide in Vienne, whose legendary approach to cooking was to market early, bring home the produce, and write a simple menu (daily and by hand) featuring only the produce that he had procured that morning. Point's simple format broke entirely with the habits of restaurants of the time, which rarely changed their menus, often printed months in advance, and froze and stocked marinated produce in order to furnish their elaborate dishes.

Although now Bocuse finds he can't take his own classic specialities off the menu, since people come from all over the world to taste them (the French Government says he makes a unique contribution to the balance of payments since so many foreigners are drawn to his restaurant), Bocuse's philosophy is still highly tied to this credence. He was one of the chefs who cast aside the rules of Escoffier, with its rich marinades and sauces, and helped usher in the development of nouvelle cuisine. But when the excesses of nouvelle cuisine became too much for him, and garnishing dishes with unlikely combinations in the form of spokes and cartwheels carried nouvelle cuisine to the ridiculous rather than enhancing his beloved produce, he implored that his name be released from the association and chose what in fact had always beeen his favourite term for his style of cooking — *cuisine du marché*, or cuisine of the marketplace. This also became the title of the most important of his books.

Cuisine du marché didn't refute the basic tenets of nouvelle cuisine. It just honed in on the one aspect crucial to Bocuse, his love for nature's produce. Therefore he sees no incompatibility when he talks about his grandmother's crème caramel recipe, or a true favorite of his, the classic French pot-au-feu, the beautifully boiled beef and vegetable braise which he considers one of the glories of French cuisine. When Bocuse is caught saying, 'But I always was a classical chef,' you'd better believe it. For a leading chef of nouvelle cuisine, no one loves provincial bourgeoise cuisine better than Bocuse.

Thanks to the high-speed train that takes just two hours from the heart of Paris to Lyon, more and more people now go to his restaurant on the banks of the Soane, at Collonges-au-Mont-d'Or. However Bocuse's fame as an ambassador of French cuisine has also tended to cause him a certain amount of criticism. He has contracts to train chefs in Japan and along with Roger Vergé and Gaston Lenôtre a responsibility to run the French restaurant and pavilion at Disney World in Florida, and both require his absence from Lyon at various times. Many people are disappointed if Bocuse is not present when they visit his restaurant, but people in the trade realise that only rarely is the cuisine of the great restaurants of France done by its masters. In general, they act as executive chefs, setting the tone of the restaurant, checking the food and design and developing the dishes. Above all, they are the working executives of their domains, enticed to their stoves only on special occasions.

I've always wondered why people find this so astounding. In the case of Bocuse's restaurant, no kitchen in the land is better staffed. There are fifty, no less, in the supporting team, and two — Paul Bocuse and Roger Jaloux, his chef-de-cuisine of eighteen years, are both Meilleurs Ouvriers de France Cuisiniers. The restaurant incidentally, has maintained its three-star rating since 1965.

The kitchen is open for you to see. Just to the left of the main room, in a small but decidedly open corridor, it is a sparkling place agleam with hundreds of pieces of polished copper, a rather mad, lacquered red ceiling and a cluster of antique knives and scales on the shelves. (The banquet room in the adjoining restaurant is even madder, for it houses one of the majestic steam-powered organs that Paul collects — wall to wall across the restaurant.) Out of the kitchen comes a stream of dishes, and you can watch for a while and see most of them made.

The menu is elaborate, meaning large, but look into it again, and you'll see how closely it reflects the marketplace. In spring when lamb is at its best it may appear in four ways, with a choice of three or four perfect vegetables of the tiniest size, served alongside and on a separate plate. The pastry will be perfect, and the fruit on a tartlet exquisite, retaining, even cooked, its fresh look and form. When you ask for the grand dessert, the entire day's workings from the pastry larder come to your table.

Bocuse's restaurant is egotistical, even garish, and often quite overwhelming, but to eat there is to gain an insight into the private domain of one of the most celebrated chefs in the world.

Rougets en Ecailles
Red Mullet Fried in its 'Scales'

Serves 4
4 red mullets, sometimes known as barbuna or *rouget barbé*
salt and pepper
2 large potatoes
5 tablespoons (Br.)/6 tablespoons (U.S.) clarified butter
butter to fry in
1 small carrot
1 small zucchini (courgette)
2 tablespoons (Br.)/ scant 3 tablespoons (U.S.) butter
300ml/½ pint (Br.)/1¼ cups (U.S.) dry white wine
3 heaped tablespoons (Br.)/4 tablespoons (U.S.) cream, preferably with 45% milk fat (heavy cream)

1. Using a sharp flexible knife, pierce the back of the fish at its head just above the backbone, and fillet the fish by running the knife along the length of the bones.

2. Fillet the second half by slipping the knife just under the backbone. Remove the bones and cut off the head. (If this is done by the fishmonger, ask for the bones and head to make the stock.)

3. Retain the skins, trim and neaten the fillets. Run your finger along the centre of each fillet against the grain of the fish to feel for any remaining bones. Remove them with tweezers. Salt and pepper the fish on both sides.

4. Peel and wash the potatoes. Cut them into 2cm/1in pieces widthwise

then, with an icing pocket nozzle or a similar round cutter of 1.25cm/½in diameter, cut these rounds into small cylinders, through the height of each piece of potato.

5. Using a mandolin if possible, or a very sharp knife, cut extremely thin slices from these potato cylinders to give the effect of fish scales. Lay the 'scales' on a plate, salt and pepper them and spoon over a couple of tablespoons of clarified butter, heated just enough to make it liquid.

6. Lay the scales of potato across the skin side of each fish fillet, starting the first layer at the head, and overlapping them in rows going right down the length of the fish, and finishing at the tail.

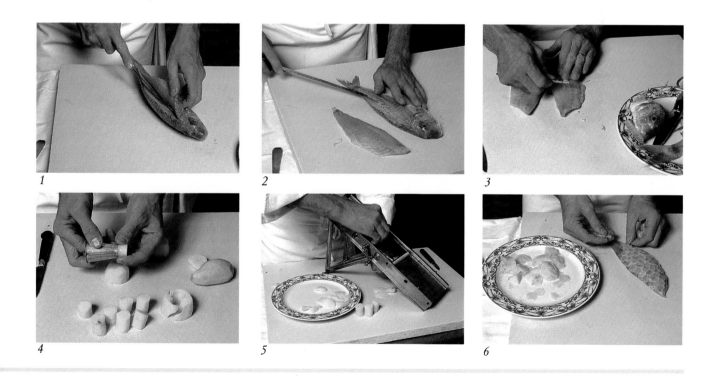

1

2

3

4

5

6

7

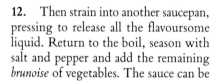

10   11   12

7. Paint with more clarified butter, then refrigerate for at least 1 hour to firm the butter completely. In this time, the starch will also solidify in the potato so it doesn't detach when frying.

8. In 2 pans large enough to hold 4 fillets each, heat enough butter to make a depth of about 5mm/¼ in. Fry the fillets, potato side down, quite speedily so that the potato crisps and colours. The fish is cooked on only one side. It takes about 2 minutes and by this time the other side has cooked through a little, though not quite fully. When turned upside down onto the serving plate, the heat will diffuse through to finish the cooking perfectly.

The sauce:

9. Chop some carrot and a little unpeeled zucchini (courgette) very finely to make a *brunoise*.

10. Chop the fish heads and bones, add half of the *brunoise* vegetables together with any remaining peeled carrot ends. Toss in a little butter, cover with dry white wine and simmer gently until the alcohol has evaporated and a good fishy sauce base is obtained (approximately 15 minutes).

11. Stir the cream into the sauce and return to the boil.

12. Then strain into another saucepan, pressing to release all the flavoursome liquid. Return to the boil, season with salt and pepper and add the remaining *brunoise* of vegetables. The sauce can be made in advance and reheated. Finish with a good smothering of snipped chives, added only at the last minute. Plate the fish and surround with the sauce.

Terrine de Foie Gras
Foie gras

Serves 10
1kg/use 2 lb fresh goose foie gras (fresh foie gras of duck can be substituted)
salt and finely ground white pepper
2 tablespoons (Br.)/scant 3 tablespoons (U.S.) port

Equipment:
1 loaf-shaped mould, pâté mould or porcelain terrine with a lid

Open out the lobes of the livers. From the top, where they are obvious from the outside of the livers, find the large veins. With a very small sharp knife, open up the lobes a little, following down the length of the veins, and carefully prise these veins out of the livers. If some pieces of liver break away, keep them to add to the terrine.

Lightly salt and pepper the livers. Sprinkle with port. Choose the appropriate size of mould or porcelain terrine to fit the livers snuggly, and place the lobes of liver in it, layering them carefully to cover the area well. Press just enough to close the airspaces, but not firmly enough to squash the livers. Cover with the lid, and place the terrine in a baking tray full of water. Cover the lot with either a large lid, or foil, then place on the stove, and bring to 75°C/170°F. Simmer at this temperature for 30 minutes.

When sterilised, remove from the baking tray, allow to cool , then leave the mould or terrine in the refrigerator for 1 day, preferably 2. When you lift the lid, the terrine, still pink in the centre, will be set in its own grease. It will now keep for up to 1 week, as long as it is kept refrigerated.

To serve:
Slice the foie gras and serve with a surround of refreshing salad of your choice. Paul has chosen a mixture of greens and radicchio, with a fanned-out presentation of artichoke base, all lightly dressed with a sherry vinegar and olive oil vinaigrette, seasoned, and with a dash of hazelnut oil in it.

Saumon à l'Unilateral
Salmon with Oil and Vinegar Dressing

Serves 4
4 salmon or ocean trout fillets of about 120g/4½ oz each. Have the fishmonger cut the pieces with their skin still on.
1 cucumber
2 or 3 baby carrots per person
9 tablespoons (Br.)/11 tablespoons (U.S.) olive oil
4 tablespoons (Br.)/5 tablespoons (U.S.) white wine vinegar
sea salt
freshly ground black pepper
chopped parsely and chives (about 6 to 7 tablespoons when mixed)

With a potato peeler or a professional mandolin, slice the unpeeled cucumber into 8 thin slices lengthwise. Set aside. Cut about 4 tablespoons of julienne from the remaining flesh of the cucumber, avoiding the seeds. Peel the carrots, leaving a short length of their green on for decorative purposes. Cook the carrots in boiling salted water, drain and set aside, then blanch the cucumber slices for a few seconds only until they soften.

Season the fish with the sea salt and black pepper. Take about 2 tablespoons of oil in a thick skillet, or better still, a non-stick skillet, just big enough to hold the fish, and heat the oil in it. Combine the rest of the oil with the vinegar, season it to taste and then set it aside.

The fish:
Cook the fish, skin side down, until it is just cooked through. There is no need to turn the fish; this way the skin will have time to become crusty and the fat, which lies just under the skin, will be rendered, just as the flesh heats through and cooks.

To serve:

Toss the cucumber slices momentarily into a pan with either hot butter or a little more oil to glaze them, add the carrot and then the uncooked julienne of cucumber. Place the fish onto the serving plates, then fold 2 slices onto each place decoratively as pictured. Spoon some julienne of cucumber over each piece of fish and sprinkle liberally with the parsley and chive mixture. Spoon the olive oil and vinegar dressing over everything and serve immediately.

Soupe aux Truffes Elysées
Truffle Soup

Makes 4 bowls

8 tablespoons (Br.)/10 tablespoons (U.S.) *matignon* (equal parts of carrots, onions, celery, mushrooms diced very finely and softened in a little unsalted butter)

200g/good 7 oz fresh raw truffles (for mere mortals, tinned will have to suffice)

80g/3 oz foie gras

1 litre /1¾ pints (Br.)/4¼ cups (U.S.) strong chicken consommé

325g/use ¾ lb puff pastry

1 egg yolk, beaten with 1 tablespoon milk or water

Equipment:

Individual oven-proof soup bowls. For the puff pastry top to hold well, use only deep, rather narrow bowls, like the traditional onion soup bowl.

Remove the woody centre from the carrots and chop all the vegetables into tiny dice (*brunoise*). Simmer gently in butter until soft to make a *matignon*. Put 2 tablespoons (Br.)/scant 3 tablespoons (U.S.) of this *matignon* into each soup bowl with the roughly sliced truffles, foie gras and the consommé, while still cold (it heats while the pastry cooks). If it is already hot, it emits too much steam and the pastry softens and falls.

On a floured board, roll out the puff pastry to about 2mm/1/16in thickness. Cut 4 circles of pastry, each 2cm/1in

larger than the diameter of the bowls. Brush the edges of the bowls with some beaten egg. Place a round of pastry over each bowl, pressing the overlap against the sides of the bowl. Place the soup bowls in the refrigerator for a minimum of 60 minutes (if it is any more, lightly place a covering of plastic film over the bowls so the pastry does not dry out). This refrigeration is necessary so the pastry does not shrink when first placed in the hot oven.

At the moment you place the soup in the oven to cook, glaze the pastry tops with beaten egg. Bake in a 220ºC/425ºF oven for 5 minutes, then reduce the heat to 200ºC/400ºF until the pastry is cooked through and golden, about 25 minutes. Serve immediately. The soup will be steaming hot.

Crème Brulée

Makes 6 individual serves
500ml/good ¾ pint (Br.)/2 good cups (U.S.) cream with 35% milk fat (whipping cream)
500ml/good ¾ pint (Br.)/2 good cups (U.S.) milk
2 vanilla beans, split in half lengthwise
9 egg yolks
200g/good 7 oz (Br.)/1 scant cup (U.S.) castor (superfine) sugar
brown sugar

Scald the milk and the cream with the split vanilla beans. Remove the beans and scrape out a little of the powdery centre to stir into the milk. Place the egg yolks in a bowl, add the sugar and whisk together, then pour in the milk and cream. Pour the mixture into small individual eared dishes or ramekins. Contrary to the usual method, Bocuse does not place these in a bain-marie, but cooks the dishes directly in a pre-heated oven at 150ºC/300ºF for 45 to 60 minutes.

Cool and refrigerate until needed. They should be very cold so that when gratinéed (glazed), the custard does not reheat and curdle. When required, sprinkle the top with a full layer of brown sugar and gratiné (glaze) under a pre-heated grill (broiler), or with a blowtorch.

Anton Mosimann

The Dorchester
London, England

'Great chefs are born, not made', goes the familiar dictum, and in Anton Mosimann, we see the living proof. Born in Switzerland to a family of restaurateurs, at eight years of age Anton was already determined to become a chef and was cooking meals for the family's adult friends. By seventeen years of age, he had become the youngest person ever to be awarded the Diplôme de Cuisinier.

Believing that a chef who took an appointment to head a kitchen too young would never have enough breadth of experience to call himself a master of his art, Anton then gave himself several years training, in more or less the same system the Freemasons had thought exemplary — he became an itinerant chef. He worked in several of Switzerland's most important hotels, others in Rome, Montreal and Japan (a year in Japan as Head Chef for the Swiss Pavilion at Expo 70 left an indelible impression on his cuisine, which he believes is reflected in almost every dish he executes today), and spent time with many of the famous modern chefs of France, among them Paul Bocuse, Michel Guérard, Roger Vergé and the Troisgros brothers, all of whom welcomed him into their kitchens.

Often starting again at grass roots, Anton determined to work his way through the pastry sections, the baking sections and even worked in butcher shops, and by the time he was twenty-five he had gained the highest diploma possible for a Swiss chef, the Diplôme de Chef de Cuisine. He was again the youngest person ever to do so.

Anton's fame spread rapidly in the English-speaking world as he took over as Maître Chef de Cuisines at the formidable Dorchester Hotel in London. Since 1975, he has led a team of eighty chefs and fifty supporting staff to greater strength than the famous old hotel has ever known for its restaurants, and now Anton Mosimann is a world celebrity with a place in the history of modern cuisine.

Today's slimmer looking Anton is the result of a man shocked one day when reading the newspaper on finding that 25,000 English people die annually of heart disease. Always a great fan of nouvelle cuisine and the light, modern style of eating that he feels contributes best to the modern life-style, Anton started wondering whether he could experiment even further with a healthy cuisine that would still be flavoursome and yet not contribute to the modern problems of cholesterol and obesity.

Consulting continually with a doctor, Anton put all his skills into creating a dietary cuisine that had no cream, no butter, no oil, no fat, and less sugar and salt. The result, his 'Cuisine Naturelle', has won world-wide acclaim and is the subject of his second book, of the same name.

Recently, Anton has joined up with well-known English food personality Lyn Hall, whose cookery school La Petite Cuisine in Richmond, Surrey is among the most respected in England. Together now as Directors of La Petite Cuisine and Cuisine Créative, Lyn and Anton work as consultants to the restaurant trade, large food companies and for television and feature films. Still working out of the Dorchester, Anton also tries to give as much time as he can to 'being on the road', giving demonstrations all over England, the U.S.A. and even Australia.

This slim and elegant-looking walking exponent of a healthier cuisine is making great progress in spreading the word. The prestigious Dorchester dining room now finds that as much as thirty per cent of the restaurant turnover is in Cuisine Naturelle. 'Steaming and poaching are wonderful methods of

Pot au Feu de Volaille

cooking' says Anton, who bases much of his natural food on good stocks. 'But eye appeal has a lot to do with what people enjoy, and the food must look wonderful on the plates. It must have flavour too, and we obtain much of that with good use of fresh herbs, some well-placed turns of the pepper mill, and retaining the wonderful texture and true fresh taste of the best and finest ingredients.'

In case you think he's turning away from his authoritative knowledge of the techniques of classical cuisine, Anton puts in hours each day with the apprentices at the Dorchester, giving them some of the most comprehensive hotel and restaurant training England can offer. Anton also still cooks and plans the menus at the Dorchester every day and coordinates the many dining services for the grand old hotel with the most prestigious address and clientele in England.

As well, in his spare time, he continues to write cookery books. He already has to his credit *Cuisine à la Carte*, *A New Style of Cooking*, *Cuisine Naturelle*, *Shellfish* which he wrote in collaboration with Holger Hofmann and, most recently, *Anton Mosimann's Fish Cuisine*. However, uppermost in Anton's mind, and utilising all the talents, skills and experience his years at the top of the trade have taught him, is the overwhelming desire to provide for eating glamorously and superbly, but within a framework fit for good health.

Dieting without despair is the subtitle here. Enjoy, and have no fear your health will suffer!

Postscript: As this book goes to press, news is that Anton has left the Dorchester to take a partnership in The Belfry, a private dining club in central London. This should certainly change the face of club dining in London.

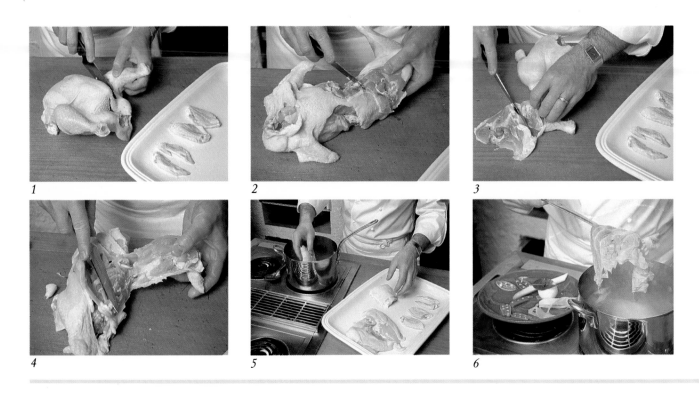

1

2

3

4

5

6

Pot au Feu de Volaille

Chicken Pot Au Feu

Serves 4

1 chicken, about 2.2kg/5 lb
about 2 litres/3½ pints (Br.)/scant 9 cups (U.S.) chicken stock
3 onions, peeled, each studded with 2 cloves
1 bay leaf
2 cloves garlic, peeled
a few peppercorns
3 stalks parsley, thyme, rosemary, tied together for easy removal
8 baby carrots, peeled but with their trimmed tops left on
12 baby turnips, peeled but with their trimmed tops left on
4 baby onions, peeled
12 baby beets if in season, peeled and with their trimmed tops left on (optional, and seasonal)
a few snow or snap peas — a couple will be cooked open, some closed
3 baby leeks, optional
2 zucchinis (courgettes), unpeeled and cut into 2 or 3 on the diagonal
¼ savoy cabbage
salt and freshly ground pepper
thyme or other herbs to garnish

Note: Depending on the season or availability, you may choose to omit some of the vegetables.

To cut the chicken:

1. Remove the chicken's wings at the second joint inwards. Cut these removed pieces into 2. Now remove the leg — drumstick and thigh — in 1 piece.

2. Remove the second leg also.

3. Cut each of the 2 legs in half at the natural joint between the thigh and drumstick.

4. Cutting from the centre breastplate of the remaining section, remove the breast (*suprême*) from the carcass at the breastplate. Chop the wing knuckle off just below the joint to neaten the appearance of the wing-tip. Repeat with the breast and wing of the second side. You now have 6 beautiful meaty pieces, plus 2 smaller sections of wing and the 2 wing-tips which should not be used.

The carcass and wing-tips may be used to make a chicken stock in the usual manner before proceeding, or you may call upon a light chicken stock from your reserves. You need about 2 litres, 3½ pints (Br.)/scant 9 cups (U.S.) in all.

5. In a large pan, bring the chicken stock to the boil, and reinforce its flavour by adding the onions studded with the cloves, the bay leaf, garlic, peppercorns and herbs. Simmer for 20 minutes then add the chicken portions and poach the drumsticks for about 12 to 15 minutes and the breasts for about 8 to 10 minutes, skimming the stock thoroughly as any scum rises to the surface.

6. Remove the chicken from the pan. Strain the stock and remove any fat that has risen to the surface with a spoon, then the residue with strips of paper towel. Return the stock to the cleaned-out pan. Add the vegetables, except for the cabbage leaves, the snow or snap peas and the beetroot. The beetroot must be boiled in water until tender (about 8 minutes) in order to prevent its colour from leeching into the dish. Keep the beetroot separate until serving time. As the vegetables are cooked, about 10 minutes in all, depending on their size, remove to a plate. Lastly, drop in the cabbage leaves and the snow or snap peas to blanch momentarily until they lose their stiffness.

7. The photograph shows how the undercooked vegetables should look to retain their flavour, colour and crispness.

8. Skin the chicken and return it to the pot for a further 5 minutes or until just cooked. Strain and keep warm with the vegetables. Boil the chicken stock rapidly to reduce by half. Adjust the seasoning only when it has reached the quantity and density required. Return everything to the pot for a final heating through, then start the arrangement of vegetables on the plate for the service.

9. Using heated dinner plates, preferably with a little depth, like old English wide soup bowls, arrange a cabbage leaf in the base of each plate, then place 1 or 2 pieces of chicken in the centre of the cabbage leaf and an assortment of vegetables around each plate.

10. Ladle a little of the flavoursome stock over everything.

7

8

9

10

Wolfgang Puck
Spago's
Chinois on Main
Los Angeles, U.S.A.

Never was a man so aptly named as Wolfgang Puck! The Wolfgang is for the Austrian birthright, a middle name (perhaps concealed by humility, but doubtless existent) can only be Armadeus for genius, and the Puck is right there in the sparkling-eyed, grinning, mischievous cherub face that presents itself to the public under the oh-so-American baseball cap that he wears at a jaunty angle throughout his working day.

Wolfgang is the great merchandiser. As much aware of the public and of the element known to the P.R. and theatrical people as 'timing' as any chef I've met, he has an unconscious 'savvy' about what works and what doesn't. He would probably have been a natural in almost any profession, as long as it put him before the public.

However, the fun-loving and show-off owner of Los Angeles's two most popular restaurants, Spago's and Chinois on Main, had a very straight, very disciplined and highly classical training in his profession. Born in Austria, Wolfgang had the most important part of his chef training in France, first and foremost with Raymond Thuillier at L'Ostau de la Baumanière in Les Baux de Provence, and later at Maxim's in Paris. In the mid-seventies after a spell working in England, Wolfgang arrived in the United States. He had a year in Indianapolis and then moved to Los Angeles as the celebrity-pleasing chef at the star-studded restaurant Ma Maison. His success there was so great that owner Patrick Terrail allowed him an associate partnership, and together they elevated the restaurant to one of the finest French restaurants in the States. Wolfgang grew little by little, first into a nouvelle cuisine chef, then blossoming more and more into a personal creativity in the light and fresh Californian style that is typical of the best chefs of this area.

It is hard to by-pass the French segment of Wolfgang's past, for he himself defines it as perhaps the most important in his life, and although it reflects the most classical period of his training, he credits Thuillier with nurturing the creativity in him that came to the fore so much later on. 'Wine-maker, lecturer, painter, writer, Mayor of the small French town of Les Baux . . . (Raymond Thuillier) is truly a Renaissance man', he declares in the introduction to his first book, *Modern French Cooking for the American Kitchen*. 'His robust and poetic approach to all aspects of his life touched and deeply influenced me. Perhaps there are more technically excellent chefs (he did not decide he wanted to cook until the age of fifty), but for me, none greater exemplifies the love of life, creation, and constant growth. I believe I always had within me the ability to excel, but Thuillier's support allowed me the confidence to express myself and accept responsibility. Most of all, he offered me the freedom to grow.'[1]

After six years of success at Ma Maison, Wolfgang was ready to marry Barbara Lazaroff, a wonderfully extremist publicist with a great flair for design and an equal to Puck as a smart self-promoter and marketer. Together they engineered one of the most extroverted and hyped-up marriage ceremonies the world has ever seen: bride, groom, horse-drawn open carriage, planeloads of wedding guests and a barrel-load of press and television photographers staged a wedding in the heavenly stone-walled medieval French village of — you guessed it — Les Baux de Provence.

If the wedding was somewhat overstated, Spago's is the opposite — quite understated. Perched over a hire-car lot in brassy Sunset Boulevard, it is a large spacious room dotted with pine-coloured benches and flowered tablecloths that give the impression of air and space. Giant flower bowls (it is hard to call them

Grilled Scallops with a Spicy Coriander Vinaigrette

vases, for they are huge, and with hundreds of dollars of long-stemmed colourful blooms in each) and the casually but somewhat eclectically dressed patrons create the colour and the ambiance of the restaurant, which most of the time can only be described as vibrant and electric. 'Going to a restaurant has become a social event — people want to feel the presence of other people,' declares Wolfgang, and to further this noisy socialising, the chefs are right there in the act too. Pizzas are the signature dish of Spago's and along the counter that runs the whole length of the restaurant are the pizza oven with its stock of wood piled high in front, the hotplates, and a large iron barbecue grill.

Wolfgang himself is also there to be seen behind the counter, baseball hat askew, while he laughingly completes yet another of his innovative pizzas, dotting it with lamb's meat sausage, goat's cheese, bits of broccoli, and *confit* of duck.

These days, his cooking is based much more on local produce than his more classical 'standards' at Ma Maison. Stir-fried scallop salad, sizzling catfish, lamb grilled over mesquite, roasted chicken breasts stuffed with yellow and red bell peppers and sweet green onion sauce, belie the classic heritage he built his talent on, but make him a hero of the local scene.

At Chinois, where the rationale was to create modern dining in the Chinese style, east meets west with a vengeance. Out at the beach and more relaxed than Spago's, the dynamics of Chinois is different. At Spago's, where seeing and being seen dictate the drama, tables are sought both for the internal and external view. At Chinois, everyone stands in queues, weaving their way through the overcrowded room less to be seen than to join their friends and sample the great cuisine. Barbara has again excelled herself in the design, which is a green-based, painted surrealist fantasy, equalled only in its boldness and strength by the noise and excitement the crowd generates. The cooking area, with bar stools around it, projects itself even more into the atmosphere of the restaurant than at Spago's. Here, Japanese chefs cut raw fish into most unclassical examples of sushi, and the wok chefs turn out such dishes as minted squab salad and Chinese duck with plum sauce. Whatever you expect when you order, you can bet it will not be quite as you imagined. For Wolfgang has a free and joyful approach to food. You can hear him laughing from the very dishes.

'My playground!', he calls them, 'my *kinderspiel*.' And while this never means you should underestimate the power of the promoter, who is out there consulting for hotels and airlines and appearing on 'Good Morning America', you can't help believing that he means it when he says, '. . . and while you're cooking, don't forget to share and laugh. Laugh a great deal, and with much love — it enhances the flavour of food.'[2]

1. Wolfgang Puck, *Modern French Cooking for the American Kitchen*, Houghton Mifflin, Boston, 1981, p xiv.
2. ibid., p xv.

Grilled Scallops with a Spicy Coriander Vinaigrette

This is a perfect summer dish which can be made as a main course, or as an appetiser without the vegetables but with mixed short-leaved salad greens.

Serves 6
30 large scallops
1 large spanish (purple) onion (often called Bermuda onion)
6 tomatoes
2 limes
1 bunch coriander (cilantro)
1 small jalapeno (hot) chilli
olive oil
vinegar
salt and pepper
1 small eggplant (aubergine)
2 baby zucchinis (courgettes)
12 broccoli flowerettes
a few fresh morels, or any available fresh mushrooms
6 baby turnips
6 tiny baby carrots

Equipment:
6 wooden skewers, soaked in water for at least half an hour

To prepare the scallops:
Remove the muscles of the scallops and trim them, removing any bits of shell and skin. (Some people also like to remove the coral part of the scallop, but it can be retained if you wish.) If the scallops are very large they can be halved horizontally. Marinate the scallops in a little chopped coriander (cilantro) and olive oil seasoned with a little white pepper. Set aside while preparing the rest.

To prepare the relish (salsa):

1. Chop the spanish onion finely. Set it aside. Remove the core from each tomato with a sharp knife. Place a fork firmly in the flesh of 1 of the tomatoes, place it in boiling water for a few minutes, remove and peel. The tomato should peel easily without removing too much flesh, but if this occurs, place it back in the boiling water for a few moments longer. Repeat the process with the remaining tomatoes, leaving the prepared tomatoes aside. Cut the tomatoes into quarters, then seed them. Roughly chop the tomato flesh. Place the onion and tomato into a bowl. Very finely chop the jalapeno chilli after removing its core and seeds, and add it to the bowl.

2. Chop the coriander (cilantro) finely and add it to the bowl.

3. Squeeze the limes into the bowl with the chopped ingredients. (If you do not have any limes you can use lemon juice or a little vinegar, but the flavour is not quite the same.) Add some olive oil, salt and pepper to the bowl and mix all the ingredients well. Set the mixture aside.

4. Thread the scallops onto the skewers, which have been soaked in water to prevent them burning.

To prepare the vegetables:

5. Slice the eggplant (aubergine) into about 5mm/¼ in slices, leaving the skin on. Brush the slices lightly with some olive oil and season with salt and pepper. Set aside. Do the same with the whole baby zucchinis (courgettes). There is no need to slice them if they are tiny. It is important that the eggplant (aubergine) slices and zucchinis (courgettes) are oiled, as they will be char-grilled later with the scallops. Cut the broccoli into flowers leaving a longer stalk than usual. Slice the morels lengthwise in half. Trim the baby turnips and carrots, removing the skin but leaving the stalks intact. Cook the turnips and carrots in boiling, salted water until just tender, then briefly place on the char-grill to brown them.

6. Char-grill the skewered scallops with the prepared eggplant (aubergine) slices, whole baby zucchinis (courgettes), the broccoli flowers and the morel halves. Turn them only once during the cooking. The grilling will only take a few minutes on either side. The scallops are ready when they have turned a milky white colour — at this point they are cooked and any further cooking will only toughen them. Remove the vegetables and scallops once cooked. Keep warm.

7. To serve the scallops, spoon the prepared relish (salsa) in the middle of each individual serving plate.

8. Remove the scallops from the skewers. Place the scallops on top of the relish (salsa), making a flower pattern, and arrange the grilled and blanched vegetables around the scallops. For this dish Wolfgang chooses to garnish the scallops with a few zucchini (courgette) or nasturtium flowers. If unavailable, use fresh sprigs of coriander (cilantro).

1

2

3

4

5

6

7

8

Lamb Chops with Cream of Shallots

The wine label on Wolfgang's house red is taken from a painting by Andy Warhol which hangs on the wall at Spago's.

Serves 6
2 racks of lamb, about 500g/use 1 lb each, or 4 individual racks of 3 to 4 cutlets each. Ask the butcher to remove

the last 5cm/2 in of the rib bones, and reserve all the trimmings, bar the fat, for a lamb stock.
olive oil
2 sprigs rosemary, plus 1 teaspoon chopped rosemary for the sauce
salt and freshly ground pepper
10 shallots, finely chopped
2 tablespoons (Br.)/scant 3 tablespoons (U.S.) unsalted butter
120ml/4 fl oz (Br.)/½ cup (U.S.) red wine vinegar

120ml/4 fl oz (Br.)/½ cup (U.S.) dry white wine
225ml/scant 8 fl oz (Br.)/1 cup (U.S.) lamb stock (see below)
3 tablespoons (Br.)/3½ tablespoons (U.S.) unsalted butter

The garnish:
2 to 3 sprigs fresh thyme, fresh rosemary, leaves of small-leafed lettuce e.g. lamb's tongue lettuce (*mâche*), oak-leaf lettuce or radicchio

The lamb stock:
the lamb bones and trimmings as above
3 to 4 tablespoons extra-virgin olive oil
1½ cups diced onion, carrot and celery
½ teaspoon whole black peppercorns
1 bay leaf

To prepare the day before:
Rub the lamb with olive oil. Add a couple of sprigs of rosemary, then cover the racks with plastic wrap and let them stand overnight in the refrigerator.

To make the lamb stock:
Brown the cut lamb bones and trimmings in a little olive oil. Add the diced vegetables (*mirepoix*), and continue browning for 2 to 3 minutes. Add the peppercorns and the bay leaf. Add water to cover, bring to a boil and simmer slowly until the stock has reduced to approximately 1 cup. Strain and reserve.

On the day:
Pre-heat the oven to 230ºC/450ºF. Place the lamb in a shallow roasting pan. Season with salt and pepper and roast for 25 minutes for the 2 racks or 10 to 12 minutes for the individual racks (medium rare). Allow them to rest in a warm spot for 10 minutes before carving.

Discard any grease from the roasting pan, add 2 to 3 tablespoons of butter and sauté the shallots for 2 minutes on a gentle heat. De-glaze the pan with the vinegar and white wine, and reduce the liquid until only about 2 tablespoons remain. Add the stock and the teaspoon of chopped rosemary and reduce by half. Cook until reduced enough to coat the spoon (approximately half the original volume). Whisk in the remaining butter, a small amount at a time. Taste and correct the seasonings. Strain the sauce.

To serve:
Slice the lamb into cutlets. Place 2 or 3 lamb cutlets on each heated serving plate. Wolfgang serves them on a bed of soft lettuce, with that most fashionable of garnishes, mashed potato.

WOLFGANG'S DESSERTS

There are four desserts in Wolfgang's photograph, each saying something about his repertoire. This is not to suggest that they all be served together.

Chocolate Raspberry Terrine

Serves 12
12 egg yolks
125g/4½ oz (Br.)/scant ⅔ cup (U.S.) sugar
550g/1 lb 4 oz dark (bittersweet) chocolate
200g/7 oz (Br.)/1 scant cup (U.S.) unsalted butter
3 tablespoons (Br.)/3½ tablespoons (U.S.) cream with 35% milk fat (whipping cream)
3 egg whites
1 tablespoon sugar
700g/1½ lbs (Br.)/4 cups (U.S.) fresh raspberries

The bitter chocolate glaze:
250g/use ½ lb dark (bittersweet) chocolate
4 tablespoons (Br.)/5 tablespoons (U.S.) unsalted butter
1 tablespoon plus one teaspoon corn syrup or liquid glucose
175ml/6 fl oz (Br.)/good ¾ cup (U.S.) cream with 35% milk fat (whipping cream)
4 tablespoons (Br.)/5 tablespoons (U.S.) cognac

Equipment:
26 x 10 x 8cm/10 x 4 x 3 in deep terrine mould, lined with baking (parchment) paper

Cream the egg yolks and sugar until very thick and mousse-like, and doubled in volume. Melt the chocolate and the butter together over hot water. Add to the yolk mixture and mix together over hot water until the mixture is thick and shiny. Remove from the heat.

Whip the cream and fold it into the chocolate mixture when cooled but still liquid enough. The better method is to start by folding a little chocolate into the cream, and then returning the cream to the rest of the chocolate.

Beat the egg whites with 1 tablespoon sugar until stiff and glossy peaks form. Whisk ⅓ of the egg whites into the chocolate mixture. Fold in the remaining egg whites.

To assemble
Pipe out of a pastry bag with a no. 4 tip. Pipe in 1/5 of the mixture into the terrine in an even layer. Arrange ¼ of the berries close together in the chocolate, leaving a 1cm/½ in border of chocolate around the edges. Repeat the layers of chocolate and berries until you have 4 layers of berries and 5 layers of chocolate, ending with a chocolate layer. Freeze for 1½ hours. Turn out of the mould. Ice with the bitter chocolate glaze.

To make the bitter chocolate glaze:
Melt the chocolate, butter and corn syrup or glucose together over a bain-marie. In a small saucepan, whisk together the cream and brandy, then simmer over a medium heat. Scrape into the melted chocolate mixture. The glaze should be warm when used, but not warm enough to harm the cake.

To serve:
Place the terrine on a rack over a plate, and pour the glaze over the terrine quickly, using a metal spatula to help spread it well. Tap it a couple of times to remove the excess. Allow it to set in the refrigerator before slicing.

Wolfgang's Marjolaine

Though this recipe is lengthy, it is not difficult, and it is well worth the effort. When making the butter cream, be sure the egg-syrup mixture is cool before the butter is added.

Serves 12

The meringue layers:
125g/4 oz (Br.)/1 scant cup (U.S.) hazelnuts, roasted for 10 to 12 minutes, then the peel rubbed off
125g/4 oz (Br.)/1 scant cup (U.S.) blanched almonds, sliced, then roasted for 5 minutes
365g/13 oz (Br.)/1¾ cups (U.S.) sugar
1 tablespoon flour
2 tablespoons (Br.)/scant 3 tablespoons (U.S.) melted butter
8 egg whites
pinch salt

Praline butter cream:
200g/good 7 oz (Br.)/1 cup (U.S.) sugar
180ml/6 fl oz (Br.)/good ¾ cup (U.S.) water
1 tablespoon hazelnuts
1 tablespoon almonds
3 egg yolks
225g/8 oz (Br.)/1 cup (U.S.) unsalted butter, softened
1 tablespoon espresso coffee
1 tablespoon hazelnut liqueur

Chocolate cream (*ganache*):
250g/9 oz dark (bittersweet) chocolate
175ml/6 fl oz (Br.)/good ¾ cup (U.S.) cream, preferably with 45% milk fat (heavy cream)

Whipped cream filling:
175ml/6 fl oz (Br.)/good ¾ cup (U.S.) cream with 35% milk fat (whipping cream)
1 tablespoon sour cream
1 tablespoon sugar (optional)

To make the meringue layers:
Reserve 2 tablespoons of sugar and combine the rest with the hazelnuts, almonds and flour. Chop finely in a food processor until the mixture resembles coarse flour.

Line 2 baking sheets 30 x 40cm/12 x 16 in with baking (parchment) paper, brushed generously with melted butter. Whip the egg whites and salt to soft peaks. Add the reserved 2 tablespoons sugar and continue to whisk. When stiff, fold in the nut mixture. Spread the meringue mixture evenly over the prepared baking sheets, in a layer about 4mm/3/16 in thick.

Bake in a 200ºC/400ºF oven for 10 to 15 minutes, until golden brown. Remove from the oven and let cool. When cool, turn the layers out on a smooth work surface and carefully remove the paper.

To prepare the praline butter cream:
In a small saucepan, cook 100g/3½ oz (Br.)/¾ cup (U.S.) sugar and 50ml/1½ fl oz (Br.)/¼ cup (U.S.) water until the bubbles are clear. Add the nuts and cook until the syrup is a dark caramel colour (the nuts will turn brown as well). Add the remaining water and cook for 1 to 2 minutes further to liquefy the caramel.

Cream the egg yolks with the remaining sugar until light and fluffy. Strain the hot caramel syrup into the egg yolk, reserving the nuts for another use. Continue to beat until the mixture is cool, and well thickened. Slowly blend in the softened butter, 1 tablespoon at a time. When incorporated, add the coffee and liqueur. Chill the butter cream until needed.

To prepare the chocolate cream (*ganache*):
Cut the chocolate into small pieces, and melt over a pan filled with hot water, then add the cream and stir over the now simmering water until smooth and well blended. Cool to spreading consistency.

To prepare the whipped cream filling:
Whip the remaining cream until stiff and fold in the sour cream. Add sugar, if desired.

To assemble:
Cut each meringue layer in half lengthwise to make 4 rectangles (12 x 35cm/5 x 14 in). Reserve the nicest for the top.

Place the first layer on a plate and spread with two-thirds of the chocolate cream. Top with the second layer and spread with the whipped cream. Top with the third layer and spread with the praline butter cream. Top with the fourth layer. Finish with a chocolate cream glaze, which is made by melting the remaining chocolate cream until it is the consistency of thickened cream. Pour it over the cake and smooth it with a spatula to form an even glaze.

Chill the marjolaine. Trim the sides if necessary with a serrated knife. Serve sprinkled with sifted powdered cocoa or icing (confectioner's) sugar.

Wolfgang's Pecan Pie

Makes 1 round tart 26cm/10 in across or 6 tartlets
350ml/11 fl oz (Br.)/1½ cups (U.S.) light corn syrup or liquid glucose
150g/good 5 oz (Br.)/¾ cup (U.S.) sugar
125g/4½ oz (Br.)/¾ cup (U.S.) brown sugar
4 eggs
2 egg yolks
2 tablespoons (Br.)/scant 3 tablespoons (U.S.) unsalted butter
sugar dough for pastry crust (⅓ quantity of recipe below)
180g/good 6 oz (Br.)/1½ cups (U.S.) pecan halves

Combine the corn syrup, sugars, eggs and egg yolks in a bowl and beat well. Heat the butter until it turns brown and has a nutty aroma. Mix it into the corn syrup mixture.

Line the tart mould with the sugar dough. Arrange the pecan halves in the bottom of the shell, then pour over the filling.

Bake in a 190ºC/375ºF oven for 45 minutes or until a skewer, inserted near the centre, comes out clean. Remove and let cool.

Wolfgang's Desserts: Chocolate Raspberry Terrine, Marjolaine, Pecan Pie, Spago's Apple Pies

Spago's Apple Pies

Makes 8 round pies 10cm/4 in across
sugar dough (1 quantity of recipe below)
8 small cooking apples (Pippin, Granny Smith or Golden Delicious)
90g/good 3 oz (Br.)/6 tablespoons (U.S.) unsalted butter
100g/scant 4 oz (Br.)/½ cup (U.S.) sugar
3 tablespoons (Br.)/3½ tablespoons (U.S.) calvados (apple brandy)
225g/8 oz puff pastry for the pastry leaves (see recipe page 171)
1 egg, lightly beaten, for eggwash

Roll the sugar dough into 2 x 28cm/ 11 in squares. Put each on a tray lined with baking (parchment) paper and chill for 20 minutes. Cut 8 circles (12cm/ 5 in across) from the dough and line tarlet tins or flan rings (10cm/4 in across, 1cm/½ in deep). Trim away the excess, which you may use instead of puff pastry for the pastry leaves. Allow the dough to rest for 30 minutes in the refrigerator before baking.

Peel, core and slice the apples 5mm/ ¼ in thick. Melt 3 tablespoons (Br.)/3½ tablespoons (U.S.) of the butter, add the apples and sprinkle with the sugar. Cook quickly so that the sugar caramelises, but the apples remain slightly crunchy. Pour the calvados over the apples and ignite it. When the flame dies, allow it to cool before using.

Divide the apples equally among the pie shells. Place ½ teaspoon of butter in the centre of each. Top each with pastry leaves, which can be cut from puff pastry or sugar dough.

Bake in a 160°C/310°F oven for 40 to 45 minutes, or until the pastry is golden brown. Let the pies rest for about 10 minutes before serving.

Sugar Dough

This is a sweet shortcrust pastry.

Makes 550g/1 lb 4 oz
250g/use ½ lb (Br.)/1 good cup (U.S.) unsalted butter, slightly softened, and cut into chunks
use 450g/1 lb (Br.)/3⅓ cups (U.S.) flour*
pinch salt
4 tablespoons (Br.)/5 tablespoons (U.S.) sugar
1½ egg yolks
1 tablespoon cream with 35% milk fat (whipping cream)

*In the United States, Wolfgang uses a mixture of pastry and plain (all-purpose) flour in equal quantities. In other countries use plain flour only.

Place the butter in the bowl of an electric mixer fitted with a dough hook, or a food processor. Add the flour, salt and sugar. Mix on a low speed (or with the pulse action of a food processor) until the butter is evenly distributed throughout the flour. Add the egg yolks and cream. Continue to mix on a low speed until the dough pulls away from the sides of the bowl.

Remove the dough, form it into a ball, then flatten it into a piece about 15cm/ 6 in round. Wrap it in plastic and chill for at least 2 hours or overnight. Use as needed.

To make by hand, use the above ingredients and follow Stephanie Alexander's step by step method on page 41.

Gay Bilson

Berowra Waters Inn
Berowra, Australia

Even if you are in Australia, the logistics of getting to Berowra Waters Inn turn a visit into a bit of an expedition. However, the Australian dining public has dubbed it, in the wonderful terms of the Michelin Guide, 'worth the detour', by heaping praise on it and making its owner Gay Bilson something of a living legend — even, as Australia's best known restaurant critic Leo Schofield called her, a 'national treasure'. Although the restaurant is open only three days a week, Gay has more plaques on the wall and top honour awards than most restaurateurs will ever cast their eyes upon.

Berowra Waters Inn is an hour and a quarter's drive north of Sydney. Regularly, the faithful trek up the Pacific Highway and wend up hill and down dale, finally negotiating the sinewy mountain track down to the peaceful little township of Berowra on the Hawkesbury River. There they park their cars and await the restaurant's punt to ford the river to the wilderness side, where the formerly humble, wooden guesthouse now turned most-important-restaurant-in-Australia, nestles on the hill.

Everyone should be extravagant at least once in their life! In Australia, where you really don't have to be a millionaire to do it, you can take the flying boat. Of course it is costly, but the breathtaking views over Sydney Harbour, the famous Harbour Bridge, the northern beaches and Pittwater; the wonderful descent into the hills at the entrance to the Hawkesbury River and taxiing between the cabin cruisers and launches plying the river are in themselves an adventure. Not to mention having the plane at your beck and call on the river to summons in a minute for the return journey. To take the flying boat may just make of a Sunday luncheon a lifetime experience.

Now that we've got you organised to get there, you're entitled to ask, 'Is Berowra Waters Inn really worth all the touting it gets? Does it really *vaut le voyage?*'

From 1973 when Gay and her former husband, Tony Bilson, opened Tony's Bon Goût, a fairly bohemian café in downtown Sydney, they have put a highly personal imprint on everything they've been associated with. At the time, they fascinated people who loved good food not by the sophistication of their dishes, but by the honest flavour of the simple dishes that they chose to serve. Since that time they have come fairly full circle. Tony developed a fine craftsmanship and technically improved to the point of being one of the best sauciers and Gay became such an expert at pastry and dessert cookery that she has produced some of the finest the country has seen. All this through the seventies and the beginning of the eighties, when they opened Berowra in an attempt to live away from the rat-race where they could develop as people as well as chefs.

With the departure of Tony to work downtown and open the café-bistro-theatre complex of Kinsela's, Gay's path took a turn as she redefined Berowra with herself at the helm. Her decision was to come out from the kitchen and take over the front-of-house and the running of the restaurant. This is not to say she has no hand in the food — she has become an extremely professional technician and oversees and develops both the style and the dishes of the restaurant, and she still often turns her fine hand to the pastry work.

Fate had a hand in consolidating Gay's new role, with the arrival of Janni Kyritsis, an empassioned cook who, in his thirties, threw up his training as an electrician to make his true love his career. After several years working with Stephanie Alexander in Melbourne, Janni moved his home to Sydney and turned up on

Crépinette of Pheasant with Pigs' Trotters and Truffles

Gay's doorstep. Voted Sydney's Chef of the Year by the *Sydney Morning Herald* in 1985, Janni is an extremely creative cook, whose greatest pleasure is the joy of research and discovery in a kitchen, and the two bring to their craft an intense artistic and intellectual approach. Together and with great rapport, they now develop recipes in tandem.

'Good restaurants are teams of people', says Gay. 'We're all working for the same thing.' It's hard work and long hours, for this team moves into Berowra at the end of each week and sleeps and cooks there for three days on end; then they all take a break before moving in again the following week. Almost everything comes from elsewhere and has to be co-ordinated, ordered and brought in by punt, although over the years Gay has built up a network of local gardeners who grow tiny vegetables especially for her. The attention to detail is minute, and all-consuming, but Gay never loses sight of the whole.

'Food,' she says, 'is only one part of what makes a terrific restaurant. I care about the surroundings and the building as much as I do about the food.' To that end, she employed architect Glenn Murcutt to do the spectacular — and spectacularly simple — transformation of the old wooden-balconied, country guesthouse. Nowadays, entry is from the sandstone basement up an iron staircase and into a long room dominated by one long line of louvre windows, a formidable linear piece of design that incorporates a bit of statutory Australiana to give a modern, abstract effect to one side of the building, at the same time allowing an unimpeded view of the cliffs opposite and the wonderful landscape of the boaters' paradise that is the Hawkesbury River. With the wattle in bloom, it has to be seen to be believed. There is something to be said for making it a lunchtime date on your first visit.

The food now is less complex than it used to be. 'The longer I cook, the more simple become my dishes,' muses Gay, in line with most sophisticated cooks. 'It's not just purism, but a greater appreciation and love of my ingredients.' 'Keeping the integral flavours is more what good cooking is all about,' says Janni. 'That doesn't mean we care less about the food — we're always going to be passionate about our sauces.'

Berowra Waters Inn currently serves a fixed-price, three-course meal, with a glass of Roederer Champagne to welcome you, an appetiser of *brandade de morue* or some other tidbit, and coffee and petits fours. The menu has a number of French classics on it (brioche and bone marrow, hare terrine, *tripes Lyonnaise*), and a number of Italian (salad of squid and pancetta, home-made noodles with pesto sauce, antipasta with tuna braised in olive oil). The choice is less personal composition than personal interpretation, always with a technical mastery rarely to be faulted, and always dictated by the season and the best possible ingredients. The desserts on my last visit reflected exactly the perfection of the February summer day — summer pudding, lemon preserve, blueberry shortcake, poached peach and champagne, cold baked figs — every one of the best fruits in the market was on this list. It is typical of the search for perfection that characterises Berowra Waters Inn.

Nowadays, this thoughtful, highly articulate ex-librarian defines herself more and more in a wider context than that of the restaurant. Gay is one of the few chefs — 'cooks' is the term she prefers — who believes there is life after food. Her conversation roves from music and architecture to books and theatre. Always ready to philosophise — about life in general and about the context of her craft — she writes articles, and is frequently on television, radio, and the lecture circuit. In 1986, at her own expense and for the joy of it, she packed her whole restaurant (chefs, ingredients, equipment and all) and rented quarters hundreds of miles away in Adelaide for the Adelaide Festival of the Arts. She has been a founding member of the group that instituted the Australian Symposium of Gastronomy but, at the same time, Gay hopes, for the betterment of Australia's restaurants as a whole, that the 'seriousness of treating good restaurants as gastronomic temples' will relax and disappear. She speaks out loudly on her feelings that restaurateurs and diners alike should realise more their own national heritage and, to that light, she now refuses to define her menu in terms of European dishes. Gone from recent menus are the truffles, the foie gras and the imported morels. On the wine list, only the inimitable French Champagne remains; the rest is an excellently selected, wide-reaching menu of Australian vintages.

Controversial to the letter, Gay continues to be criticised, and to be copied. As the bicentenary starts a new phase in Australia's history, Gay and Janni will be among the forerunners leading to a new era in Australian cuisine.

Crépinette of Pheasant with Pigs' Trotters and Truffles

Crépinette is the French word for caulfat (pork membrane, part of the amniotic sac) and, by extension, a small rissole of pork that is wrapped in caulfat. Gay's pheasant *crépinette* with truffles makes the traditional *crépinette* into a luxury dish. It may be made with guinea fowl or pigeon instead.

Serves 6 to 8
2 pheasants of about 1.5kg/3¼ lb each
3 large pigs' trotters
500g/use 1 lb pork and veal mince
1½ eggs (beat 3 with a fork, then halve)
¼ cup truffle juice (from a can)
1 large truffle, chopped, plus slices for garnish
salt, pepper, thyme
½ teaspoon *quatre-épices* or allspice
75ml/2½ fl oz (Br.)/⅓ cup (U.S.) brandy
caulfat to bind the *crépinette* (available from specialist butchers)
chicken stock to poach the pheasant
a *mirepoix* of vegetables and water to cook the pork trotters

The sauce:
450 ml/¾ pint (Br.)/2 scant cups (U.S.) chicken stock, enriched by the pheasant poaching; or demi glace the pheasant carcasses, chopped
dash truffle juice
150ml/¼ pint (Br.)/scant ¾ cup (U.S.) red wine
salt and pepper
80g/3 oz (Br.)/5 tablespoons (U.S.) butter
1 teaspoon brandy

Note: The pheasants and trotters can be cooked the day before, the sauce prepared except for the final binding with butter, and the *crépinettes* refrigerated and ready to roast on the day.

1. Poach the pheasants gently in chicken stock until just firmed. Remove the breast and thigh meat and chop fairly coarsely. You should have about 850g/1¾ lb (Br.)/6 cups (U.S.) pheasant meat. Reserve the carcasses.

2. Cook the trotters with a *mirepoix* of onion, carrot, celery and herbs, wet with water. Cool, remove the meat, dice. Include some of the rind section to give flavour and texture. You should have about 600g/1 lb 6 oz (Br.)/4 cups (U.S.) meat from the trotters.

3. Mix the meat in a bowl, and add the additional mincemeat, then the flavouring ingredients including the truffle juice, chopped truffle, *quatre-épices*, thyme, salt, pepper and the egg to bind it. Mix together well.

4. With your hands form the meat into rissole shapes (each should just fit neatly into the palm of the hand). Lay these on the spread caulfat at regular intervals.

5. Cut the caulfat between the rissoles and roll each rissole in the caulfat to hold the shape. Arrange in an ovenproof dish, drizzle with a little melted butter and bake in a 180ºC/350ºF oven for 25 to 30 minutes.

6. **The sauce:** Chop the pheasant carcasses, place them in a pan with either the chicken stock or demi glace, the red wine and truffle juice. Reduce to a shiny, strong glaze, then strain into a saucepan, pushing to extract the maximum of flavour and juices. Add the sliced truffle, brandy, salt and pepper and bind with the butter to give a sheen.

To serve:
Place a *crépinette* in the centre of a plate. Sauce well and arrange a sliced truffle to fall on top and in the sauce. Gay serves it with peeled, boiled broad beans drained and then tossed lightly in butter.

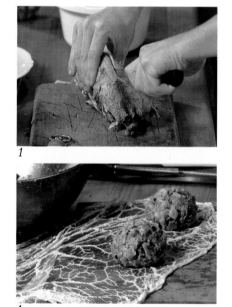
1

2

3

4

5

6

Orange Bavarian Cream with Caramel Sauce

Serves 8 to 10

The *génoise* spongecake:
3 eggs
100g/scant 4 oz (Br.)/½ cup (U.S.)
sugar
75g/2½ oz (Br.)/good ½ cup (U.S.)
plain (all-purpose) flour
50g/scant 2 oz (Br.)/3 tablespoons
(U.S.) unsalted butter

The bavarian cream:
3 egg yolks
110g/4 oz (Br.)/good ½ cup (U.S.)
sugar
300ml/½ pint (Br.)/1¼ cups (U.S.)
milk
rind of one orange
juice of half an orange
2½ leaves or 2½ teaspoons granulated
unflavoured gelatine
450ml/¾ pint (Br.)/2 scant cups
(U.S.) cream with 35% milk fat
(whipping cream), lightly whipped

The caramel sauce:
250g/9 oz (Br.)/1¼ cups (U.S.) sugar
approximately 375ml/12 fl oz
(Br.)/good 1½ cups (U.S.) water

Equipment:
24cm/10 in round cake tin or
springform mould. Then the same
sized mould or cake circle without a
base.

The cake:
Whisk the eggs and sugar in a large
bowl over a saucepan of steaming water

until light and fluffy. Continue until the mixture firms slightly, remove from heat and, after beating a moment further, add the sifted flour. Fold the flour in carefully with a wooden spatula, then add the melted butter, folding carefully.

Pour into a greased cake tin or springform mould, then bake in a 190ºC/375ºF oven for 30 to 35 minutes or until a skewer comes out dry. Cool then slice horizontally into 1cm/½ in slices. You will need only 1 slice, the others can be frozen for later use.

Place the cake slice into the base of a cake circle (or upside-down springform mould without its base) placed on a sheet of greaseproof (parchment) paper on a baking tray with a flat surface (not warped!).

The bavarian cream:
Scald the milk, sugar and rind. Place the egg yolks in a large bowl, strain the rind from the milk and pour over the egg, whisking all the time over a saucepan of steaming water until light and fluffy. Gay insists the secret behind the lightness of her dessert is in the beating at this stage, and she uses a large balloon whisk. Try to aerate the mixture as much as possible to ensure this magical lightness. Add the gelatine, softened first in the orange juice. Beat in well, then remove the bowl from the steam and continue beating until the mixture cools, lest it poaches the egg. Then set over ice, stirring occasionally, until the mixture approaches the texture of whipped cream. Fold in the whipped cream. Pour the mixture on top of the cake slice in the cake circle or spingform mould without its base, and refrigerate until set (at least 6 hours).

The caramel sauce:
(This can be made in advance and stored in the refrigerator.) Add one third of the water to the sugar. Set over heat and stir to dissolve the sugar; then boil to a dark but not bitter caramel, brushing down the sides of the pan with water to remove any crystals. When the caramel darkens, add the rest of the

water to stop the cooking and bring the caramel to sauce consistency. Be careful, as it splashes when you add the cold water. Bring back to the boil to see the mixture well blended, then remove from the stove and allow it to cool.

To serve:
Unmould the dessert by wrapping a warm towel around the cake circle or springform mould, running a knife around the inside edge, then lifting it off. Serve either whole or sliced and plated, with the caramel sauce. Gay decorates with a julienne of sliced, glazed orange peel.

Janni's Tuna Braised in Olive Oil

Serves 10
1kg/use 2 lb fresh tuna in 1 piece
3 large cloves garlic, finely chopped
1 teaspoon ground coriander seeds
4 tablespoons (Br.)/5 tablespoons (U.S.) chopped Italian parsley
2 teaspoons chopped fresh coriander (cilantro)
salt and ground white pepper
approximately 750ml/1¼ pints (Br.)/3 cups (U.S.) virgin olive oil, plus little extra
flaked sea salt

Roll the tuna in the spices and herbs and place it in a baking dish, in a fairly tight fit. Cover completely with olive oil, then cover the dish with foil. Place in a 150ºC/300ºF oven for 45 minutes. Allow it to cool, then refrigerate the tuna in the oil for at least 8 hours. Remove it from the oil and cut 10 slices with a thin sharp knife. Drizzle the slices with extra virgin olive oil, and grind a little white pepper and a pinch of salt over them. Garnish with Mediterranean accompaniments such as roasted peeled capsicum (bell pepper), fried eggplant (aubergine), blanched garlic cloves, or olives.

Antony Worrall-Thompson

Ménage à Trois
London. Bombay. New York...

A s someone who more than once has hosted Princess Diana and her friends in his fashionable London restaurant, Ménage à Trois, Antony Worrall-Thompson has to be listened to when he tells you he considers himself cheeky and arrogant.

Maybe...but, despite the occasional flash of attempted pomposity, when I worked with him on a scorching Melbourne summer's day, he impressed me as a sensitive chef, quietly and relaxedly working in my unfamiliar kitchen. If he was hot and overworked he certainly wasn't complaining. So much for arrogance!

An untrained chef, and a somewhat unconventional restaurateur, Antony has very speedily made his mark on the London dining scene with a restaurant of unusual concept that has made everybody sit up and take notice...beating their foreheads and emitting an inevitable cry of envy, 'Why didn't I think of that?'

Two simple observations determined his restaurant's format: Observation one — Antony, the self-declared ladykiller, takes out his ladies and notices just how often they prefer to order two entrées instead of an entrée and a main course. Observation two — with the advent of nouvelle cuisine, Antony, the paying client, begins to resent paying twice the price for half the portion. So he reasoned: 'I will open a restaurant serving only entrées and desserts. They will be at least the same size portions, and at half the price.' Making his intentions quite clear — and if his cheekiness is anything to go by I can imagine he stated his case loudly and clearly in all the right places — Antony opened Ménage à Trois with a fanfare of publicity and attracted just the right, trendy clientele — including the most right of them all, the Princess of Wales. He has taken London by storm, serving

every elegant, tiny and visually beautiful combination his artist's eye can think up.

The words 'visual' and 'edible' govern every dish. Plates are never overfilled with clumsy elaboration; garish, flavourless garnishes are abandoned in favour of tiny delicacies, beautifully plated. Tony has an extraordinary eye for the graphic, and every dish he serves in the restaurant has his designer's eye behind it. Amazingly enough, the dishes are very easy to copy since, feeling that as an untrained cook he couldn't handle too much à la carte, last-minute panic, Antony devised recipes which, like all those he presents here, are to all intents and purposes pre-prepared, requiring only last-minute assembly and maybe a quick *coup de feu* to bring them up to temperature for serving.

The 'visual soups' (to use Tony's own words) are a case in point. They are certainly the most appealing-looking soups you will ever come across. We have only two here, but that is enough to see how his mind works. First, choose the main ingredient and work out the plating and the atmosphere you want the soup to have. Then build a soup base (in advance), trim and cut the vegetables, and blanch and set them aside (in advance). They are then ready to make into beautifully presented servings at the last moment. Each morsel however must be carefully looked after so it retains its freshness — quick blanching in flavoursome waters (vegetable stock rather than water) and speedy transfer to iced water to stop the cooking and preserve the freshness and colour of each ingredient is imperative. Then all that is required is last-minute assembly, right on the serving plate.

This same thematic approach is carried to the beef salads, and so too to the plating of the fruit dessert. Absolutely simple, employing only raw fruit and a tiny amount of pre-prepared granita, it gives you the impression that anyone can do it. But as usual, Antony

Cream Soup of Mussels and Saffron

thought of it first. His eye for colour, his presentation and the interesting combinations of flavours make the difference. Up to date at all times, and right in tune with what the public is interested in at any given moment, Tony foresees trends, creates trends and then frames them with great ease in the cosmopolitan, bustling atmosphere of his restaurant in Beauchamp Place, Knightsbridge.

Antony graduated from hotel management school with more cheek than good marks, and staged his own rise to stardom by bluffing his way into taking over when the head chef at the local hotel didn't turn up. Unable to cook, but using all his management skills, he found the easiest way was to tell the second chef what to do so he could sit back and learn how to do it. But when Tony learns, he learns fast, and as he is usually three steps ahead in the creativity department, he uses each new-found skill more quickly and better than most of his teachers. He is now one of the most admired young chefs in London, with a restaurant already franchised in Bombay, another in New York, and one planned for Washington. Although he swears that what he likes best is the behind-the-stoves part, not the business part, he still finds time to commute from one to the other, planning the menus, employing staff, organising and creating the right atmosphere.

Meantime, Tony has rented a factory and, from a business suitably named 'Mise en Place', is selling the products of the restaurant (terrines, soups, sauces, pastries, prepared dishes, etc) to Harrods and a few other upmarket London stores. He is also running a catering business from there — strictly large affairs — but with the same loving approach to the small, beautifully plated dishes of the restaurant. His cookbook, released in 1985 and aptly called *The Small and Beautiful Cookbook*, has sold a storm, riding high on the then revolutionary concept of the restaurant.

But Tony doesn't sit still. Recently, he has fought to have his skills acclaimed, since untrained chefs have it hard to imprint their importance on other chefs, even if they have the support of the public. With the help of Michel Roux and Michel Bourdin, the Executive Chef at the Connaught, in 1987 Antony, after a couple of rejections on the grounds of his lack of training, finally became a member of the English affiliate of the Académie Culinaire de France. When the first Meilleur Ouvrier de Grande Bretagne took place in December 1987, Antony submitted menus and got through the preliminary rounds, overtaking even important, French-trained chefs. Studying like crazy all the intricacies of the classic French theories of Carême and Escoffier, he prepared himself for the finals, to be judged by a panel of ten judges, among them Paul Bocuse and Alain Chapel (all Meilleur Ouvriers de France come for the occasion, for the award is administered and judged by its peers). Antony doffed his chef's cap, executed a perfect *Timbales de Sole Carême* in the classic manner and then, in the section where they give the chefs a basket of food to prepare with their own ingenuity, he completely won over the élitist French panel. On that historic day, Friday 4 December, Antony Worrall-Thompson was one of only three chefs to be named the first ever Meilleur Ouvrier de Grande Bretagne (the others were Michel Perraud of the Waterside Inn and Michael Aldridge of the Connaught). Until then, Michel Roux had been the only Meilleur Ouvrier de France in Britain, having earned his award in France.

Vindicated! But then straight on to the next thing, for ideas and seeing them set into motion is what most interests Antony's (over)active mind. He is presently designing a part creole, part American grill restaurant for another consortium in Bombay, has found quarters for the Washington branch of Ménage à Trois, and is looking for another franchised Ménage à Trois in Australia. Plans are also well advanced for a second book — this time on the social eating of the English. With chapters on Henley, Glyndebourne, Ascot, traditional festivals and their traditional menus, it is part history, part send up, part recipe book and part Worrall-Thompson suggestions for cooking some updated and stylish food for these traditional occasions.

But that's only the news for today. Turn around twice, and no doubt there'll be more.

Cream Soup of Mussels and Saffron

Serves 6 to 8 .
75g/2½ oz (Br.)/5 tablespoons (U.S.)
unsalted butter, clarified
2 shallots, finely chopped
2 cloves garlic, finely chopped
2 teaspoons chopped fresh ginger
500ml/good ¾ pint (Br.)/2 good cups
(U.S.) dry white wine
1 tablespoon soy sauce
2kg/4½ lb mussels, cleaned well
1 stalk celery, diced
½ small head fennel, diced (in season)
white of 1 leek, diced
1 small potato, diced
1 small carrot, diced
500ml/good ¾ pint (Br.)/2 good cups
(U.S.) fish stock
1 bayleaf
1 sprig thyme
1 pinch saffron stamens, soaked in 1
tablespoon warm water
300ml/½ pint (Br.)/1¼ cups (U.S.)
cream with 35% milk fat (whipping
cream)
salt, white pepper and freshly grated
nutmeg

The garnish:
white of 1 leek
1 carrot
1 tomato, peeled and seeded
25g/1 oz (Br.)/2 tablespoons (U.S.)
unsalted butter

1. Heat the butter in a large soup pot. Add the chopped garlic, shallots and the ginger. Cook over low heat until soft but not browned. Remove half the mixture to a second pot. Add the wine and soy to the first pot and bring to the boil.

2. Add the mussels and cook, covered, for about 5 minutes, turning them from top to bottom, until they are open.

3. Shell the mussels, set them aside, and strain the liquid into the second saucepan. Add all the vegetables bar those for the garnish, the fish stock, bayleaf and thyme. Bring to the boil and simmer for 25 minutes or until the vegetables are tender.

4. Meanwhile, shred the leek and carrot into a fine julienne of about 10cm/ 4 inches in length. Peel and seed the tomato and cut it into strips as long as the size permits. Blanch the leek and carrot in boiling water until softened; then remove them with a slotted spoon

and put them into cold water to cool them quickly so they keep their colour well. Drain and set aside as garnish.

5. Remove the bayleaf and sprig of thyme. Put the soup into a blender and process to a purée, then strain it to be sure it is well creamed. Add the saffron stamens and stir while reheating, adding the cream. Do not allow it to boil. Season with salt, pepper and freshly grated nutmeg.

6. Arrange the presentation vegetables in a circular nest in the centre of the soup bowls with the mussels, divided up between the number of bowls, nestled in the middle. Ladle the hot soup over the nest, thus heating the central ingredients. If the presentation ingredients have been done a long time in advance, they may be quickly heated by pan frying them in a little butter before arranging in the soup bowls.

Note: Antony warns that the soup bowls should be put in the warming oven before arranging the presentation ingredients in the bowls when you make his style of 'visual soups', a hint that we would be wise to follow with any soup presentation, as a cold bowl can cool soup very quickly.

1

2

3

4

5

6

Minestrone of Shellfish and Vegetables Perfumed with Fresh Basil

Serves 6
390ml/13 fl oz (Br.)/1⅔ cups (U.S.)
dry white wine
1 shallot, finely chopped
2 cloves garlic, crushed
2 tablespoons (Br.)/scant 3 tablespoons
(U.S.) finely chopped fresh ginger
450g/1 lb mussels
4 large tiger prawns, yabbies (fresh
water cray) or other locally available
crustaceans
16 medium scallops; or 8 large scallops,
sliced in half horizontally
750ml/1¼ pints (Br.)/3 cups (U.S.)
vegetable stock (see below)
1 carrot, sliced
1 spring onion, sliced
1 leek, sliced
a few broccoli flowerettes
a few cauliflower flowerettes
12 snow peas
1 tomato, peeled, seeded and diced
a few leaves basil for décor
salt and freshly ground black pepper

The vegetable stock:
400ml/⅔ pint (Br.)/1¾ cups (U.S.)
dry white wine
4 tomatoes, peeled and seeded
1 carrot, peeled and sliced
2 leeks, washed and sliced
1 stalk celery, sliced
1 onion, peeled and spiked with 2
cloves
4 cloves garlic, sliced
bouquet garni
1 teaspoon white peppercorns, crushed
1 tablespoon mushroom peelings

To make the vegetable stock:
Put all the prepared ingredients into a large saucepan. Cover with water, bring to the boil and simmer for approximately 2½ hours, remembering to skim the surface regularly. Pass through a fine sieve lined with a piece of wet muslin to catch all the debris. This will make about the amount required above, or alternatively top with a little water.

To prepare and cook the vegetables and shellfish:
Boil the wine, shallot, garlic and ginger for 3 minutes. Add the mussels, cover the pan and cook over a brisk heat until the mussels have opened. Shell the mussels, discarding any that have not opened. Strain the juice through a fine muslin, and reserve.

Cook the chosen crustaceans — tiger prawns, yabbies (fresh water cray), etc in about 350ml/11 fl oz (Br.)/1½ cups (U.S.) of the vegetable stock for 2 minutes or until cooked. Remove and drop into cold water to stop the cooking. Poach the scallops in like manner. Shell the crustaceans and halve them lengthwise. Halve the scallops horizontally if large. Set aside.

In the same liquid, cook the broccoli and cauliflower flowerettes and the snow peas, passing each into cold water to stop the cooking and preserve the colour as you proceed. Drain each and set aside. Strain the cooking liquid into the mussel stock.

The soup:
Boil the mussel liquid and remaining vegetable stock together. Add the carrot, spring onion and leek and cook for 5 minutes or until the carrot is tender. Season with salt and pepper to taste.

Everything up to here is made in advance, and now awaits serving time, when Tony assembles his 'visual soup', by arranging the vegetables attractively in the dish, and adding the liquid.

To serve:
Arrange the seafood and the vegetables, including also the diced tomato, decoratively in the plate. Pass briefly into a very hot oven to heat a little, then spoon the hot soup over them. Finish with a few leaves of basil for décor.

Fresh Summer Fruits with Cassis Granita

Serves 8

The granita:
450ml/¾ pint (Br.)/2 scant cups (U.S.) sugar syrup*
1 bottle white wine
2 tablespoons (Br.)/scant 3 tablespoons (U.S.) cassis
juice of an orange
juice of 4 limes (or 2 lemons)

*Sugar syrup: (Best to make it in larger quantities to have on hand.) Bring 1 litre/good 1½ pints (Br.)/4¼ cups (U.S.) water to the boil with 1.3kg/3 lb (Br.)/good 6 cups (U.S.) sugar. Remove from the heat and cool before placing in a storage jar. For ease of use keep the syrup in the refrigerator to speed up the freezing process.

The fruit:
Antony chose from the best fruit available on that day in the markets, and suggests you make up the variety according to local availability. On his platter there are blueberries, watermelon, kiwifruit, strawberries, apples, mangoes, tamarillos, starfruit, fortunellas and pieces of pineapple.

The coulis:
Choose whichever fruit pulps the best to make up 3 coulis. Antony chose strawberries, mangoes and blueberries.
sugar to taste
cassis for the blueberry coulis
mint sprigs for décor

To make the granita:
Mix all the ingredients together. Place in a shallow dish that can stand the temperature of the freezer (an ice-cube tray or enamel baking dish is ideal). A shallow dish is best as it gives you a greater surface area than a narrow, deeper dish, and the increased surface area will enable the granita to freeze at a quicker rate. Place the granita in the freezer compartment. A true granita texture is achieved by occasionally stirring the granita mix during the freezing process, thus allowing the granita to freeze in flakes rather than in a solid block, as it will if left to freeze undisturbed.

To prepare the fruit:
Peel the fruit or not, depending on the type of fruit and your preference. Cut attractively and arrange on the serving plates to make an appealing presentation.

To make the coulis:
Purée each fruit chosen for a coulis, and sugar to taste while in the blender or food processor. Enhance the flavour of blueberry coulis with a little cassis liqueur. Store each coulis in a small plastic jug.

To serve:
Take 1 small plate per person and carefully pour some of each of the 3 coulis onto it. Allow them to run together and then pattern them by pulling the end of a spoon handle, or a skewer, through each to intermingle the colours. At the last moment, place 2 or 3 spoonfuls of granita in the foreground of each person's fruit. Serve each person with an individual plate of coulis in which to dip the fruit.

TRIO OF BEEF SALADS

Plated together, this little trio of beef salads makes an appealing, refreshing and flavoursome starter for a summer meal. The proportions below are for 4 to 6 people only if you are serving small portions. If serving only one of the recipes at a time, you will need to double the recipe to have enough for the number of servings stated.

Beef Tartare on Avocado

170g/6 oz beef fillet (tenderloin)

The flavouring ingredients:
6 capers, finely chopped
1 anchovy fillet, mashed
1 small shallot, finely chopped
2 tablespoons (Br.)/scant 3 tablespoons (U.S.) olive oil
1 teaspoon balsamic vinegar
dash Worcestershire sauce
1 raw egg yolk
½ teaspoon Dijon mustard
tabasco to taste
salt and freshly milled black pepper

The garnish:
1 avocado
sieved hard-boiled egg yolk

Finely dice the beef, then set aside on a plate.

Mix the raw egg yolk with the mustard; add the olive oil slowly, stirring well with a wooden spoon to emulsify the mixture. Add the remaining flavouring ingredients, varying the seasoning to your taste. Change to a fork and mash the beef into the mixture to blend the flavours through the beef. It should finish up the consistency of paste.

To serve:
Cut the avocado into 2, remove the stone, peel, and cut each half into thin slices. Using 2 small spoons (ice-cream spoons are good, otherwise teaspoons), spoon the beef out into small *quenelle*-shaped portions. Serve *quenelles* of the tartare on or next to some fanned-out slices of avocado. Sprinkle with sieved egg yolk as garnish.

Beef and Veal Carpaccio on Salad Leaves with Parmesan Flakes

85g/3 oz beef fillet (tenderloin)
85g/3 oz veal fillet (tenderloin)
green salad leaves of your choice
virgin olive oil
balsamic vinegar
salt and freshly milled black pepper

The garnish:
parmeggiano cheese, cut from the piece into flakes with the blade of a potato peeler or small sharp knife

Cut the beef and veal into thin slices, then beat with a meat mallet to make fine whole slices.

In a small bowl, blend a little virgin olive oil and balsamic vinegar to make a dressing, and season to taste with salt and freshly milled pepper.

To serve:
When ready to serve, toss the salad leaves in the dressing and arrange on the plates. Drape the beef and veal over the salad. Drizzle with a little more oil, grind a little pepper over it all, and garnish with the flakes of parmeggiano.

Oriental Beef with Cucumber

170g/6 oz beef fillet (tenderloin)
cucumber pickle (1 quantity of recipe below)

The flavouring ingredients:
6 drops chilli oil
1 clove garlic, finely chopped or crushed
1 teaspoon lime juice
1 teaspoon Thai fish sauce (naam pla)
1 teaspoon oyster sauce
1 teaspoon clear honey
1 teaspoon soy sauce
½ cup coriander (cilantro) leaves
1 chilli, seeded and finely chopped
2 tablespoons (Br.)/scant 3 tablespoons (U.S.) shredded mint leaves
sesame seeds

Cut the raw beef into small thin pieces,

as for Chinese cookery. Make up the recipe of cucumber pickle.

Blend the first 8 of the flavouring ingredients together in the food processor until smooth, holding back just a few of the coriander (cilantro) leaves for garnish later.

Half an hour before serving, toss the beef pieces into the flavouring ingredients with the shredded mint and chopped chilli tossed through. Serve over the cucumber pickle, sprinkled with sesame seeds and the few remaining coriander (cilantro) leaves.

Cucumber Pickle

100g/3½ oz (Br.)/¾ cup (U.S.) cucumber, cut in julienne

The flavouring ingredients:
2 heaped teaspoons clear honey
1 tablespoon cider vinegar
1 red chilli, finely chopped
1 heaped tablespoon finely chopped peanuts
2 heaped teaspoons finely chopped Spanish (red) onion
2 heaped teaspoons shredded coriander (cilantro) leaves
2 heaped teaspoons shredded mint leaves
2 teaspoons Thai fish sauce (naam pla)

Combine the flavouring ingredients in a bowl, and just before serving, toss the cucumber julienne through the mixture to flavour it.

François Minot

Relais et Châteaux Hôtels
France

'The way to a man's heart is through his stomach.' It may be an old adage but it's one that many people have not yet been quite able to laugh off. 'The way to a man's heart is knowing how to bake a good pie.' More specific, but certainly not advice to be laughed at. My own mother is one who often uses the term 'man's food', meaning all those hearty dishes that men seem to love, and she often laments the fact that modern, busy women (my generation) don't seem to make dishes any more that take a long time to cook.

Whether it's the percentage of working women nowadays, or whether we're just a little better off and can afford the prime roasting cuts and the better quality grilling cuts, she has a point — the modern cook is fast becoming something of a short-order cook, and the stews, casserole dishes and pies that grandmother used to make are becoming much less prevalent in our time. My friend François Minot is too Burgundian to let a thing like this pass unnoticed, and he sets this pigeon pie before you just to make amends.

I first met François when he came to Australia briefly in 1976 on a promotional tour with Joseph Olivéreau, President of the fabulous Relais et Châteaux hotel group, for which François is the culinary adviser; and since then he and his wife Monique have become such great friends that I can thank them not only for many hospitable stays in their home, but for continual insights — and forays — into many of the great restaurants of France. As part of his job, François spends his time moving between the beautiful, privately owned châteaux that have linked themselves together to form this chain, overseeing any problems in their kitchens, hiring new chefs, updating or upgrading menus, or simply making their cuisine more reflective of the region to which they belong.

François gained his reputation from 1962, when he became the successor to Alexandre Dumaine at the legendary Hôtel de la Côte d'Or in Saulieu. Along with Point of the Hôtel de la Pyramide in Vienne, and Pic at Valence, Dumaine was one of the three most quoted chefs of this century's France.

Born into a Burgundian family with a long lineage of chefs on both the paternal and maternal sides, François could hardly have conceived of any other career. On his father's side, he became the fifth generation to wear a chef's toque, while on his mother's side, the family were pâtissiers from father to son, and up until 1910, his maternal grandfather was *Chef Entremetier* of the Russian Tsar. François' apprenticeship was undertaken with Léon Trimouillat, student of the great Escoffier, and from this tutelage in Dôle, he moved into the large hotel brigade of the Concorde St. Lazare in Paris under Alexandre Monnier, also a master of the grand old style and an enormously talented chef who went on to take over the brigade of the Plaza-Athénée in the 1950s.

For his military service, this rich background was enough to assure François the position of Chef of the Military Headquarters of the French Army in Morocco, followed by a bout at the stoves of the French Embassy in Rabat. Returning home, François was taken on by Dumaine, who soon accepted him as his spiritual son, and as Dumaine became more crippled with diabetes in his latter years, François oversaw the great man's kitchen, eventually succeeding him upon his retirement. François remained at the reigns of the Hôtel de la Côte d'Or for twelve years, earning two Michelin stars, three chefs hats from Gault et Millau, the title Maître Cuisinier de France, the Commanderie des Cordons Bleus, and an Oscar from the Club des Gastronomes of Belgium, as well as a formidable

Pâté Chaud de Pigeons

reputation as one of the most respected chefs in France.

After years at the helm of a restaurant that took up so many hours of his day, and with a young family craving his attention, Minot let himself be persuaded by Olivéreau to take up the position of Technical Advisor to the Relais. François finds the Relais job fascinating as he moves from place to place all the time, one day advising on a new restaurant joining the prestigious group in England or the South of France, another day doing a series of dinners promoting the group in far-off countries like Australia or the United States; one day establishing a menu of French specialities in Rio, another day a menu of local specialities in Bordeaux or Savoie.

Since the Relais boasts at least twelve of the three-star Michelin-rated restaurants of France among its members, François is also highly qualified to demonstrate and discourse on the latest trends in France. On one of my visits to France, François, having spent two days talking at length on what is appearing on French restaurant tables since the 'fall' of nouvelle cuisine — and from time to time illustrating this by demonstrating dishes that seemingly combined the eye appeal of nouvelle cuisine with one of the most reclaimed elements, the classic sauces — François ended the discussion with a long discourse on French regional cuisine.

A proud Burgundian, François champions the region that has given so many great dishes to the nation. There was a time when the Burgundian princes were wealthier and more esteemed than the kings of France, owning territory from what is now the border between Italy and their own great province to the countries of Flanders and Belgium. It was a nation of dukes and princes, with an enormous and very wealthy '*haute bourgeoisie*', and it was from these palatial tables that some of the very grand dishes of the region stemmed.

One that is less known outside the province than the more peasant-like *coq au vin, boeuf bourguignon* or *pochouse*, is this outstandingly beautiful pigeon pie. It is certainly a long and fairly difficult dish to make, but it's ideal for the gaming season, for the dish can be made with quails, pigeons, wild duck or other feathered game. If there's not a shooter in the family, much is now available commercially. I commend it to you as worth the effort, and I commend it particularly to those in whom I can arouse just a twinge of guilt with this one question: 'What have you cooked lately expressly for the man in your life?'

1

2

3

4

5

6

Pâté Chaud de Pigeons
Burgundian Hot Pigeon Pie

Serves 8 to 10

8 to 10 pigeons, quail or wild duck, preferably of about 300g/11 oz each
100g/3½ oz (Br.)/scant ½ cup (U.S.) shallots or pickling onions, chopped
thyme, bay leaf, nutmeg, salt, pepper
100ml/3 fl oz (Br.)/scant ½ cup (U.S.) brandy
100ml/3 fl oz (Br.)/scant ½ cup (U.S.) madeira
½ bottle dry white wine
50ml/1½ fl oz (Br.)/¼ cup (U.S.) Pernod
juice of a lemon
50ml/1½ fl oz (Br.)/¼ cup (U.S.) Noilly Prat or other dry vermouth
50ml/1½ fl oz (Br.)/¼ cup (U.S.) olive oil
1kg/use 2 lb continental-style smoked, thick-cut bacon
100g/3½ oz chicken livers
200g/7 oz (Br.)/good 2 cups (U.S.) finely chopped champignons (baby mushrooms)
2 eggs
200ml/scant 7 fl oz (Br.)/1 scant cup (U.S.) cream with 35% milk fat (whipping cream)
50g/scant 2 oz (Br.)/good ⅓ cup (U.S.) flour
600g/1 lb 6 oz puff pastry
1 egg beaten with 1 tablespoon water (eggwash)

Equipment:
Use either a loaf mould, pâté tin, or a round, thick-based mould of 22 to 24cm/9 to 10in diameter. François chose to make it in a round, aluminium sauté pan because, as this makes it more difficult, he could add a few tips on how to mould pie pastry to a round shape when there is depth in the mould.

One day in advance:
To debone the pigeons:
1. Discard the wings up to the fleshy part just before the first joint, and then remove the flesh from the carcass in 4 pieces — 2 drumstick and thigh sections, and 2 breast and wing sections.

2. Then remove the bones from these sections, with one neat cut along each bone, so that each piece can be flattened out into a schnitzel shape. Flatten slightly with a meat hammer to increase the size.

3. Marinate the deboned pigeon with half the shallots or pickling onions, the wine, half the brandy, all the Pernod and vermouth, the lemon, the oil and half the madeira. Add salt, pepper, the thyme and bay leaf. Keep the bones if you want to serve the hot pâté with a light *jus*, but this is optional.

The next day:
The *farce à gratin* (stuffing):
4. Cut the bacon in cubes, fry it in a little olive oil, then add the chicken livers and brown them, before adding the remaining shallots or pickling onions, the champignons (baby mushrooms), salt and pepper. Keep the heat on very high, to cook off any juices that may come from the champignons (mushrooms), then add the rest of the brandy and the madeira and boil until all the liquid is cooked away.

5. Cool this mixture and pass through the fine grill of a mincer (meat grinder). It is possible to use a food processor, but the texture is not as good and the stuffing is more inclined to crumble.

6. Transfer now to a bowl and incorporate 2 eggs and the cream. Season with salt and pepper. This mixture may also be made a day in advance and refrigerated until it is needed.

To roll the pastry:
7. Roll the pastry out to a thickness of 5mm/¼ in. If lining a circular mould with some depth, you have to roll it in such a way as to create a pocket in the pastry. To do this, roll to about one and a half times the diameter of the mould, then fold the pastry in half, flouring the folded centre well so the 2 widths cannot stick to each other. Stretch the side edges of the pastry upwards (away from you) to create a slight curve in the folded edge.

8. Roll the pastry out further, extending the depth of the pocket by rolling more on the middle section than on the top and bottom ends. Check that the pastry is floured well so it doesn't stick together in the central area (although by this time the side edges should be welded).

9. When it appears that the diameter is approximately 4cm/2 in larger than the diameter of the mould, place the pastry in the buttered sauté pan. You should be able to line the mould without undue gathering at the top of the walls of the pan. Too much gathering makes the sides of the finished pie look unattractive. Line the mould, pressing pastry well into the corners of the pan so as to give a sharp, neat edge to the finished pie. Allow a 2cm/1 in overlap and set aside the remaining pastry to be re-rolled later for the top crust.

7

8

9

10

11

12

To assemble the pâté:

10. Remove the pigeon from the marinade, lay all the pieces one by one on a wooden board and spread a thin layer of the stuffing on each. Roll each into a *paupiette* (beef olive shape) but do not fix them with a pin or any trussing. Spread some stuffing carefully on the base and walls of the pastry, then place the rolled pigeon around to cover the base of the pie. Finish with the remaining stuffing.

11. Fold the overlap of pastry inwards, then roll out and cut the remaining section of pastry into a disc, slightly smaller than the diameter of the mould. Combine the remaining egg with a tablespoon of water and beat with a fork, to use as an eggwash. Paint the overlapping pastry with the eggwash, so as to glue the top crust to the base. Pose the disc of pastry on top of the pie, then use a fork or pastry pincers to crimp the top crust to the bottom crust.

12. Make a decorative pattern on top of the pie. Cut a 1cm/½in circular hole in the centre of the pastry to allow steam to escape. (This hole also acts as a guide to when the pie is cooked — the visible juices must be yellow, not pink.) Finish by sticking (with eggwash) 5 to 6 pastry leaves on top of the pie then paint the entire surface with the remaining eggwash.

Bake in a 220°C/425°F oven for 90 to 115 minutes (depending on the size of the mould), checking from time to time. If it browns too quickly or too much, cover the top with a piece of buttered greaseproof (parchment) paper. When cooked, remove from the oven, and shake the pan to ensure the pie is not caught at the sides or on the base. Cover with a plate, hold very firmly, pray, upturn the pie onto the plate, then quickly upturn it again onto the serving platter so it finishes right side up.

Served hot or cold, the pie will cut like a cake. However, when hot, it is beautifully succulent, and should be tried this way at least once.

The sauce (optional):

If the pie is to be eaten hot, a pigeon sauce can be served as an accompaniment. To make this, sweat a few diced vegetables *(mirepoix)* in a pan, add the pigeon bones, stock or a demi glace, and reduce this with a little white wine until you have a strong *jus*. Strain, season and finish with a little brandy or madeira.

Huîtres au Champagne

Hot Oysters in Champagne

Serves 6 to 8
6 to 9 oysters in their shells per person
3 shallots or small pickling onions, finely chopped
⅓ bottle champagne
600ml/1 pint (Br.)/2½ cups (U.S.) cream with 35% milk fat (whipping cream)
5 egg yolks
pepper

Remove the oysters from their shells and place them in a frying pan with any juice that comes with them, topped with about 3 tablespoons of the champagne. Scrub the shells and place them on serving plates.

In a saucepan, place the finely chopped shallots or pickling onions, the remaining champagne, the cream, egg yolks and a little pepper from a few turns of the mill. Whisking well so that it cannot curdle in the base of the pot, heat until the egg starts to thicken the mixture. Do not allow it to get hot enough to scramble the egg. Meantime, cover and gently heat the oysters. They must only warm or they toughen.

Replace the oysters in their shells and spoon over a little sauce onto each. Serve immediately. In our photo the oysters were placed under a griller (broiler) to gratiné (glaze). As this is difficult to do at home for large numbers, and as the mixture tends to curdle if it is not gratinéed (glazed) under very high heat, you may prefer simply to dust the oysters with a small shaking of paprika.

This dish may be made more elaborate with a vegetable — poached spinach (English spinach), a little grated zucchini (courgette) or chopped mushrooms — cooked until softened in a little butter, then placed under the oyster.

Gratin d'Oranges aux Poivrons

Oranges, Gratinéed with Candied Capsicum (Bell Peppers)

Serves 8

200g/7 oz (about 1 large) red capsicum (bell pepper)
200g/7 oz (about 1 large) green capsicum (bell pepper)
40g/1½ oz (Br.)/¼ cup (U.S.) glucose
800g/1 lb 12 oz (Br.)/4 cups (U.S.) sugar
300ml/½ pint (Br.)/1¼ cups (U.S.) water
approximately 1 orange per person, peeled carefully into quarters, with a minimum of membrane
100g/3½ oz (Br.)/½ cup (U.S.) flaked almonds, toasted
750ml/1¼ pints (Br.)/½ cup (U.S.) flaked almonds, toasted
750ml/1¼ pints (Br.)/3 cups (U.S.) cream with 35% milk fat (whipping cream)
100g/3½ oz (Br.)/½ cup (U.S.) vanilla sugar
150ml/¼ pint (Br.)/scant ¾ cup (U.S.) Grand Marnier or Cointreau

Blanch the capsicums for 3 minutes in boiling water, refresh and drain. Cut into rings. Put the sugar and water in a saucepan with the glucose. Bring to the boil, ensuring that the sugar has all melted. Cook to 'hard ball' (130ºC/250ºF), then add the capsicums (bell peppers). Cook for approximately 35 minutes until the capsicums become glacéed. Let them cool in the liquid. It is best to cook the capsicums well in advance and keep them, well covered with syrup, in a sealed jar.

Marinate the prepared oranges in Grand Marnier or Cointreau. Whip the cream with the sugar, but not too firmly.

To serve:
Place some orange quarters in a small dessert plate. Sprinkle with the almonds and some glacéed capsicum. Add a thin layer of the whipped cream and gratiné (glaze) under a grill (broiler), or with a blowtorch.

John Desmond

Itinerant Teacher
Paris, France

Medieval craftsmen held that learning from a variety of masters was not only desirable, but essential to developing their skills. Such an apprenticeship forced them to long, often arduous travels, but it was a prerequisite of their guilds and only then had they earned the right to be called master.

This philosophy seems to have filtered down the ages to John Desmond who, in the name of his craft, trained first in Hotel Management at a school in Ireland, and even now continues to work in the kitchens of the greats in France and England and hone his skills at such renowned classes as those run by Lenôtre school in Paris. For John is, as well as a teacher, a perennial student.

A young Irishman in love with cooking, John has become internationally renowned. With his soft spoken accent and gentle nature he is in constant demand. For years now he has given classes in the U.S.A., Canada, Ireland, England and Australia, but these days he manages his schedule so that it allows him to spend about one third of the year at his home base in Paris. For many years he gave classes at La Varenne; now he also runs a catering business from his home.

Putting his philosophy into practice, John deliberately sets aside time (perhaps another third of the year) to broadening his own experience, and over the years, has moved from The Ritz on the historic Place Vendôme in Paris, to the Pavillon Royal, and then on to gain further experience at the three-star restaurant Taillevent, under the very precise task master and brilliant chef Claude Déligne.

John's delight in the unique flavours of South West France soon prompted him to seek a place in the kitchens of André Dauguin, owner of the two-star restaurant Hôtel de France, at Auch, and hero-chef of the area; and his time there has left John with a special interest in the foods of the region. André is a great personality chef, a champion of the cuisine of the South West, which is built upon bean and bread-based soups, interesting Moorish-influenced spicing, and cooking and preserving in goose fat. But he has also a remarkable flair to combine these traditions with a modernist's approach to lightening the region's somewhat hearty cooking, and it was not long before the stimulation of working beside him left its mark on John.

With this kind of experience behind him, John decided that his main emphasis in teaching would be to pass on his well-practised technical skills of French classical cuisine and the 'haute-cuisine' he learned under the great masters. He based many of his early classes on communicating manual skills, techniques, and what the French so aptly call 'trucs'; but the more time he spent in France, the more his classes tended also to include recipes tuned to the love he was fast gaining for the regional cuisines of his adopted country.

With his year broken up into threes, John's life is reminiscent of the itinerant craftsman of medieval days — only he treks the world in a pair of jeans and gym shoes, tasting his way through a myriad of cuisines — learning as he goes, paying his way, studying his craft. A great way to learn; and what a way to live!

Feuilletés de Coquilles Saint Jacques

To Make Puff Pastry:

1

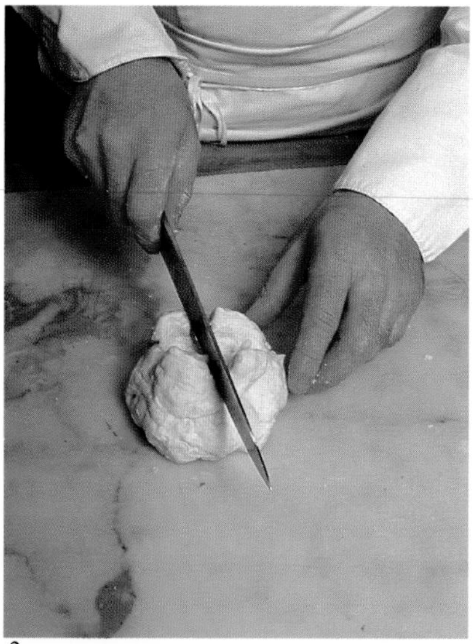

2

3

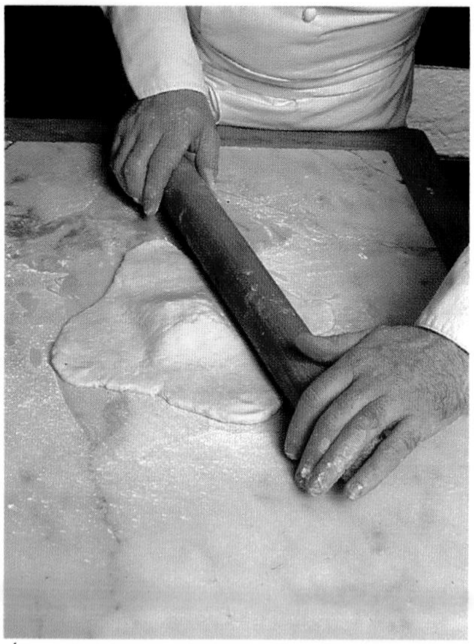

4

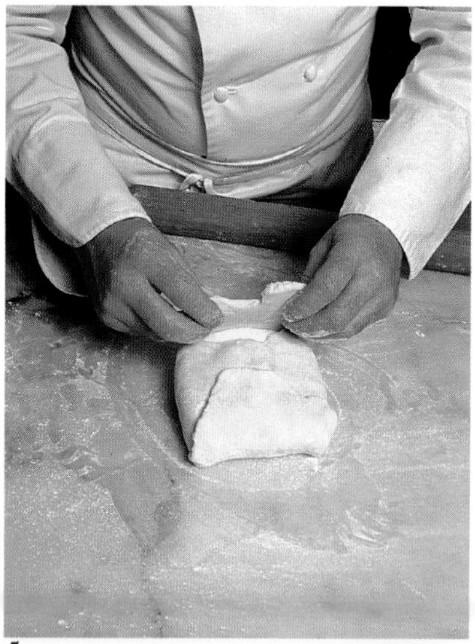

5

6

7

8

9

Pâte Feuilleté
Puff Pastry

250g/use ½ lb (Br.)/scant 2 cups (U.S.)
plain (all-purpose) flour, sifted
pinch salt
50g/2 oz (Br.)/3 tablespoons (U.S.)
butter, softened or even melted, for the
détrempe
200g/7 oz (Br.)/1 scant cup (U.S.)
butter, in the block
125ml/4 fl oz (Br.)/½ cup (U.S.) water

1. Place the flour on your workbench top, preferably a cool surface like marble. Make a well (hole) in the centre and in it place the water, salt and the smaller weight of butter. Using your fingertips, mix together all the ingredients in the well (hole). Bit by bit incorporate all the flour from the edges. (Up to here it may be done in the food processor or a mixer fitted with a dough hook, if preferred.) Knead the pastry until it comes together in a ball.

2. Cut a heavy incision in the form of a cross in the top of the dough ball, and open out the 4 corners of this incision so as to open the centre of the ball slightly. This helps even the texture and the temperature of the dough as it rests. In this shape, resting the dough for 20 minutes instead of the usual 2 hours should suffice. Wrap it in plastic film and refrigerate.

3. Wrap the block of butter in plastic film. Re-form its shape to a flattened rectangle of about 10 x 12cm/4 x 5 in by pounding it with a rolling pin. It should now be about 2cm/1 in thick.

4. Starting from the 4 corners that were made by the incision, roll the ball of dough (known as the *détrempe* before the block of butter is added) from each corner, leaving the central portion of the *détrempe* in its original thickness.

5. Place the block of butter in the centre of the *détrempe* and fold over the flaps inwards to neatly enclose the butter. Turn the package over, and tap to equalise the shape.

6. Make an impression at each end of the package with the rolling pin. This is to ensure the ends do not unfold or roll unevenly during the rolling of the layers of the pastry. Roll the pastry into rectanges of about 36 x 12cm/14 x 5 in.

7. Fold the far end of the pastry toward you one-third of the way down the length. Fold the other end back up. Tap lightly with the rolling pin to help the 3 layers stay together, then grasp the pastry and turn it around a full right angle. Recommence rolling, stretching the pastry this time in the other direction.

8. When this second rolling is completed to a rectangle the same length as before, fold again into 3.

9. Make an impression with 2 fingers to show you have rolled it twice, wrap it in plastic film and rest it in the refrigerator for 20 to 30 minutes. The pastry is now said to have done 2 'turns'.

Repeat from steps **6** to **9** twice more, resting in between each 2 turns, thus giving the pastry 6 turns in all. Rest the pastry again, and only then is it ready to roll out and use. With this alternate rolling and folding, the pastry now contains 1459 layers (leaves) of dough, thus earning it the name *mille feuilles* — one thousand leaves.

Feuilletés de Coquilles Saint Jacques
Feuilletés of Scallops with Tomato and Basil Sauce

Serves 8
400g/good 14 oz puff pastry (see step-by-step method above)
300ml/½ pint (Br.)/1¼ cups (U.S.) fish stock
300ml/½ pint (Br.)/1¼ cups (U.S.) cream with 35% milk fat (whipping cream)
2 large fleshy tomatoes
450g/1 lb scallops
basil
salt and freshly ground black pepper

Roll out the puff pastry into a rectangle of 5mm/¼ in thickness, cut into 8 rectangles of 8 x 12cm/3 x 5 in. Place on a heavy baking sheet. Refrigerate for a minimum of 1 hour, or freeze for 20 minutes before baking.

Reduce the fish stock to half, to concentrate its flavour. Add the cream and bring to the boil. Reduce again to sauce consistency, or when it coats the back of the spoon.

Skin and seed the tomatoes and chop into small dice. Set aside on a small plate.

Bake the puff pastry in a 200°C/400°F oven for 20 to 25 minutes or until brown, crisp and well risen. Bring the sauce back to the boil. Add the diced tomato. Chop the basil and add it to the sauce about 3 to 5 minutes before serving. Place the scallops into boiling water and let stand in the hot water off the heat.

When the pastry is cooked, remove and cut the top off each piece. Place the bottom part of the pastry on individual serving plates. Add the scallops. (You may prefer to put a little hot spinach in each shell and then lay the scallops on top). Coat with the sauce. Place the pastry tops jauntily on top.

A SOUFFLE WORKSHOP

John's three soufflé recipes provide us with something of a soufflé workshop, exploring the techniques of various styles of soufflé making. The ultra-light, modern-style pear soufflé is based on a purée of fruit. Blow-away light and highly aerated, it is lifted by a much higher quantity of egg white than the classical-style soufflé, and contrasts with the lemon soufflé recipe which is done with the more traditional *crème pâtissière* base. To further explore the parameters, John places the lemon soufflé in a crêpe to demonstrate a very elegant manner of serving a soufflé.

Our 'soufflé workshop' does not cover John making a cold soufflé, the term given to the cold, gelatined dessert which, in fact, is technically a mousse. It gets its name from the presentation technique of having the mixture set into a bowl edged with a paper border so that when the paper is peeled away, the mousse sits above the height of the bowl to give a soufflé-like appearance. Since they are light and aerated and just as 'blow away' as the translation of the word 'soufflé' suggests, they probably do deserve their name as one of the soufflé styles, but for the most part they are known on menus as mousses if they are served in any way but with this soufflé appearance.

Similarly the *soufflé glacé* or iced soufflé is technically a parfait but for the purposes of our 'workshop' is included as a soufflé. The *soufflé glacé* is an ice-cream so rich in cream and sugar syrup that it can set without risking crystallisation, and thus needs no churning and can be moulded. Presented in a soufflé bowl with a false border to allow the parfait mixture to be poured to a greater height than the true edges of the mould, the parfait gets its name *soufflé glacé* from the appearance when the paper is peeled free. John cooked for us a beautifully presented iced soufflé

with a caramel sauce. It is extremely light, for the recipe also uses a portion of *meringue italienne*, a grand tool of the chefs but often left out in home kitchens because of the extra time (and skill) involved in its preparation.

The Desmond hints for success with soufflés:
• Weigh everything for utmost accuracy.
• Have eggs at room temperature and separated only just before needed, so they don't dry out.
• Where sugar is ever placed directly onto egg yolks, beat immediately. If you let it sit on the yolks it cooks the egg and produces lumps that will not dissolve in the beating.
• Use a copper bowl to whip egg whites, but be sure it is grease free by first scrubbing it with vinegar and salt, then rinsing it in cold water. This scrubbing, just before use, also rids the copper of any toxic effects that the egg whites would pick up in the whipping.
• Finish the egg whites by incorporating a little sugar in the last few moments of beating. This strengthens the whites and allows the soufflé to wait, fully assembled and in the bowl, an hour or two before putting it in the oven. A soufflé with badly beaten egg whites needs to go into the oven immediately; the sugar helps firm them and ensure you've done a better job.
• Always fill a soufflé bowl to its full height, then pass a metal spatula over the top to flatten the top and to cast off any excess. Finally, run your thumb around the edge of the bowl to stop the edges sticking and to allow an even rise.
• To whip cream well requires a chilled bowl. Place it in the freezer for a moment before starting.
• For caramelising sugar, the best sugar is lump sugar, which is not quite so refined. A dash of lemon juice in the water and sugar that is to be caramelised also helps avoid crystallisation.

Soufflé aux Poires d'Alsace
Alsatian Pear Soufflé

From the three-star Paris restaurant Taillevent

Serves 10
60g/2 oz (Br.)/¼ cup (U.S.) butter
100g/scant 4 oz (Br.)/½ cup (U.S.) sugar
1kg/2 lb 4 oz raw pears (about 5 pears)
100ml/3 fl oz (Br.)/scant ½ cup (U.S.) water
1 extra raw pear, kept separate
200ml/scant 7 fl oz (Br.)/1 scant cup (U.S.) pear alcohol
40g/1½ oz (Br.)/⅓ cup cornflour (cornstarch)
100ml/3 fl oz (Br.)/scant ½ cup (U.S.) water
200g/good 7 oz. (Br.)/1 cup (U.S.) sugar
100ml/3 fl oz (Br.)/scant ½ cup (U.S.) water
450g/1 lb egg whites
pinch of salt
50 to 100g/scant 2 to scant 4 oz (Br.)/¼ to ½ cup (U.S.) sugar
icing (confectioner's) sugar for decoration

Equipment:
Individual soufflé dishes, 300ml/½ pint (Br.)/1¼ cup (U.S.) capacity.

Soften the butter and brush it evenly on the inside of each soufflé dish with a pastry brush. Pour 100g/scant 4 oz (Br.)/½ cup (U.S.) sugar into one dish, turning it to coat the inside evenly with sugar. Pour the excess into the next dish and continue this procedure until all the dishes are coated.

Peel and core the larger quantity of raw pears. Slice them thinly and place them in a heavy saucepan with 100ml/3 fl oz (Br.)/scant ½ cup (U.S.) water. Cook over a low heat until the pears are soft. Purée them in a food processor and return them to the saucepan.

Peel and core the remaining ràw pear, dice it finely, place it in a small bowl and cover it with the pear alcohol.

Put the cornflour (cornstarch) and 100ml/3 fl oz (Br.)/scant ½ cup (U.S.)

water in a small bowl and stir to dissolve completely. Add the mixture slowly to the pear purée, whisking constantly, and return the pan to a low heat.

Combine 200g/good 7 oz (Br.)/1 cup

(U.S.) sugar and 100ml/3 fl oz (Br.)/scant ½ cup (U.S.) water in a heavy saucepan and cook over a low heat until the sugar is dissolved. Raise the heat and boil until the sugar reaches the soft ball stage (about 120°C/235°F). Whisk the mixture into the pear purée and cook over a low heat for a couple of minutes. At this stage the mixture can be kept covered in the refrigerator.

When ready to make the soufflé, heat the pear purée mixture gently. Pour in the alcohol from macerating the pears. Heat the oven to moderately hot (190°C/375°F). If using a machine to beat the egg whites, be sure the bowl and whisk are clean. Put the egg whites in the bowl and add a little salt. Beat on high speed until frothy. Turn the machine down to medium and continue beating. When the egg whites grain at the sides of the bowl, as usually happens to egg whites beaten in a mixer, add 50g/scant 2 oz (Br.)/¼ cup (U.S.) sugar to the side of the bowl. When the whites form stiff peaks, add the remaining 50g/scant 2 oz (Br.)/¼ cup (U.S.) sugar and turn the machine to high to tighten the whites. Whisk a quarter of the egg whites into the pear mixture. Using a wooden spoon, fold in the remaining egg whites as gently as possible, folding from the centre to the sides of the bowl and gently turning the bowl in the opposite direction. Fill the soufflé dishes only halfway, sprinkle with half the diced pears, then add the rest of the soufflé mixture to fill the dishes to the top.

Smooth the surface with a spatula. Run your thumb around the top along the inside edge of the dish, forming a ridge. Sprinkle the remaining diced pears on top. Lower the oven heat to 178°C/345°F and place the soufflés on a baking sheet near the bottom of the oven. Bake for 11 to 14 minutes. Just before serving, sprinkle with icing (confectioner's) sugar.

Soufflé Glacé au Liqueur Sauce Caramel

Iced Liqueur Soufflé with Caramel Sauce

Serves 10
1 vanilla bean
250ml/8 fl oz (Br.)/1 good cup (U.S.) milk
75g/2½ oz (Br.)/good ⅓ cup (U.S.) sugar
120g/4½ oz egg yolks
75g/2½ oz (Br.)/good ⅓ cup (U.S.) sugar
100ml/3 fl oz (Br.)/scant ½ cup (U.S.) liqueur of your choice
400 to 450g/use 1 lb *meringue italienne* (use 1 quantity of recipe below)
500ml/good ¾ pint (Br.)/2 good cups (U.S.) cream with 35% milk fat (whipping cream)

The caramel sauce:
200g/good 7 oz (Br.)/1 cup (U.S.) sugar
100ml/3 fl oz (Br.)/scant ½ cup (U.S.) water
drop of lemon juice
cold water
150ml/good 5 fl oz (Br.)/scant ¾ cup (U.S.) hot water
cocoa and icing (confectioner's) sugar for decoration

Equipment:
1 large soufflé dish, 1.2 litres/good 2 pints (Br.)/5 cups (U.S.) or individual ramekins, 125ml/4 fl oz (Br.)/½ cup (U.S.) in capacity

Split a vanilla bean and scrape the seeds into the milk in a heavy saucepan. Add 75g/2½ oz (Br.)/good ⅓ cup (U.S.) sugar and the bean and bring it to the boil. Take the pan from the heat, cover and leave to infuse for 10 to 15 minutes. Remove the bean and bring the milk back to the boil.

Whisk the egg yolks with 75g/2½ oz (Br.)/good ⅓ cup (U.S.) sugar with a mixer until light and doubled in volume.

Whisk in half the hot milk, then return this mixture to the remaining milk in the saucepan. Cook over a low heat, whisking constantly, until the custard thickens. (This custard will thicken quickly because it has double the usual amount of egg yolks.) Remove from the heat, strain into a bowl and let cool, whisking occasionally.

When the custard is cool, add the liqueur of your choice. Wrap a strip of doubled aluminium foil around each ramekin or the soufflé dish extending about 4cm/1½ in above the rim of the dish. Tie with string or use tape to secure the collar.

Make up the *meringue italienne*, following the recipe below.

Whisk the cream until it holds soft peaks.

The custard, *meringue italienne* and whipped cream should all be of about the same consistency before being combined. Fold the cooled *meringue italienne* into the cold custard, then fold in the whipped cream. Pour the mixture into the soufflé dish or ramekins, filling them to the rim of the collar, and freeze.

The caramel sauce:
Put the sugar and 100ml/3 fl oz (Br.)/scant ½ cup (U.S.) water in a heavy saucepan and heat gently until dissolved. Bring to the boil and cook over a high heat until light brown. Immediately add a drop of lemon juice and dip the pan in cold water to stop the caramel from cooking further. At once add the hot water to make a sauce of syrupy consistency; stand back because the caramel will sputter. Heat gently until the caramel has dissolved and leave it to cool.

To serve:
1 hour before serving, take the soufflés out of the freezer and put them in the refrigerator. Just before serving, peel off the collars and sprinkle each soufflé with sifted cocoa and then icing (confectioner's) sugar.

Soufflé Glacé au Liqueur Sauce Caramel

Meringue Italienne
Italian Meringue

Makes about 400 to 450g/1 lb
120g/4½ oz egg whites
50g/1½ oz (Br.)/¼ cup (U.S.) sugar
250/9 oz (Br.)/1¼ cups (U.S.) sugar
100ml/3 fl oz (Br.)/scant ½ cup (U.S.)
water

Put the egg whites and ½ tablespoon
of the smaller quantity of sugar in the
mixer bowl. With the mixer on high
speed, whisk for 30 seconds or until
frothy. Turn the speed down to low and
continue beating the whites, adding the
rest of the smaller quantity of sugar
gradually if necessary to prevent the
whites from graining.

Meanwhile, put the 250g/9 oz (Br.)/1¼
cups (U.S.) sugar and water in a heavy-
based saucepan and heat gently until the
sugar has dissolved. Raise the heat to
high and boil without stirring.

Wash down any sugar crystals at the
sides of the pan with a brush dipped
in cold water. Boil the syrup until it
reaches the soft ball stage (120ºC/235ºF).
To test, you can dip your finger first
in cold water, then into the syrup, and
then back into the basin of cold water.
The mixture should form a soft ball
when rolled between your fingers.

Set the mixer at high speed and continue whisking the egg whites until stiff,
gradually adding any remaining sugar.
With the mixer still at high speed, slowly pour half the syrup down the side
of the bowl; turn the mixer down to
medium speed and add the remaining
syrup. Continue beating at low speed
until the meringue is cool.

Meringue italienne can be kept in a bowl
in the refrigerator for 2 to 3 days.

Pannequets au Citron
Crêpes Stuffed with Lemon Soufflé

Serves 8
2 crêpes per person (see recipe below)
400g/good 14 oz *crème pâtissière* (use ½
quantity of recipe below)
grated zest and juice of 1 lemon
8 egg whites
icing (confectioner's) sugar
crème anglaise (see recipe below)

Make crêpes, and set aside 2 per person.

Make the *crème pâtissière* as in the recipe
below, and stir in the zest and juice of
the lemon. Whip the egg whites to a
firm snow and gently fold into the mixture. Place 3 to 4 tablespoons of lemon
soufflé mixture on one half of each crêpe,
fold the second half lightly over the
soufflé mixture and bake on a well-
buttered baking tray or individual ovenproof plates for 12 minutes at
190°C/375°F.

To serve:
Dust well with icing (confectioner's)
sugar and take to the table immediately. Serve surrounded by *crème anglaise*.

Crêpes Roxelane

Serves 10 (makes 20 crêpes)
150g/good 5 oz (Br.)/1¼ cups (U.S.)
plain (all-purpose) flour
100g/3½ oz eggs
20g/¾ oz egg yolk
10g/⅓ oz (Br.)/½ tablespoon (U.S.)
sugar
pinch salt
250ml/8 fl oz (Br.)/1 good cup (U.S.)
milk
100g/3½ oz (Br.)/½ cup (U.S.) butter
250g/use ½ lb fresh or frozen
raspberries
1 tablespoon kirsch
powdered sugar
800g/1 lb 12 oz *crème pâtissière* (use 1
quantity of recipe below)
40g/1½ oz egg yolks
rind of 3 lemons
300g/scant 11 oz egg whites

pinch salt
50g/scant 2 oz (Br.)/¼ cup (U.S.)
sugar
icing (confectioner's) sugar

Equipment:
Crêpe pan

The crêpe batter:
Sift the flour into a bowl and make a
well (hole) in the centre. Add the
100g/3½ oz eggs, 20g/¾ oz egg yolk,
10g/⅓ oz (Br.)/½ tablespooon (U.S.)
sugar and pinch of salt. Mix these centre
ingredients briefly, then gradually whisk
in the flour until you have a homogeneous mass. Gently whisk in the milk to
make a smooth batter.

Melt the butter and stir it into the batter.

Heat the crêpe pan until very hot. Add
3 tablespoons (Br.)/ 3½ tablespoons
(U.S.) batter and turn the pan quickly
to coat the bottom evenly with batter.
Cook over medium-high heat until
brown on the bottom, then turn the
crêpe and brown the other side. Transfer the crêpe to a plate and continue
cooking the remaining batter in the same
way, piling the crêpes onto a plate as
they are done.

The raspberry sauce:
Push the raspberries through a strainer
or purée them in a blender or food
processor; strain to remove the seeds.

If using frozen raspberries, thaw them first. Add the kirsch and powdered sugar to taste.

In a heavy saucepan, heat 800g/1 lb 12 oz *crème pâtissiè*re with 40g/1½ oz egg yolks, whisking constantly, just until hot. Remove from the heat and grate in the rind of 3 lemons. Heat the oven to 175ºC/340ºF. When ready to assemble, lay the crêpes on the workbench.

Add the egg whites to a cleaned bowl (a copper bowl gives the best result) only when ready to beat them; they should be at room temperature. Add a pinch of salt and whisk the egg whites quickly until frothy. Continue whisking slowly until the whites form stiff peaks. Add 50g/scant 2 oz (Br.)/¼ cup (U.S.) sugar and whisk vigorously to tighten the egg whites so that they become very stiff and glossy. Whisk a quarter of the egg whites into the lemon mixture. Using a wooden spoon, fold in the remaining egg whites as gently as possible, folding from the centre to the sides of the bowl and gently turning the bowl in the opposite direction.

Place a heaped tablespoon of soufflé mixture on each crêpe. Fold the crêpe over and place on a large, buttered ovenproof platter. Do not let the crêpes overlap.

Bake in the oven for 7 to 10 minutes. Just before the end of the baking time, sprinkle the crêpes with icing (confectioner's) sugar. Bake for another minute, remove from the oven, pour raspberry sauce around the crêpes and serve immediately.

Crème Anglaise
Custard

500ml/good ¾ pint (Br.)/2 good cups (U.S.) milk
1 vanilla bean
60g/2oz (Br.)/scant ⅓ cup (U.S.) sugar
120g/4½ oz egg yolk
60g/2 oz (Br.)/scant ⅓ cup (U.S.) sugar

Pour the milk into a heavy-based saucepan. Split the vanilla bean and scrape the seeds into the milk (if you do not like the little black specks, leave the vanilla bean whole). Add 60g/2 oz (Br.)/scant ⅓ cup (U.S.) sugar and bring to a rolling boil. Remove from the heat, cover and leave to infuse for 10 minutes. Remove the bean and wash it to re-use. Reheat the milk to boiling. Skim if necessary.

Whisk the egg yolk and 60g/2 oz (Br.)/scant ⅓ cup (U.S.) sugar until creamy. (This is best when done by machine.) Whisk in half the boiling milk, then return this mixture to the saucepan with the rest of the milk. Heat gently, whisking constantly, until the custard thickens slightly and begins to leave a light film on the side of the saucepan; if you draw a finger across the side of the saucepan, it will leave a clear train. (Do not overcook or boil the sauce or it will curdle.) Remove from the heat at once and strain into a large bowl, whisking it now and then.

Crème anglaise can be frozen.

Crème Pâtissière
Pastry Cream

Makes about 800g/1 lb 12 oz
500ml/good ¾ pint (Br.)/2 good cups (U.S.) milk
1 vanilla bean
60g/2 oz (Br.)/scant ⅓ cup (U.S.) sugar
120g/4½ oz egg yolk
60g/2 oz (Br.)/scant ⅓ cup (U.S.) sugar
40g/1 ½ oz (Br.)/⅓ cup (U.S.) plain (all-purpose) flour

Pour the milk into a heavy-based saucepan. Add the vanilla bean and 60g/2 oz (Br.)/scant ⅓ cup (U.S.) sugar and bring it to the boil. Remove from the heat, cover and leave to infuse for 10 minutes.

Beat the egg yolk with 60g/2oz (Br.)/scant ⅓ cup (U.S.) sugar until light. Add the flour to this mixture, but do not whisk it or the pastry cream will become elastic.

Remove the vanilla bean and bring the milk back to the boil. Whisk half the milk into the egg yolk, sugar and flour mixure, then return this mixture to the saucepan with the rest of the milk. Continue to whisk over a moderately high heat; in less than 1 minute it should thicken. Pour into a large container and let cool, whisking occasionally.

Crème pâtissière can be kept in the refrigerator for 3 days. It should not be frozen.

Ken Hom

Author, T.V. Personality
Hong Kong. Berkeley, U.S.A.

Have wok, will travel. Ken Hom, an affable American-born Chinese, and probably the most well known of all the exponents of Chinese cookery, certainly makes the world his playground. His visiting card has three addresses on it — Berkeley (California), Paris and Hong Kong; his excellent television series that made him 'Chinese cookery teacher to the English-speaking world' is made in Britain; he demonstrates his art in regular visits to towns all over the U.S.A. and England, and to American tourists in Hong Kong; and he makes an annual trek to places as far off as Australia and New Zealand. Wherever he goes, his books precede him and are stacked up in department stores world-wide to announce he's on his way.

Nowadays, Ken travels with only a cleaver — the woks get there before him. Having demonstrated on all varieties of stove from tentative Chinese iron tripods to commercial stoves, Ken has now designed his own wok — in strong but very fine carbon steel, of the particular gauge that he decided would meet all domestic requirements, and with a flat base so that it could be used with electricity. These too, are stacked in the department stores before his arrival around the world.

All this international living for a boy born on the wrong side of the tracks in Tucson, Arizona! Ken's father, an Hawaiian-born Chinese who met his Cantonese mother in Hong Kong and took his bride to mainland America though she didn't speak a word of English, died when Ken was only eight months old. His mother moved to Chicago, took a two-room apartment in Chinatown and worked in a Chinese food canning company to support herself and the baby. Until Ken was twenty, he grew up in an all-but-Chinese environment, earning money in an uncle's restaurant from the time he was eleven so he could have pocket money and continue his education. And continue his education he did, right through to Berkeley University, where he studied art history, all the time paying his way by giving classes in Chinese cooking to his friends and anyone else he could find who was interested.

One of the opportunities that came his way was to teach a group that wanted lessons in Italian cooking. Armed with a friend's book on Italian cuisine, Ken quickly practised up on pasta dishes and gave the courses. And it was another crazy piece of luck that first took Ken to France, and was equally foreboding for his future. As a graduate of art history and an avid photographer, Ken was asked to visit Europe and photograph great works of art for the Art Department at Berkeley, a job that was followed up by similar demands from other United States and English universities. And so Ken's love affair with France began, and with it, his love affair with French cuisine. He devoured dishes and pondered over the differences in cooking techniques, often trading lessons in Chinese cookery for lessons in French.

Ken has a tremendous thirst for knowledge of all the different culinary worlds that he encounters on his trips. He's not keen on bastardising the authentic dishes of regional Chinese cooking, knowing the difference when someone cheats and the produce is not the same, but he's lived in enough cultures to know that the palates, the markets, the produce and the food habits of different people can never be the same and, unlike most cooks, he's willing to consider the best in each one.

It was a small step then, to Ken's love of inventing recipes which employ the techniques of one cuisine with the ingredients, or differing techniques, of another. Now, in his repertoire you'll find dishes such as ginger-

Stir-fried Crayfish with Capsicum

flavoured fish ragoût served with a garlic-flavoured mayonnaise studded with Sichuan peppercorns and chilli; and chicken marinated in soy, cut the Chinese way then barbecued with a mint and parsley-coated *persillade*. His latest book, *East Meets West*, is the culmination of this philosophy.

Ken's first book, published in 1981, was a large, illustrated volume called *Chinese Technique*. It had enormous international sales, for it was the first comprehensive book that described step-by-step the fundamental techniques of Chinese cooking. Literally hundreds of photos helped his readers know and understand how to wield a cleaver; apportion a chicken or a squab; bone a chicken; star-cut a carrot; cook in a claypot, a wok or a steamer; make a wonton or an eggroll; and blow up, bake and serve a Peking duck. It is doubtful any book on Chinese cookery has ever surpassed it as a foreign student's Chinese cookery bible.

By then acknowledged as 'one of the world's greatest authorities on Chinese cooking' by no less than the *New York Times* food critic Craig Claiborne, Ken was searched out by a team of B.B.C. London television producers who had been wanting to instigate a Chinese cookery programme, but had had difficulty in finding someone with the right balance of knowledge, charm and flair to put it across. This culminated in 'Ken Hom's Chinese Cookery', which played on the B.B.C. and affiliated B.B.C. channels in England, and over a hundred public broadcasting channels in the U.S.A., Australia, New Zealand and Hong Kong. The B.B.C. published an accompanying book that has sold millions of copies. Since then, Ken has published a book on vegetables and pasta and another, probably the one that most expresses Ken's personal leanings in the culinary world, his wonderful *East Meets West*.

The kitchen in Ken's home — the low-slung ceiling made even lower by an array of hanging pots, woks and assorted strainers — is almost entirely taken up with a large island work bench surrounded by six or eight umpire-height red canvas director's chairs. Guests walk past the other rooms of his rather modest cottage and find themselves sitting with Ken in this friendly room, for chatting around the preparation area, sipping wine or leafing through a book from his immense collection is the way Ken likes to spend his days. At once the office, the preparation area and the place to catch up on a letter, the room tells much of Ken's personality. The man has come a long way, but his life-style has changed little. Friend to all in the Berkeley neighbourhood, he is well known and well liked. He still rides a bike and refuses to drive, jeans and a T-shirt are his 'at home' garb, pottering around the local markets and talking to the local vegetable growers is still his passion, and open house on Sunday or cooking up a storm for an enormous number of people on his days off are his ways of sharing his time with the people he loves.

So if he arrives at work at the T.V. studio in his Gianni Versace designer coats; if he stalks Hong Kong with the rich from his Peninsular Hotel base while shepherding tourist groups through the markets or into the sultry, dusty suburban area of Mongkok to identify for them the 'real' Hong Kong; if he spends Christmas in Paris and speaks several languages and jets around the world like there's no tomorrow; and if he was listed on *Esquire* magazine's 1984 register of Outstanding Americans Under the Age of Forty; those who have visited his kitchen, feasted on his banquet of hospitality or simply sat with him while he looked them straight in the eye and grinned his charming, sincere grin, know that the grandiose life-style is like water off a duck's back.

The real Ken Hom is alive and well and living — serenely and calmly, just as Confucius would have wished a wise Chinese to do — in Berkeley, U.S.A.

  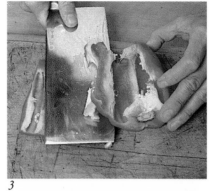

1   2   3

4   5   6

Stir-fried Crayfish with Capsicum

Serves 4

1 crayfish of about 1kg/2¼ lb
1 x 4cm/1½ in piece of fresh ginger
2 tablespoons (Br.)/scant 3 tablespoons (U.S.) black beans.*
1½ tablespoons (Br.)/2 tablespoons (U.S.) garlic
1 red and 1 green bell pepper (capsicum)
4 to 5 spring onions
2 to 3 medium hot chillis, as desired
6 to 8 asparagus, depending on thickness
3½ tablespoons (Br.)/4 tablespoons (U.S.) peanut oil
150ml/good 5 fl oz (Br.)/scant ¾ cup (U.S.) Chinese rice wine (*schao chiew*)
200ml/scant 7 fl oz (Br.)/1 scant cup (U.S.) chicken stock or water
1 teaspoon sugar
1½ tablespoons (Br.)/2 tablespoons (U.S.) light soy

*These are fermented in salt and spices and are sometimes sold canned under the name 'black beans in salted sauce'.

They are cheap and readily available in Chinese stores.

1. Peel and finely chop the piece of ginger. As ginger is fibrous, never do this with a food processor. Chop the spring onions and garlic.

2. Diagonal cut the asparagus in the Chinese manner to lengths of about 3cm/1½ in. Stop cutting at the tail end where it is tougher and resists the knife.

To prepare the bell peppers (capsicums):

3. Firstly cut off both ends. In cutting the top end, the stalk simply falls free. Make a lengthwise cut in the pepper (capsicum) but through one side only, thus you can unravel the pepper into one whole continuous-length piece. Holding the cleaver parallel to the chopping board separate the inside core and seeds while rolling the pepper (capsicum) around — this process removes the inside rubble and white membranes in one action. Now cut down the natural divisions and you end up with 2 to 3 large lobes. Chop the prepared flesh into squares for this dish. As Ken says, the

preparation is really important; done well it will save you a lot of time. In Chinese cooking a lot of time can be spent in cutting and preparation; quite different from Western cooking, where the cooking is the larger part of the work.

Prepare the chillis using the same technique. You can use the smaller, hotter (birds' eye) chilli if you wish but it has a tendency to overpower the more subtle seafood flavours present in this dish.

To cut the crayfish:

4. (If dealing with a live cray is bothersome, the cray can be drowned first in fresh water. This takes about 15 minutes.) Hold the crayfish firmly against the cutting board and with a large knife pierce the carcass between the eyes and cut in half lengthwise.

5. Remove the intestine. Discard the lungs; keep the mustard (the pink/yellow smooth part).

6. Hold the pieces together in their original shape and cut medallions along the tail end towards the head. These should be just over 1cm/½ in thick.

7

8

9

10

11

12

7. Cut the two head pieces into 2 or 3 each, keeping the legs on the body. These less meaty pieces are used because shell adds colour and flavour to the dish. However, remove 'feathery' pieces from around the gills.

To cook the dish:
8. Heat about 1 tablespoon of peanut oil in a wok. Swirl around to coat the surface. Add the cray to the pan and sauté, moving it about constantly. If the pan gets dry, or if the cray seems to be browning too quickly, stop the heat build-up by adding a little water or rice wine. Partially cook the cray for a further 5 to 7 minutes before adding anything further. Remove the head pieces for the garnish, then remove the partially cooked cray. Rinse out the wok; dry, and return to a high heat.

9. Heat 2 tablespoons (Br.)/scant 3 tablespoons (U.S.) oil, add the garlic and toss, then almost immediately the ginger and blackbeans. Dilute with a couple of tablespoons of rice wine. Add the peppers, chilli and spring onions and about 200ml/scant 7 fl oz (Br.)/1 scant cup (U.S.) of chicken stock or water.

Cook for 2 minutes to allow the vegetables to soften.

10. Add the asparagus; add a teaspoon of sugar to balance the flavours; add the light soy. Cook a further few minutes to allow for the asparagus.

11. Then stir in the mustard (the pink/yellow smooth part) momentarily, breaking it up with the back of a spoon to flavour the sauce. Return the crayfish to the wok and heat it through.

To serve:
12. Ladle onto a large platter using the head pieces and tail for decoration or serve on individual dishes.

Sun-dried Tomato Spring Rolls

Makes about 20
60g/2 oz soya bean thread noodles
225g/½ lb (about 2 large) boneless chicken breasts, cut into thin strips about 8cm/3 in long

2 teaspoons olive oil
1 tablespoon finely chopped fresh marjoram, sage or oregano
2 tablespoons (Br.)/scant 3 tablespoons (U.S.) finely chopped fresh chives
2 tablespoons (Br.)/scant 3 tablespoons (U.S.) chopped sun-dried tomatoes
salt, and ground black pepper
½ x 450g/1 lb packet of rice paper spring roll wrappers (*banh frang*)
750ml/1¼ pints (Br.)/3 cups (U.S.) peanut oil for deep frying

Soak the bean thread noodles in warm water for about 15 minutes, or until soft. Drain and cut into thirds. Place in a teatowel and squeeze to remove excess moisture.

Combine the chicken pieces, herbs, chives and sun-dried tomatoes, and moisten with the olive oil. Add the noodles, mix well, season with salt and pepper. Cover and refrigerate for 1 hour.

To make the spring rolls:
Fill a large bowl with warm water. Dip a rice paper wrapper in and out of the water to soften. Place on a teatowel and spoon about 2 tablespoons (Br.)/scant

3 tablespoons (U.S.) of the chicken mixture on the edge of the rice paper. Roll the edge over the mixture once, fold up both ends of the rice paper, parcel-style, and continue to roll to the end. The roll should be compact and as tight as possible. Make up the rest of the mixture in the same way. You should have between 15 and 20 spring rolls. The spring rolls can be made ahead to this point and may stay refrigerated, covered with plastic wrap, for up to 4 hours.

To cook the spring rolls:
Heat the peanut oil in a wok or frying pan until it is moderately hot (about 180ºC/350ºF). Deep fry the spring rolls 2 or 3 at a time, as they have a tendency to stick to one another. When golden brown, remove, drain on paper towelling, and serve at once.

Warm Peach Compôte with Basil Leaves

Serves 4
125g/4½ oz (Br.)/scant ⅔ cup (U.S.) sugar
225ml/scant 8 fl oz (Br.)/1 cup (U.S.) water
1kg/use 2 lb peaches. White are nicer; freestone (yellow) or nectarines are easier to slice
1 vanilla bean
3½ tablespoons (Br.)/4 tablespoons (U.S.) butter, cut into small pieces
15 to 20 basil leaves

Dip the peaches in boiling water, momentarily, for easier peeling. Peel and slice from the stone. In a medium-sized skillet, combine the sugar and water and bring to the boil, stirring until the sugar dissolves. Add the peaches and vanilla bean, split in 2 lengthwise. Simmer for 2 minutes. Remove the vanilla. Whisk in the butter, a few pieces at a time, and the basil leaves, whole unless very large. This dish can be served hot, warm or cold, but Ken prefers to serve it at once.

Marcella Hazan
Author. Cooking Teacher
Bologna and Venice, Italy
New York, U.S.A.

'**B**alance is what it's all about,' says Marcella Hazan in the low-voiced, gutteral tones that are her trademark. 'Italian cuisine is one of the great cuisines of the world, and one of the healthiest, because of its balance. We whet the appetite with a small variety of antipasta — mixed seafood, meat or smallgoods, olives, and often vegetables (perhaps pickled, perhaps braised, perhaps preserved in oil); then a simple pasta or broth. We follow with a simply cooked fish or meat dish, most often small in portion, and usually with a vegetable served apart, but one only; then cheese and fruit. Desserts are rare, bread never has butter, and olive oil is the most natural produce in the world, with no saturated fat, no cholesterol! If we're a little thick in the waist line, then it's only because it's so damn good!' And the wonderful laugh of Marcella Hazan takes over, the eyes sparkling with delight. Being serious for long doesn't come easily.

Much of the atmosphere of Italy seems to centre around food. Of course there are the wonderful hillside landscapes, but the best of them are terraced with vineyards or olive groves. There are wonderful museums, art galleries and churches, but most of them have tables outside, with people relaxing at the cafés that line the piazzas, with a glass of wine, a sandwich of *porchetta* or a plateful of *prosciutto*. Farmers harvesting in the field rest seated against a tree with a great lump of bread cut from a loaf held aloft in mid-air and carved in thick slices with a large knife; and in the city, people stop in the streets for the best coffee in the world, a quick pick-me-up zabaglione or a slice of *panettone* from the Motta cafés.

Marcella Hazan has documented the food of her native country better than any other writer in three books that have made her the most celebrated author on Italian food in the English-speaking world. Born in the town of Cesenatico, she is a native of Emilia-Romagna, the cradle of Italian gastronomy and the source of its richest cuisine, but through years of research and thousands of hours spent in households all over the country, she has done more than anyone else to extricate and preserve old family recipes from regions throughout Italy.

Marcella's cooking is the cooking of the home. She is a gutsy cook, with the all-important element being flavour. For her, fussy presentation is not what food and eating is all about. Of the earthy, fundamentalist school, she believes if a dish is to tantalise, it should be ladled out steaming hot onto a large platter and rushed speedily to the table while the steam is still imparting the loveliest aroma. Marcella wants you to salivate, not admire; she wants you to say 'it tastes good', not 'it looks pretty'. This is not a chef's food, this is a woman's food, a mother's food in fact.

Marcella cooks like a woman, holding leeks and artichokes to her body as she cuts and peels, slicing unevenly, slowly, using paper towelling, smoking as she goes. The feel of the ingredients, the taste, the texture, and above all the aroma, guides the addition of a little more of this, a little more of that. She is much more apt to say 'a handful of this' than '75g of this', and her books are probably as easy as they are to follow only because when she is writing a book, her husband Victor wisely has her stalked and followed with a pencil and a pair of scales.

In class Marcella doesn't want to know about that, and in the Bologna school where she has taught every summer since 1976, her main intent has been to infuse into her students her love and intuition for Italian tastes and flavours, rather than her recipes. She herds them to the markets, to restaurants, to tastings, and expects them to improvise Italian dishes not just copy

Risotto ai Gamberi

them before she allows them any sort of diploma. The result is that she has done wonders at toppling people head over heels in love with her food and her country.

Interesting that this instinctive approach to cooking is the one that dominates Marcella's style, for in fact she is science trained. A graduate in natural sciences and biology from the University of Ferrara, she was for many years a teacher and researcher and to this day, her mind is far too inquiring to allow food to overwhelm her passion for the world. She learned her cooking in a domestic situation, 'part of the pleasures and responsibilities of marriage', she calls it and in her latest (she swears her last) book *Marcella's Kitchen*, she says, 'When I step into my kitchen I am still the woman who learned to cook to please her family and her friends.'

Nowadays, Marcella leaves most of the cooking in the *Accademia Marcella Hazan* to her son Giuliano, supported by a team of professional pastry cooks and chefs; but she also accepts students in small groups in her 16th century palazzo in Venice, where she and her Italian-American husband live. Victor, great champion of his wife, translator and business manager, works with Marcella and complements her course with his knowledge of wine. His own book *Italian Wine*, an excellent guide to the subject, is warmly dedicated to her, as is Marcella's first book to him.

If you cannot be taught by Marcella personally, she is an author whose personality breathes in her books. She is there cajoling you along, reminiscing, warning you where you'll slip up, and holding up a scolding finger to assure you that the best element in the kichen is commonsense. 'You cannot live without eating. No. And if it's something you have to do, why don't you do it well?'

1 2 3

4 5 6

7 8 9

Risotto ai Gamberi

Risotto with Shrimps

Serves 8

200g/7 oz (Br.)/1½ cups (U.S.)
shrimps
5 tablespoons/6 tablespoons olive oil
1 very small onion, chopped
2 medium cloves garlic, chopped
225ml/scant 8 fl oz (Br.)/1 cup (U.S.)
dry white wine
4 tablespoons (Br.)/5 tablespoons
(U.S.) Italian parsley, chopped
1 x 425g/use 1 lb can of Italian peeled
tomatoes
1 small hot chilli pepper
400g/good 14 oz (Br.)/2 cups (U.S.)
Italian Arborio rice
1.5 litres/2½ pints (Br.)/6 cups (U.S.)
home-made fish broth* or failing that,
water. With the wine and tomato
juice, the dish does make up
successfully with water.
1 to 2 tablespoons extra virgin olive oil

*Marcella's Fish Broth: Bring to the boil
in a large pot 1 carrot peeled, 1 small
onion peeled, 1 stick celery, ¼ green
pepper, 1 very ripe tomato, and 1 small
potato peeled, together with 1 kg/use
2 lb fish bones and scraps, covered with
cold water. Allow the broth to gently
simmer for 10 to 12 minutes, removing
any scum. Strain the broth into a clean
bowl. It can be frozen until required.

1.   De-vein the shrimps. Chop half of
the shrimps roughly; leave the remaining
half whole. Set aside.

2.   In a large pot, heat the olive oil
and add the chopped onion. Cook until
softened but not brown, then add
the chopped garlic. Add about half of
the chopped parsley.

3.   Add the chopped shrimp and allow
to cook for about 3 minutes, turning
frequently, then add the wine and
the can of tomatoes, using only half the
tomato liquid. Bring to a slow simmer.

4.   Slice the chilli pepper open, de-vein
and seed it, slice it and add it to the
mixture. Bring the fish broth or water
to the boil and have it on the stove nearby
at a rolling boil.

5.   Add the rice, turn up the heat to
medium high, and keep the pan uncovered.
Stir the rice thoroughly a few
times so that the contents of the pan
will coat the rice grains.

6.   Add a ladleful of the hot broth or
water and stir the rice well, making sure
that all the rice is mixed with the hot
broth. When the broth has been almost
absorbed by the rice add another ladleful
of the simmering broth. Stir constantly
to prevent it from sticking to the
pan. Continue to add ladlefuls of the
hot broth, as each is absorbed, repeating
the procedure until the rice is done.
If you run out of the hot broth, hot
water can be added.

7.   Two things become apparent to the
beginner here. How do I know when
to add more broth? How do I know
when the rice is done? The Italians have
an expression for the former. They keep

the rice *'al onde'* — 'on the wave', meaning
it should roll around the pot like
the swell of the waves in the sea. If it
gets any drier, add more broth. This
way it will never dry out enough to
stick to the bottom. The resultant risotto
is also served this way, never any drier.
As to deciding when the rice is ready,
it cannot be guessed, it must be tasted.
The Italians serve it firm but tender,
when no chalky centre is apparent. Marcella
insists too on the importance of
maintaining a high heat; quick evaporation
gives a much better result.

8.   Add the remaining shrimps and
parsley, and toss them through the
risotto for a few minutes to allow the
shrimps to cook through.

9.   Stir 1 to 2 tablespoons of extra virgin
olive oil into the risotto. Pour into
the serving plate or bowl and serve
immediately.

Carciofi alla Romana

Carciofi alla Romana
Braised Globe Artichokes

Serves 6
6 large globe artichokes
lemon
3 tablespoons (Br.)/3½ tablespoons
chopped parsley
1 clove garlic, finely chopped
½ teaspoon crumbled mint leaves
salt
8 tablespoons (Br.)/10 tablespoons
(U.S.) olive oil

To prepare the artichokes:
In this dish the artichokes are served with the stems still on, so take care not to snap them off whilst preparing them. The artichokes are prepared by firstly removing the outer leaves. This is done by bending them back and snapping them off. You should be snapping the leaves off so that the whitish, tender bottom part of each leaf remains. You do not have to pull them off all the way to the base, but you will notice that as you move deeper into the artichoke base the leaves will start to snap higher from the base. Keep pulling off the outer leaves until you reach the leaves that are green only at the tips and have a whitish base that comes up about a third to half of the length of the artichoke.

With the artichokes on a chopping board cut the tops of the artichokes off from the bases. Cut off only enough to remove the green tipped part.

Looking at the edge you have just cut you will notice that in the centre of the artichokes there are some very small leaves with a purple tinge to them, with prickly tips curving inwards. Using a knife with a rounded end, cut off all these leaves and scrape away at the fuzzy choke that should now be exposed. At this point you may find it easier to use a teaspoon to remove all of the choke part, being careful not to scrape away any of the heart or edible parts. You should end up with artichokes that have an outer circle of tightly packed leaves surrounding a hollowed-out section.

On the artichoke bases, pare away the green outer parts of the snapped-off leaves as you would peel an apple. This step will expose the white of the artichokes and remove the tough fibrous green part.

Taking care not to break the stems, trim away the outer green layers to the bases of the artichokes, again leaving only the white part exposed. Drop the prepared artichokes into a bowl of water into which you have squeezed the lemon and add the lemon halves. Leave the prepared artichokes in the lemon water to prevent discolouring until ready to use.

To cook the artichokes:
In a bowl combine all of the ingredients and mix well. Using two-thirds of the mixture fill each of the artichoke cavities with a spoonful of the mixture pressing it well.

In a heavy-based saucepan or casserole dish with a tight-fitting lid, place the artichokes with the cavity facing down and the stems poking upwards. It is important that the pan is large enough to hold all the artichokes in this manner. Rub the rest of the garlic mixture onto the outside of the artichokes. Add all the oil and a little water to cover one third of the artichoke bases, not the stems.

Moisten 2 pieces of kitchen paper wide enough to cover the top of the casserole, place the paper over the top of the casserole and then put the lid on top. The paper is moistened to allow the steam to remain in the pot and hence to cook the artichoke stems by steaming. Fold any excess paper back over the lid to prevent it from catching fire during cooking.

Cook the artichokes over a medium heat for about 35 to 40 minutes, or until they can be easily pierced with a fork. Cooking time varies according to the freshness of the artichokes. You may have to add a couple of tablespoons of water if it boils away; on the other hand, if they cook before the water has had a chance to boil away, remove the lid and boil the water rapidly away.

To serve:
Gently remove the artichokes to a serving plate, being careful not to knock the stems off from the bases. Apart from being edible, the stems also lend themselves to a different serving presentation. Reserve the cooking oil and juices from the pot and, prior to serving, pour over the artichokes. This dish is best eaten either lukewarm or at room temperature.

Finocchi Fritti
Fried Fennel

Serves 6
3 fennel bulbs
salt
2 eggs, lightly beaten
200g/7 oz (Br.)/2 cups (U.S.) fine, dry breadcrumbs, re-toasted in a hot oven or a dry frying pan for added crispness
vegetable oil for deep frying

To prepare the fennel:
Cut off the tops of the fennel bulbs. Trim away any parts that are discoloured and neaten the base, taking care not to trim it too close as only this base part holds the sections together. Cut the bulb lengthwise (through its height) into slices about 8mm/3/8 in thick. Rinse the slices carefully under running cold water, then cook them in boiling salted water until the core is tender but still firm, about 6 to 10 minutes. Drain.

On 2 separate plates place the breadcrumbs and the lightly beaten egg. When the fennel is cool enough to handle, dip a slice into the egg, allow any excess egg to drip off, then place it in the breadcrumbs, patting them on with your fingertips to coat the fennel well. Repeat until all the slices have been done, setting the crumbed slices on a plate.

In a large frying pan heat enough oil to allow the slices to float. Fry a few at a time until golden, turning once to brown the second side. Drain on paper towelling. Salt before serving.

Fragole all'Aceto Balsamico
Strawberries with Balsamic Vinegar

Serves 6 to 8
1 kg/use 2 lb strawberries
4 to 6 tablespoons (Br.)/5 to 7
tablespoons (U.S.) sugar, depending
on the ripeness of the strawberries
2 to 3 tablespoons balsamic vinegar

Wash the strawberries before hulling
them, to prevent excess water from seep-
ing in. Then hull the strawberries and
cut the larger ones in half. Place in a
serving bowl.

An hour before serving, lightly toss the
strawberries in the sugar, giving time
for the sugar to dissolve and form a light
syrup.

When ready to serve, add the balsamic
vinegar and toss gently to combine all
the ingredients. (Balsamic vinegar not
only adds a richness of colour and a pungent aroma, it seems to have a magical
touch in rendering unripe strawberries
the flavour of ripe ones.)

John Sedlar

St. Estèphe Restaurant
Manhattan Beach, U.S.A.

French meets American Indian and Hispanic in suburban Los Angeles? What's this? *Haute* blue corn tortillas? *Nouvelle* American Southwest? 'Perhaps only laid-back California can produce such a combination,' I mused as I took the forty dollar taxi drive to this airport suburb, wondering exactly why I chase my tail around the world following crazy tips from equally crazy confrères who think they're one up on spotting 'the best-with-the-latest'; and whether in fact it could be true that 'there's nothing new under the sun'.

But what John Sedlar produces at the St. Estèphe is definitely new, and definitely worth the foray into the South Bay.

The association with France is not just in the restaurant's name, for John has been steeped in French training and spent his last year before opening his own restaurant in the employ of one of Los Angeles's most inspirational French chefs, Jean Bertranou at L'Ermitage. However John is also of Spanish descent, was born in Santa Fe, New Mexico, and was raised on the dishes of the region — tamales, pinto beans, pork and hominy stew, blue corn and chillies. 'I'm a full-blooded son of the Southwest,' he explains.

John got into the restaurant trade by accident. When he left school at fifteen, he got work at a local garage and washing dishes at a local restaurant. Somewhat intrigued by the latter and spurred on by curiosity rather than ambition, he graduated there from the sink to the stoves. Later drifting to Los Angeles, John started in a well-run and highly rated restaurant called Silo, came to the notice of the critics and suddenly found himself voted Best Chef of South Bay. Taking stock, he made a decision then to become more professional and treat his seven or eight years in kitchens as a true career, and he chased the position at L'Ermitage

to consolidate his experience. He found working under Bertranou the turning point of his career, and the move to the prettily plated, light, appealing dishes of nouvelle cuisine highly stimulating.

When John and his partner, his life-time friend Steve Garcia, opened their little shop-front restaurant in the neat, clean but highly unlikely shopping mall of Manhattan Beach, wedged in between supermarkets and discount stores, they were a highly competent, French, nouvelle cuisine restaurant— well thought of, but one of many. Their attention to detail was proud: John is basically a great saucier with a subtle palate and, not incidentally, a great dessert maker, turning out delicious desserts that are rich rather than sweet, and wonderfully light textured despite their luscious looks. Steve handles the front of house with warmth and charm, an excellent foil to the possible pretension of their now highly stylised food.

Guided by his gifted palate, a loving affection for the foods of his childhood, and the subtle sense of humour that allows him to send up his own nostalgia, John started to introduce some French-influenced versions of the foods of his native region. The Pueblo Indians were good farmers and good cooks, although the dishes resulting from their love of cornmeal, chillies, beans and the like were coarser and more peasant like than the foods John had been trained to cook.

Quietly, and often fearing the clients would laugh him out of town, the first strains of his flirtation with the foods of his youth began to appear on the menu, under unlikely French titles like *Mosaïque Kachina des Caviars Américains, servie avec des Oeufs Hachés* (Kachina Mosaic of American Caviars served with Chopped Egg and Endive Feathers) and *Coquilles St. Jacques 'Nacho', servies avec 'Gorditas', Sauce Crème de Roquefort* (Scallop Nachos served with Gorditas and a Roquefort Cream Sauce). It's all ridiculous, and

Salmon Painted Desert

wonderful — and I wonder sometimes if the calm, collected, but twinkle-eyed chef keeps the menu in French just for the joy of passing an hour with the series of giggles that must be necessary to put in place such outrageous translations!

Outrageous translations, but outrageous food? Emphatically not! For behind all this stands a craftsman, an excellent young chef. If the plated food is teasingly placed into the shape of an Indian rug or decorated with cornmeal pasta in the shape of an Indian arrow, it is nevertheless the flavour which, above all, stands out. When John uses his celebrated 'squeeze bottles' to draw lines, arrows or Indian 'war paint' through the sauce, amazingly it is still the interchange of flavours that is paramount. When the streak of chilli or avocado purée meets the tongue, intermingled with the garlic and goat's cheese sauce that surrounds the chilli rellenos, they give a thrilling lift to the palate that is as calculated as the way they look on the plate. And if the chocolate chilli rellenos has a moulded chilli-shaped form, it also has the most traditionally prepared filling of hazelnut butter cream, the highest quality espresso coffee *crème anglaise* and the best chocolate 'war paint' in town.

If Manhattan Beach, California is a long way from home, then John shares some of his secrets in the book he wrote in 1986, *Modern Southwest Cuisine*. The photos speak loudly of the unique graphic effects he produces on his plates, and his recipes will let you experience the wonderful flavours that hide behind them.

The dishes presented here are some of the 'classics' of the restaurant. Fireworks is served as an appetiser with the apéritif and, both visually and in its choice of flavours, sets the tone for the rest of the meal. The Chilli Rellenos are John's very French-influenced version of the Indian classic, stuffed Jalepeno pepper, which was traditionally roasted, peeled and filled with tasty cheese and a ground meat mixture known as *picadillo*. In John's version the peppers are stuffed with a succulent *duxelles* and served with goat's cheese and garlic enhancing the sauce. Salmon Painted Desert was so-named because the pattern made by the two colours of what John calls his 'Indian paint' reminded him of the striated colours of the mesas in the New Mexican desert. The dish is typical of the illusions he creates with the unique, innovative style that he calls 'Modern Southwest Cuisine'.

1   *2*   *3*

4   *5*   *6*

Salmon Painted Desert

Serves 6

The red (chilli) Indian paint:
1 tablespoon oil, preferably peanut or other bland oil
2 cloves garlic, finely chopped
125ml/4 fl oz (Br.)/½ cup (U.S.) red chilli powder, mild to medium hot
175ml/6 fl oz (Br.)/good ¾ cup (U.S.) water

The green (sorrel) Indian paint:
1 bunch sorrel, or use ¾ cup pre-puréed sorrel, available sometimes in jars. (You can substitute spinach [English spinach].)
2 cloves garlic, finely chopped
oil, preferably peanut or other bland oil
salt and pepper

6 x 150g/use 6 oz salmon steaks
salt and freshly ground pepper

The shallot sauce:
125ml/4 fl oz (Br.)/½ cup (U.S.) dry white wine
3 shallots, finely chopped
450ml/¾ pint (Br.)/2 scant cups (U.S.) cream, preferably with 45% milk fat (heavy cream)
salt and ground white pepper

Equipment
2 plastic 'squeeze bottles' with nozzles and a steamer

The red (chilli) Indian paint:
1. Heat the oil and gently pan-fry the garlic so it cooks through but doesn't brown. Add the chilli powder and straight away, the water. Bring to the boil; blend the colours.

2. Strain through a *chinois* (strainer). Recuperate the sauce, check the seasoning, and pour into a squeeze bottle.

The green (sorrel) Indian paint:
Take the stalks from the sorrel and devein the leaves. Heat the oil in a pan and fry the garlic. Add the leaves to the frypan to soften them a little, then transfer it all to a food processor. Purée to a fine paste, sieve, season with salt and pepper and place in the squeeze bottle. If using the pre-puréed paste, cook the garlic, add the paste momentarily, then proceed to the food processor.

In the second picture, the green paint, which was made first, is in the bottle so you can see the finished effect.

You need ¼ to ½ bottle of each purée to decorate the dish. They may be made in advance and set aside until needed. They need not be hot.

3. Combine the chopped shallots and wine in a saucepan and bring to the boil. Reduce to about half the volume, so the alcohol goes from the wine, and the shallots have given up their flavour. Add the cream, return to the boil and continue reducing to about 1½ cups, stirring from time to time.

4. Sieve the sauce to remove the shallots. Keep warm. Heat the serving plates, but not enough to spoil the sauce.

5. Season the salmon steaks with salt and pepper. Bring the steamer to a rolling boil, then place the steaks on the steamer rack and lower gently into the steamer to cook, about 5 to 7 minutes,

depending on size. When cooked, lift them carefully with an egglift, and put them on the plates as in step **9**.

6. While the salmon is cooking, ladle the sauce into the centre of each serving dish. Tilt the dish to make the sauce run over the plate and cover the central area of the dish.

7. Take the squeeze bottle of green Indian paint and make sure it is pouring properly by quickly squirting a little onto a plate or paper. Then, with a steady hand, paint horizontal lines of green paint over the sauce, each line spaced about 5mm/¼ in apart. The lines should be painted over only two-thirds of the plate, leaving the last third for the fish. When the green lines are drawn, draw red ones with the red Indian paint from the other squeeze bottle in between the green ones. The number of lines of each colour you need depends on the size of the plate and your ability to space them equally. Normally the count should be between 3 and 5 of each, preferably the latter.

8. Using the back of a knife, or a skewer, pull through these lines at right angles, also in equal spaces, cutting the painted lines and pulling the lines towards you, thus creating a pattern as in the photograph.

9. Place the salmon in position in the space left for it, but before doing so, blot off any excess moisture by resting the egglift momentarily on a teatowel. This should prevent any water weeping into the sauce.

7

8

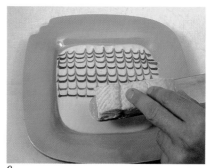

9

Fireworks

The appetiser that John serves to all his
clients while they have their drink. His
fun fireworks, with a corn chip to pick
up the avocado and chilli 'paints' that
taste just like tingling dips, has a coun-
terpart in an equally decorative dessert,
Neon Tumbleweeds, which tangles fruit
purées poured from a squeeze bottle
among a jumble of fruits, this time with
a sweet bizcochitos to pick up the
flavours. Conceived with humour as a
parody of his southwestern themes, both
are flavoursome to eat as well as bringing a smile to all his guests.

Serves 6

The avocado paint:

1 avocado
a vinaigrette made from 2 good
tablespoons (Br.)/3 tablespoons (U.S.)
olive oil, 1 tablespoon sherry vinegar,
salt, black pepper, mixed together
50ml/1½ fl oz (Br.)/¼ cup (U.S.)
milk or, if obtainable, 'half and half' (a
mixture of cream and milk)

The red Indian paint:

about ¼ squeeze bottle of red paint (as
in the Salmon Painted Desert recipe
above)
5 tablespoons (Br.)/6 tablespoons
(U.S.) diced, peeled and seeded tomato
the cooked kernels scraped from 1
boiled corn on the cob
corn chips

Take the avocado flesh from its skin.
Combine it in a food processor with
the vinaigrette and the milk or 'half
and half' (the latter makes it a little
creamier) and purée to a paste. Sieve it
and place it in a squeeze bottle. This
paste can be kept in the bottle in the
refrigerator for 2 days. If it oxidises and
greys a little on the top, squirt this part
off before using the paste. Make up the
red Indian paste and have it ready in a
second squeeze bottle.

Squirt a tumbling pattern of the 2 pastes
onto the plate. Scatter the tomato and
corn decoratively around. Place the corn
chips attractively in place. Serve extra
chips if necessary, to be used as you
would for a dip, to lift these lively,
flavoursome pastes to the tongue.

Red Chilli Rellenos with Garlic *Chèvre* Sauce

Serves 6

The *duxelles*:
1 tablespoon unsalted butter
1 kg/2lb 4 oz (Br.)/good 11 cups (U.S.) champignons (baby mushrooms), finely chopped
125mls/4 fl oz (Br.)/½ cup (U.S.) cream, preferably with 45% milk fat (heavy cream)
salt and finely ground white pepper

The sauce:
125mls/4 fl oz (Br.)/½ cup (U.S.) dry white wine
3 cloves garlic, finely chopped
450mls/¾ pint (Br.)/2 scant cups (U.S.) cream, preferably with 45% milk fat (heavy cream)
150g/good 5 oz *chèvre* (goat's cheese)

salt
6 red Anaheim peppers (sometimes known as banana peppers, roasted, skinned and seeded)
about ¼ squeeze bottle red paint (as in the Salmon Painted Desert recipe)

To prepare the *duxelles*:
Heat the butter in a frypan and add the finely chopped champignons (baby mushrooms). Keep on a high heat, stirring until all the liquid evaporates. Add the cream and season to taste. Simmer for a further 20 minutes until the mixture thickens into a fairly pasty, thick mixture. Set it aside.

To prepare the sauce:
Combine the chopped garlic and wine in a saucepan and boil until reduced by half, stirring from time to time. Stir in the cream and *chèvre* (goat's cheese) and blend together with a whisk or

wooden spoon until the sauce is amalgamated. Pass through a sieve. Season with a little salt and set aside.

To make the chilli rellenos:
Slit open the peppers carefully and spoon 2 good tablespoons (Br.)/3 tablespoons (U.S.) of the *duxelles* into the centre. Fold them close again and re-form their shape. Transfer them carefully to a buttered baking tray (sheet) and bake, covered with a damp kitchen towel, in a 220ºC/425ºF oven for about 10 minutes, or until heated through.

To serve:
Spoon the sauce into the centre of the plate and tilt the plate so the sauce covers the entire base. Place the chillis carefully on the sauce, and then finish by making the Indian pattern along the side of the plate with the red Indian paint squirted from the squeeze bottle.

Alice Waters

Chez Panisse Restaurant Berkeley, U.S.A.

When talking about Alice Waters one wonders whether one is talking about a chef, a restaurateur, a woman . . . or a revolution. Totally untrained in the field of cooking, Alice herself admits to being a 'political entity'. The inspirational work she has done in changing America's attitudes to food, its eating habits, food-buying habits, even its agricultural activities, has made her the doyenne of the modern American food movement. The Messiah is alive and well, and living in the diminutive bird-like frame of a radiant, silk-skinned, intense woman in Berkeley, California.

If Alice's political radicalism was a product of the sixties, when she took time out from her Bachelor of Arts in French cultural studies to shout from the barricades against the Vietnam war, for freedom of speech, or to stage a lay-in against the use of napalm; it is still highly relevant to the intensity with which she runs her restaurant, and to the dogmatism with which she pronounces every single bean or carrot fit to be served in the restaurant that night.

No one doubts that her restaurant is a political statement. In a country in which convenience foods and frozen foods reign paramount, Alice's dedication to searching out and serving only the smallest, only the pesticide free, only the best tasting and only 'worthy' natural produce has been a radical, even revolutionary step. It has not only caused her to have an enormous personal following in the restaurant but also in the Agricultural Departments of California, where she helps with research and development; and in the fields, where former flower children, bohemians and dedicated enthusiasts grow particular vegetables, salad greens, herbs, suckling pigs, and even make goat's cheeses especially for her. A friend from her university days recalls her firmly declaring, 'I do not want to be part of a revolution fuelled by people fed on peanut butter and jelly.' The statement may well have been the catalyst for her adult life.

Another catalyst was undoubtedly her first visit to France. Designed to be part of her field study for her degree, the trip became a year of wonderment for Alice, who declares in her first book *The Chez Panisse Menu Cookbook* that, in that year, 'I experienced a major realisation: I hadn't eaten anything, comparatively speaking, and I wanted to taste everything.'[1] On her return, she literally cooked her way from end to end through Elizabeth David's book, *French Country Cooking*, acknowledging that 'it was so important that I was driven, as if I had a sense of mission'.[2]

Alice's involvement with France was all consuming, but within a few years it had a narrower focus, and the Mediterranean became her obsession — a fantasy that was perhaps crystallised into an obsession by the marvellous trilogy of films of the thirties *Marius, Fanny* and *César* by Marcel Pagnol (on whose novels were also recently based the films *Jean de Florette* and *Manon des Sources*). Panisse, the old sailmaker in the films, seemed to Alice to epitomise the charm and character of her beloved Provence, and gave her the name for her restaurant; Fanny, the name for her daughter, and for the stand-up coffee bar she devised in 1984. Just a few miles down the road from Chez Panisse, Café Fanny serves good coffee and bakery products, wine by the glass and take-away luncheon finger food.

Chez Panisse came into being in 1971 in a tiny two-storey wooden building in Shattuck Avenue, where it remains today. It was started with a group of friends with like personal commitment, and they all 'slaved away' without much technical knowledge (much less formal training) believing in an end product that should be simple, perfectly cooked and subtely flavoured.

Salmon Carpaccio

Alice's love of Mediterranean produce was easy to transfer to the local Californian produce because the climates were similar and California was, even at the time, considered the 'salad basket' and produce-growing centre of America (though Berkeley itself was perhaps at the time more attuned to eating pulses and brown rice than morel mushrooms, coriander and *mesclun* salad greens).

However, Alice soon discovered that what she meant by fresh, was over and beyond the concept generally understood by the surrounding professional producers, and what she meant by flavoursome led her into almost immediate confrontation with prevailing standards. The battle to produce smaller, more flavour-intense ingredients began then, and has much to do with the advent of the miniature vegetables California now sells to the world, but which many, perhaps even Alice, would say carry her original intention to the point of the ridiculous. If she disagrees with her description as the patron saint of California Cuisine — believing it to be more a catchword of media hype than a definable style of cooking — Alice would quite happily acknowledge her role in restoring the role of the vegetable, and a respect for the fresh and the seasonal, to the American restaurant industry. She is much more comfortable with these concepts.

From the beginning at Chez Panisse the friends, most of whom had equity in the restaurant, worked with a five-course *prix-fixe* menu, and one that changed daily. The format endures, and to this day eating at Alice's restaurant is like eating in a private home. Your dinner is at the whim and the choice of the hostess. In the seventeen or so years since its conception, they are said to have served a hundred people five nights a week (there are two sittings, one at 6 pm, one at 8.30 pm) without repeating a menu, and bookings can usually only be obtained a month in advance. As it was in the beginning, is now and ever shall be, in Alice's words, 'Here at Chez Panisse we spit roast, we grill. We treat the food simply. We don't make elaborate masking sauces.'

In 1980, April Fool's Day to be exact, Alice extended the range of the restaurant by building an upstairs bistro-type café that allows clients to choose their menu and to come and go all day. Students sit over food chosen from an à la carte menu centred mostly around innovative modern versions of the pizza and dishes that can be grilled over a mesquite fire. It is extraordinarily good value, and caters to upwards of two hundred and fifty people a day.

So the myth of Alice Waters goes on, with Alice like some highly dedicated amateur (in the true sense of the word) in the eye of the storm of her own fame, still caring about and guided by the very same dream that began it all. She is drawn to people, and chooses her staff from among those she instinctively likes, remaining friends with them, and leaving those she has trained to spread the word in restaurants, produce markets and farms all over the country. In 1982 after a fire devastated Chez Panisse, Alice, who is said not to have made a penny out of the place until her business consultant father took over the reins in the early eighties, saw this extended family rally together and get her on her feet again and her restaurant back and running in a matter of weeks.

Alice Waters is a legend to the restaurant public of America. The Gault et Millau Guide, famous for the French bloody-mindedness that sees nothing worthy in the food business outside France, listed her in 1987, along with Fredy Girardet, as the only non-French in their list of the world's top ten chefs. In fact Alice cooks very little now, although the talk of the town are the mini-*dégustation* meals she makes for her young daughter Fanny! Whilst still supervising everything, she leaves the restaurant kitchen in the hands of Paul Bertolli and the pastry to her great friend and long-time collaborator Lindsey Shere. But Alice's Provençal dream is still her guide. It's a singular dream, and one that has given great consistency to her vision.

1. Alice Waters, *Chez Panisse Menu Cookbook,* Random House, New York, 1982, p ix.
2. ibid., p x.

Salmon *Carpaccio*

In this recipe, made by Paul with Alice hovering and commenting, they used a 2.7kg/6 lb chinook salmon from the Pacific North West of America. Canadian or Scottish salmon are the most reliable substitutes in the northern hemisphere, and in the southern, use the Atlantic salmon, nowadays bred in hatcheries. Ocean-run trout, or large river trout are the next best substitutes, and Alice also suggests using fresh tuna.

The amount of fish here is excessive, but the restaurant only buys in large fish. Each of the fillets weighed 450g/ 1 lb and made 12 servings of *carpaccio.* To serve 6 or 8, buy only the head section (where the meat is thicker). Alice however, can think of lots to do with any leftover fish — make salmon *rillettes,* poach it in a hot *court-bouillon,* bake it in baking (parchment) paper, or cook it into a ragoût.

Serves 8
Pepper relish:
45g/1½ oz (Br.)/about 2 shallots, finely chopped
as many different coloured bell peppers (capsicums) as you can find (use about

¼ to ½ of each colour)
1cm/½ in piece of cucumber, peeled and seeded
juice of half a lemon
salt and pepper
2 tablespoons (Br.)/scant 3 tablespoons (U.S.) olive oil

Flower confetti:
These are the flowers that Alice used, providing the vital colours:
rocket flowers (tiny white flowers with yellow centres)
borage flowers (blue)
nasturtiums (dark orange-yellow)
calendula (marigold)
mustard flowers (yellow)
dwarf pansies (purple)

To prepare the fish:
1.   Remove the head and fins. With a large, very sharp knife, start along the backbone at the (removed) head end, and cut cleanly along the length of the bone to remove the top fillet.

2.   Turn the fish over and repeat to remove the fillet on the other side. Paul cuts directly through the stomach bones so they come away with the fillet, instead of wending his knife up and around them. The stomach bones are then cut

away from the fillet as in picture 2. This cut, which is also the traditional method for making smoked salmon, leaves a neater line.

3.   Lay the fillets in turn flesh side upwards on the bench, and using the weight and flexibility of the knife, cut away this line of rib-cage bones in 1 neat cut.

4.   Use pincers to remove the bones that remain along the centre of the fillets. There is 1 per division (lobe) of flesh, and they can be felt by running your finger along the centre of the fillet against the grain of the flesh.

5.   Skin each fillet in turn by holding the tail of the fish and, using the flexibility of the fish knife by lying it flush with the board between the skin and the flesh, slicing the fillet free from the skin with a sawing action. Paul then removes the head section, by cutting the fish in half lengthwise.

6.   Halve the fillet lengthwise, then, using a flat hand to support the fish so it doesn't mash, cut into 5mm/ ¼ in slices. You should get 8 slices from each half, each half weighing in at about 225g/8 oz.

1

2

3

4

5

6

7

8

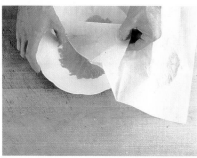

9

10

Wild Mushroom Ragoût with Grilled Polenta

Serves 6

50g/scant 2 oz (Br.)/½ cup dried *cèpe (porcini)*, boletus or other dried wild mushrooms
475ml/good ¾ pint (Br.)/2 cups (U.S.) rich veal or beef stock
450g/1 lb fresh wild mushrooms (chanterelles, morels or other)
5 tablespoons (Br.)/6 tablespoons (U.S.) unsalted butter
2 shallots, finely chopped
1 clove garlic, finely chopped
salt and pepper

To prepare the mushrooms:
Soak the dried mushrooms in hot water to cover, for 30 minutes. Drain and reserve the liquid. Rinse the fresh mushrooms under water if they are gritty. Cut the fresh mushrooms into 5mm/¼ in slices.

7. Cut 8 pieces of baking (parchment) paper (40 x 30cm/16 x 12 in), fold in half and crease well. Open again and brush lightly with olive oil. Place 1 piece of fish on half of each piece, and fold the other half over it smoothly. Make sure there are no creases. Holding the paper firmly, pound it so that the fish spreads to about 2½ times its size, and is evenly translucent when the paper is held to the light. Protected from the air in its paper the fish can be refrigerated for 3 to 4 hours without spoiling.

To prepare the relish vegetables:
8. Chop the relish vegetables very finely. In a small bowl, combine them and dress with the juice of about ½ a lemon, salt and freshly ground black pepper, plus 2 tablespoons (Br.)/scant 3 tablespoons (U.S.) olive oil.

9. Peel, **don't pull** the paper from 1 side of the fish, checking constantly with your finger that nothing attaches. Then upend the paper onto the serving plate, and pull away the other side. (Press it down first, so the action of it sticking to the plate helps you.)

To serve:
10. Scatter approximately 1 tablespoon of relish over the salmon. Chop the flowers and scatter this 'flower confetti' over the dish, but only just before you go to the table.

To cook the ragoût:

Melt the butter over a medium heat, until the butter just starts to brown. Sauté the dried mushrooms for a few minutes before adding the sliced fresh mushrooms. Lightly brown the mushrooms over a high heat. Add the shallots, garlic, salt and pepper; stir the mixture for a moment. Strain the stock and the liquid from the dried mushrooms and add to the ragoût. Continue to cook until all the liquid has reduced a little and the mushrooms are just tender.

To serve:

Adjust the seasoning and serve with slices of grilled polenta (see recipe below), sprinkled with chopped parsley.

Grilled Polenta

180g/good 6 oz (Br.)/1 cup (U.S.) polenta
750ml/1¼ pints (Br.)/3 cups (U.S.) light chicken stock
1 teaspoon salt
½ teaspoon black pepper
3 tablespoons (Br.)/3½ tablespoons (U.S.) unsalted butter
2 tablespoons (Br.)/scant 3 tablespoons (U.S.) fresh grated parmesan cheese
extra virgin olive oil

Bring the chicken stock to the boil and stir in the polenta, using a strong wire whisk to prevent lumps from forming. Add the salt and pepper and continue to whisk occasionally for about 10 minutes. When the polenta has become rather stiff, stir in the butter and the parmesan cheese. Spread the polenta into a buttered baking dish (sheet) of about 20 x 20cm/8 x 8 in. Let it cool until it has set firm, then cut it into serving squares or triangles. Brush the polenta on both sides with olive oil and season it with salt and pepper. Grill the polenta over a hot fire, for about 5 minutes on each side, or pan fry it in a little olive oil.

Walnut Spice Cake

Alice would like to compliment her pastry chef, Lindsey Shere, for this recipe. Lindsey's long association with Chez Panisse has accounted for their many wonderful desserts.

250g/9 oz (Br.)/2 cups (U.S.) finely ground walnuts
40g/1½ oz (Br.)/⅓ cup (U.S.) fine dry breadcrumbs
2 teaspoons grated orange zest
1⅓ teaspoons grated lemon zest
1⅓ teaspoons baking powder
⅔ teaspoon cinnamon
1/8 teaspoon ground cloves
3/8 teaspoon salt
6 eggs, separated
130g/4½ oz (Br.)/⅔ cup (U.S.) sugar
⅔ teaspoon vanilla extract
1 to 2 tablespoons water
¼ teaspoon cream of tartar
icing (confectioner's) sugar

Equipment:

23cm/9 in round spring-form pan, buttered and lined with baking (parchment) paper, then floured

Combine the walnuts, grated zests, baking powder, spices and salt. Beat the egg yolks and half of the sugar until they will hold a firm ribbon. Beat in the vanilla and the water.

Beat the egg whites with the cream of tartar until they just hold a soft shape; then beat in the remaining sugar until they hold their soft shape again. Alternately fold in the egg yolk and walnut mixtures in 3 additions until just combined.

Pour into the prepared pan and bake in a 180ºC/350ºF oven until a cake tester comes out clean and the top of the cake springs back when lightly touched (approximately 55 minutes).

Cool completely in the pan. When ready to serve, turn out of the pan and peel off the baking (parchment) paper. Powder the top of the cake lightly with icing (confectioner's) sugar. Serve with *crème anglaise* (see recipe page 177) and sliced blood oranges.

Iain Hewitson
The Last Aussie Fishcaf
Melbourne and Sydney
Australia

ain Hewitson, the New Zealand boy from the bush with the big grin and the highly outspoken opinions, came to Australia in 1973, and within months the word got around. Here was a lad who could cook, and could stand and tell you about it too . . . though he wouldn't be looking at you while he talked — he has to be fidgeting, cutting the meat, plating the food, installing the new tandoori oven, sipping or pouring the champagne, or just checking who's coming in the door.

Get Iain on a subject he's adamant about — something like the merits of nouvelle cuisine, or 'Is there a real Australian cuisine?' and if so, 'Where should it be going next?'; or worse still, what the restaurant critic wrote about the restaurant he reviewed last week, or whether the rules to the latest culinary competition are fair (and the judges competent to judge it) — and out will come the real Iain. Out too, will come a well-worded column, or one of his famed letters to the editor, for Iain's acidity is not just in the sauce, but well on hand in his choice of words when something goes against his grain.

After three years spent changing the image of 'pub food' at the Lemon Tree Hotel in Melbourne, Iain became a leading exponent of nouvelle cuisine. When later, he was head of the stoves at Clichy, also in Melbourne, his *menus-dégustation* were ten-courses long, and his *prix-fixe* menu one of the first in the country. A popular left-bank style restaurant with unpretentious prices in an unpretentious suburb, Clichy became the haunt of Melbourne food and wine buffs, even though Iain had no intention of telling them what they were going to eat, nor how he would manage to get it out to eighty-five people. At his best he was excellent, at the worst you needed to take a book to read, hoping that the one dish that would make it all worthwhile

would be the next one. Looking back, he would probably agree that what he served at Clichy was substantially based on the new genre chefs of France, without a great deal of personal input, except the talent he has always had for making things taste good.

Meantime, Iain was studying — cookbooks lined the walls — and he has since become, technically, a better and better cook. The professional Iain of today began to emerge when his instinct took him from the larger restaurant and geared him to renovate a very personable old house, the front two rooms of which he painted pastel pink, decorated simply with large bunches of flowers, beautiful glassware and tableware, and floor-length pink tablecloths. The result was a very personal, elegant small restaurant seating only thirty-five. Iain named it Fleurie and says he realised that there, 'I could really have time to personally tend every dish that left the kitchen.'

Some of the best food in Melbourne came from that kitchen, as the copy-cat food gave way to Iain's own style and creativity, based on a stronger confidence in himself and an assured technical skill. The chef had graduated.

But to leave it at that would be to disregard the entrepreneurial Iain. As he began to take what he was doing at Fleurie in his stride, up came the head again — to look onward and out — and he spied, just around the corner from Fleurie, a coffee lounge that was losing money. Yet another formula was working its way into his consciousness!

Champagne Charlies was, to my mind, a brilliant concept — one of the country's first attempts to broaden the impact of good food and bring it to a cheaper venue. Champagne Charlies was to have the best wines and French champagne by the glass. (Iain knows and loves his wines. He had for years been a great propogandist for Beaujolais, pioneering

Ballotine of Chicken

Australia's participation in the traditional game of getting the first bottle of Beaujolais Nouveau into the country. The Clichy Cup for the first person to open the new season's wine at the table at Clichy became legendary. It was also to have a very affordable menu, without compromising the quality of food. Simple dishes were to be served, and a fairly eclectic mix at that. The starter would be the same for everyone in the restaurant (usually some form of salad, hors d'oeuvres or a ratatouille), followed by a choice of main courses, including offerings from the tandoor oven Iain so loves. *Naan*, Indian tandoori bread, was to be the official bread of the restaurant. On one side of the room was a table with cheeses and desserts placed along it, and the customers were to choose from what was available. And for all this, when the doors opened, the price of a meal was about double that of going to the cinema. It was one of the best value restaurants in town, and with no bookings taken, Champagne Charlies opened every night to queues.

The original idea was to franchise Champagne Charlies, and Iain still cooked nightly at Fleurie. Only in 1987 did he give up Fleurie, and in 1988 Champagne Charlies, and that had to do with the phenomenal success of yet another of his unique ideas.

The Last Aussie Fishcaf was so simple in concept it would have been hard to guess at the enormous appeal it was to have almost immediately. In a large barn of a room, Iain picked up a theme of the fifties and, with neon tubing and old laminated café tables, reconstructed the 'diner' of the past. With a bar and stools along one side, and a juke box playing the music of the fifties and sixties on the other (Iain brings in professional dancers to start the jiving and rock and rolling), the Fishcaf does most of its business in excellent, crisp-battered fish and chips, served on large plates cleverly clad in butchers' paper, with copious quantities of tartare, chutney and *raita* as sauces.

The food buffs however, can also have a piece of salmon with a *beurre blanc* sauce, Thai-style fish salad, fish curry, or Beluga caviar for the best price in town. The first courses are equally inviting, and the desserts range from huge sundaes with multiple balls of different home-made ice-creams to excellent tarts.

The place buzzes day and night, and is a haunt of the young, Yuppies and the man and woman about town. If you don't want formal dining, this is the best food you'll ever get in a non-restaurant restaurant.

The Last Aussie Fishcaf then, was fated to become the Second Last Aussie Fishcaf, as Iain set out to repeat the success in Sydney — maybe the most important thing a good chef could do for his country. For isn't it time that there was good food everywhere, rather than just in the most expensive restaurants?

And as he does so, boy, is the grin on his face even wider than before.

VARIATIONS ON A THEME

The following dishes have all been prepared with one basic forcemeat mixture. Each has quite a different flavour, presentation and look. Iain's intention is not that you should make one mixture and subdivide it — he would never serve these things on the same menu — but just that you should understand the versatility of certain basic mixtures, so you can be freed from eternal dependence on the cookbook. If you can make a further five things out of the basic mixture, Iain will be delighted.

Basic Forcemeat Mixture

100g/3½ oz (Br.)/1 scant cup (U.S.) white breadcrumbs
1 onion
2 cloves garlic
150ml/¼ pint (Br.)/scant ¾ cup (U.S.) cream with 35% milk fat (whipping cream)
250g/use ½ lb lean veal
125g/use ¼ lb pork
125g/use ¼ lb pork fat
250g/use ½ lb chicken breast
3 eggs
pepper
1 teaspoon allspice

Place the breadcrumbs in a large bowl. Chop the onion and garlic finely. Pour the cream into a small saucepan, add the garlic and onion, and bring to the boil. Pour over the breadcrumbs. Mix well.

Mix the meats together and mince through the medium disc of a mincer (meat grinder). (If you use a food processor, process to a fine grind but be careful not to let it go to a pulp.) Add 3 eggs, a teaspoon of allspice and ground pepper. Test the seasoning. Add this mixture to the cream and crumb mixture.

Optional additions:

Choose from the following additions, varying them to gain different effects according to the dishes you wish to make: pink peppercorns, any type of chopped fresh or dried mushrooms (the latter pre-soaked), truffles, chopped blanched spinach (English spinach), fresh herbs, pistachio nuts. Of the dishes Iain has made, he prefers pink peppercorns in the ballotine, pistachio nuts in the leek terrine, and in the sausages he often uses chopped spinach (English spinach), fresh herbs or pink peppercorns, according to his mood.

Ballotine of Chicken

For this recipe, use the basic mix with your preferred addition. Use only fresh chickens. 1 chicken serves only 2 people, but the legs will serve for another meal.

Serves 4

2 chickens (the legs will be set aside for another use)
basic forcemeat (one quantity of recipe above)
melted butter to roast the ballotines
salt

The sauce:

250ml/8 fl oz (Br.)/1 good cup (U.S.) vermouth
250ml/8 fl oz (Br.)/1 good cup (U.S.) chicken stock
125ml/4 fl oz (Br.)½ cup (U.S.) dry white wine
250ml/8 fl oz (Br.)/1 good cup (U.S.) cream, preferably with 35% milk fat (whipping cream)
salt and pepper
about 2 tablespoons hollandaise sauce, butter, or herbed butter

The vegetables:

(These may be varied with the season, and your preference)
12 snow peas *(mange tout)*, topped and tailed
10 to 12 champignons (baby mushrooms)
75g/2½ oz (Br.)/½ cup (U.S.) shelled peas
half a small onion, thinly sliced
8 to 10 small green beans, sliced
50g/scant 2 oz (Br.)/3 tablespoons (U.S.) butter to sauté the vegetables

To bone out the breasts:

1. Remove the drumsticks and thighs in 1 piece and set them aside for another use. Laying the chicken on its side, remove the wings at the knuckle joint.

2. Slit the skin down the spinal column. With a sharp knife, ease the skin from the carcass. The right-handed will find the carcass under the knife, and the (intact) flesh in their left hand.

3. The point of the breastbone is the place where the knife is closest to the skin. Go carefully here. Free the flesh and continue around the chicken until the flesh is totally removed from the carcass.

To stuff the ballotines:

4. Spread the breast open on a board and flatten slightly with the flat side of a meat hammer. Then place a long cylinder-shaped quantity of stuffing in the centre of the chicken breast.

5. Fold the chicken breast around the stuffing, slightly overlapping the fold so it does not burst any stuffing.

6. Tie the chicken breast into the tubular ballotine shape, parcel style. Leave overnight in the refrigerator so that it settles into its shape and does not shrink back when cooking. This resting time also matures and firms the forcemeat so that it holds its shape when cut.

1

2

3

4

5

6

7

8

9

10

wrapped in spinach (English spinach), or long batons of marinated veal fillet, ham or sliced lengths of chicken breast. The forcemeat may also have other ingredients chopped through it, such as spinach (English spinach) to create a different forcemeat texture from the colour of the chicken fillets or other meats that are studded through it.

Sausages

Any of the ingredients listed as **'optional additions'** can be added to the basic forcemeat mix for an interesting stuffing for sausages. Follow the step-by-step instructions for making sausages on page 67 or try to persuade a butcher to take your mixture and fill skins for you.

To cook sausages, Iain's way:
Bring a pan of 2 parts milk and 1 part water to simmering point. Place the sausages in a fry basket and lower into the liquid. Simmer gently for 15 to 20 minutes. They are ready when firm to the touch. Remove, allow to cool, then peel away the skins. Coat with melted butter and breadcrumbs in a baking dish, and set aside until ready to eat. Then heat them in a 180ºC/350ºF oven for 10 minutes. They can be served with apple, hot potato salad, most cream sauces and most *beurre blanc* derivatives. Iain often serves these bland style sausages with a tomato-flavoured hot vinaigrette, and garnishes them with cucumber.

To cook:
7. Stand the ballotines in a baking dish, and brush them very well with melted butter. Salt, but do not pepper them. Bake in a 230ºC/450ºF oven for 25 minutes. Like all rolled meats, let them rest for 5 minutes before cutting.

8. Cut the strings, and slice the meat into 1cm/½ in slices, discarding the ends for a more perfect presentation.

The sauce and garnish:
9. Cut the vegetables into attractive-sized pieces, either julienne or diced a little larger than the peas. Here, Iain has used snow peas (*mange tout*), freshly shelled peas and sliced champignons (baby mushrooms). Place the vermouth, chicken stock and dry white wine in a saucepan. Bring to a boil and reduce to a third. Add the cream, and reduce by another third.

10. Sauté the vegetables in butter until softened, add the reduction and finish the sauce in either of the following ways. The beginner can simply reduce until it coats the spoon (sauce consistency), but Iain insists that to give it body, the sauce should be mounted with a spoonful of hollandaise sauce (chefs are

able to have this on hand). At home, it may be easier to mount with butter or better still, butter in which you have blended chopped fresh herbs.

To serve:
Spoon some of the sauce and vegetables onto the plate before placing 2 slices of the ballotine in the centre of the plate, per person. Iain has garnished with a sprig of rosemary.

Terrines

A simple terrine may be made using the basic forcemeat simply as it is written above. Better still, the mixture can be studded with pistachio, ham pieces, or pink peppercorns to give it flavour and substance. A leek terrine is more interesting and is easily made by lining a pâté mould with bacon and layering 9 thin leeks (half cooked in boiling water) into the forcemeat in 3 layers of 3. Bake in a bain-marie of hot water covered with a lid or foil in a 210ºC/415ºF oven for 45 minutes. Remove from the oven and press with a weight. For other variations, the leeks can be subsituted with a row of prunes

Indian Marinated Fish

Serves 6 to 8

The fish:
1 kg/use 2 lb fish fillets — for
preference choose a large-lobed white-
fleshed fish such as trumpeter, turbot,
snapper, any of the cods, or ling
flour to dredge the fish
clarified butter or ghee to fry

The marinade:
3 teaspoons tumeric
1½ teaspoons chilli powder
salt and freshly ground black pepper
1 tablespoon Brinjal chutney
1 tablespoon hot mango chutney
3 cloves garlic, finely chopped
3 slices fresh ginger, finely chopped
2 tablespoons (Br.)/scant 3 tablespoons
(U.S.) peanut oil
lemon juice to make a moist paste

To marinate the fish:
In a bowl, mix together all the marinade
ingredients, seasoning with salt and
pepper to your taste. Blend in enough
lemon juice to moisten it to the
consistency of paste, so that it can be
rubbed over the fish.

Cut the fish into the size of your choice.
This may be large cubes or, as Iain
prefers, thick slices so that 2 or 3 combine to make a suitable serving. Rub
the marinade well into the fish and leave
for 2 to 3 hours before proceeding.

To cook the fish:
When needed, dust the fish with flour,
then pat off the excess. Heat some clarified butter or ghee and sauté the fish
until lightly browned on the outside,
and the flesh on the inside is fairly
opaque, that is, just cooked.

Transfer the fish to the serving plates
and serve with pickled vegetables (see
recipe below) and the chutney of your
choice.

Pickled Vegetables

The vegetables:
2 cucumbers
250g/use ½ lb green beans
10 small hot red chillis
15 small pickling-size onions
3 red bell peppers (capsicums)
2 to 3 tablespoons peanut oil
1 tablespoon brown mustard seeds

The spicing:
1 teaspoon turmeric
about 3 tablespoons salt
4 tablespoons (Br.)/5 tablespoons
(U.S.) sugar
170ml/5½ fl oz (Br.)/¾ cup (U.S.)
white vinegar
150g/6 oz (Br.)/1 cup (U.S.) peanuts,
shelled

To prepare the vegetables:
Cut the unpeeled cucumbers in half and
scoop out the seeds. Cut into slices
5cm/2 in long. Top, tail, and remove
any strings from the beans. Cut into
similar lengths. Open the red chillis and
remove the seeds and filaments, then
cut into a fine julienne. Halve the onions, and cut the red bell peppers (capsicums) into thin lobes 5cm/2 in long.

To prepare the pickling liquid:
Heat the oil in a small skillet and fry
the mustard seeds until they pop. Reduce
the heat and add the vegetables then
the turmeric and salt. Stir fry for about
2 minutes until the vegetables soften
a little and take on the glaze of the oil,
then add the sugar and vinegar. Bring
to the boil, add the peanuts, and remove from the heat.

To store:
Pack the vegetables into jars and seal
while still hot. Cool and store at room
temperature. The mixture is best after
3 days. It keeps indefinitely, but progres-
sively loses its crispness, so is best used
within 4 to 6 weeks.

Gérard Pangaud

Aurora
New York, U.S.A.

At an early age, Gérard Pangaud established a fine reputation for himself as one of the up-and-coming young chefs of France.

He was the archetypal Parisian and, after training in Paris and working a while in Antibes and Germany, he quickly returned to base and started a tiny restaurant near the Paris Stock Exchange. Gathering himself a clientele and a name as a talented youngster, Gérard later opened the larger restaurant that bore his name, on the outskirts of Paris at Boulogne-Billancourt and easily filled his sixty seats nightly. Although classically trained, Gerard's aim was to cook modern dishes, interesting and innovative, for his ambition ran high and he was out to make himself a name.

Gault et Millau first drew the public's attention to Pangaud when they called him a 'master of his craft' and described his restaurant as 'indisputably the best on the outskirts of Paris'; and the Michelin Guide followed by awarding him a second star.

An effervescent and extroverted character, Gérard was ideally suited to the role of *vedette* or star that is the aspiration of many of today's zealous young showman chefs. A seeker of publicity, he became the media's darling very young and attracted lots of coverage for his restaurant, as well as invitations to cook for important and prestigious dinners.

It wasn't long before the two-star-rated restaurant was itself drawing the stars, and Nana Mouskouri, Candice Bergen, Sylvie Vartan and Roman Polanski among others became his regular clients. Stars lead to stardom, and Gérard was signed up by a management company. He speaks excellent English and his promoters soon had him travelling the world demonstrating his style of French cuisine, particularly in the United States.

Gerard's high profile served him well. Among other accomplishments of which he is justifiably proud, Gérard was asked in 1982 to create dishes for the Williamsburg Summit which was attended by Ronald Reagan, Margaret Thatcher, François Mitterand, Pierre Trudeau and Helmut Schmidt. The lobster and pigeon recipe which he created for them drew praise from all.

Then in 1984 Joe Baum, the man often referred to as the Godfather of the New York restaurant scene, spied Gérard. Having successfully created Four Seasons, Windows of the World at The World Trade Centre and The Rainbow Room, with its eleven-restaurant complex, Baum had a new scheme — to open a restaurant with a truly high-class French cuisine — and he managed to entice Gérard to New York as his chef. After ten months, during which time Gérard was fully involved in the developmental phase of the restaurant, Aurora opened to the public in December 1985. Gérard is now a partner, and the restaurant, complete with cherry wood panelling, a large central bar and chandeliers which change colour during the span of the meal, is highly regarded.

In New York Gérard is in his element, cooking before his public from a semi-open kitchen. His flirtation with the press is as successful as it has always been and currently, along with Bernard Le Coze at Le Bernadin, he is respected as one of the two best French chefs in New York.

He continues to serve some of the innovative dishes that helped make his name, like his Hot Oysters with Saffron and Caviar, and Saddle of Rabbit with Basil; but he admits to a new-found love of the local ingredients. He talks enthusiastically of his 'inspirations Franco-Americain' which have led him to broaden the ingredients he combines and invent modernistic dishes.

For Gérard Pangaud, New York is home now, and his career has never looked brighter.

Selle de Lapin au Basilic

Selle de Lapin au Basilic
Saddle of Rabbit with Basil

Serves 4
1 rabbit of about 750g to 1kg/use 1½ to 2lb

The stock:
The shoulder and the leg bones of the rabbit
1 onion
1 small carrot
½ stalk celery
3 to 4 stalks parsley
3 peppercorns
water to cover

To cook the rabbit:
bouquet garni made with 3 stalks parsley, sprig thyme, bay leaf, 3 large sprigs basil
40g/1½ oz (Br.)/3 tablespoons (U.S.) butter
about 600ml/1 pint (Br.)/2½ cups (U.S.) rabbit stock
100ml/3 fl oz (Br.)/scant ½ cup (U.S.) dry white wine
100ml/3 fl oz (Br.)/ scant ½ cup (U.S.) Noilly Prat or dry vermouth
3 shallots, chopped finely
1 clove garlic, crushed
1 tomato, peeled, seeded and diced
150ml/¼ pint (Br.)/scant ¼ cup (U.S.) cream, preferably with 45% milk fat (heavy cream)
salt and pepper
a further 10 to 12 fresh basil leaves
about 450g/1 lb tagliatelle, cooked and drained

1. Cut the rabbit into 3 portions, namely the leg section, the shoulder (including the rib cage and front legs) and the saddle (the centre back piece including the 2 fillets). Remove the kidneys; discard the lungs and the liver.

2. Separate out the 2 legs and remove the bones from each with the aid of a small knife. Add these bones to the shoulder section and make a rabbit stock with these pieces of rabbit and the peeled and chopped vegetables. Cover with water, bring to the boil, and simmer for 2 hours, skimming when necessary. When drained, you should have about 600 to 800ml/1 to 1¼ pints (Br.)/2½ to 3½ cups (U.S.) of stock.

3. Place the 2 kidneys in the underside section of the saddle, and roll the belly flaps around to encase them.

4. Tie firmly into a parcel.

5. Roll the legs back into their natural shape and tie them firmly, too. You now have 3 pieces of rabbit meat for the dish. Tie the herbs into a bouquet garni.

6. Pierce the fillet on the back of the saddle with a knife in order to break the tendon. This helps prevent the meat from shrinking.

7. Place a nob of butter in the pan, add the rabbit, garlic, shallots, white wine, vermouth, rabbit stock and the bouquet garni. Bring the ingredients to the boil, transfer them to the oven

and cook at 190°C/375°F for about 20 minutes. The meat should still be slightly pink. In the meantime, cook and drain the pasta. Remove the meat and keep it warm. Return the pan to the stove and reduce the liquid rapidly to half its volume. Then add the cream and diced tomato. Reduce again to a nice syrupy sauce consistency.

8. Remove the bouquet garni and lightly purée the sauce, leaving a little texture in the ingredients. Season with salt and pepper and add the chopped basil.

9. Untie the meat pieces. The flaps of the saddle are sliced into fairly wide julienne pieces, the fillets are removed from the bone and sliced.

10. Slice the kidneys and the leg meat.

11. Heat the pre-cooked and drained pasta with a little butter and enough of the sauce to keep it from sticking.

12. Place a bed of pasta on each of the dinner plates; toss the more raggedy pieces of rabbit through the sauce and spoon it over the pasta. Decorate with the remaining rabbit slices.

1

2

3

4

5

6

7

8

9

10

11

12

Alain Senderens

Lucas-Carton
Paris, France

Alain Senderens has been dubbed the most controversial chef in Paris. Often spoken of as a genius, his work is unique and hard to categorise. In a time when one can go from one three-star restaurant to another in France and find similar 'trendy' dishes and ingredients recurring from menu to menu, Alain Senderens will place before you a list of startling dishes, the like of which you've never imagined before.

Long championed by Gault and Millau, the more conservative Michelin Guide acknowledged Alain's importance when they gave him their coveted third star in 1978, while he was at his much-lauded restaurant, l'Archestrate. Just after he had retired as head of the Michelin Guide, André Trichot spoke reverently of Alain, whom he said he considered the most innovative of all the French chefs. He lauded him particularly for his influence in 'lightening' French cuisine and making it healthier.

With Alain's cuisine, things taste as they really should. He has lead the movement to bring vegetables back into restaurants and, using them differently and always cooked to perfection, he has given many people a new appreciation of vegetables. For Alain, steaming is a favourite cooking method, as he believes it allows the real flavour of the ingredients to come through. Following this theory, he has shocked many by serving a lobe of foie gras wrapped and steamed in a cabbage leaf, with shavings of rock salt and coarsely ground peppercorns the only accompaniments.

Despite his innovative, very personal style, Alain Senderens did have a classical background. Born in the south west of France, Alain trained at the Hotel Ambassadeur in Lourdes, then went to Paris at the age of twenty-one, first to La Tour d'Argent and then to the traditional Lucas-Carton. Alain was sous chef when the Hilton Orly opened and then in 1968 branched out to become his own patron/chef at l'Archestrate.

A passionate reader of all things gastronomic, Alain named l'Archestrate after the most famous gastronomic figure of Ancient Greece. He has an enormous collection of cookbooks, and adapts many recipes from ancient manuscripts. One of his recent specialities is a duck dish, in which the breast is heavily crusted with coriander, carvi, peppercorns, spices and honey, served with a sweet and soured demi glace and a splendid purée of fresh dates flavoured with mint, ginger and carvi. This height-of-new-fashion dish was an ancient Roman-style preparation that Alain adapted to his own style! Alain's love of medieval cookery and the delight he takes in reading old manuscripts stimulates him immensely but, unlike other chefs, who so often state categorically that 'there is nothing new under the sun', Alain insists that there are still thousands of combinations yet to be discovered.

In 1985, after long negotiation, Alain and his wife Eventhia took over the famous restaurant where Alain had worked earlier in his life, Lucas-Carton. This wonderful turn-of-the-century establishment right in the heart of Paris on the Place de la Madeleine, has undoubtedly one of the most beautiful interiors of all the fine old Paris restaurants. Its wonderful sculpted lemon wood wall panels and classic 1900 furniture, signed by Majorelle, are still in perfect condition. The restaurant is classed as an Historic Monument and is breathtakingly beautiful.

Eventhia, who is as much a presence in the front of the restaurant as is Alain in the kitchens, set out to change the décor as little as possible, but to complement it with beautiful table settings. The most delightful and possibly the largest bowl of long-stemmed flowers you have ever seen greets diners at

Tarte Tatin aux Mangues

the restaurant entrance, an individual silver bowl with just one peonie rose sits on each table, the napery is white damask and the cutlery is heavy jade-handled bistro cutlery with sculpted silver edging, custom made to maintain the turn-of-the-century atmosphere. The remarkable Eventhia, whose flair for design led her to bathe the ceiling of l'Archestrate in Chinese lacquer red, has put a royal blue bow tie on all the waiters — a touch of the modern artistry typical of this woman renowned in France as much for her chic as for the charm with which she greets her guests.

A year or two ago, when the real estate value of this extraordinary property cast doubt on the future of Lucas-Carton, many people worried whether the restaurant could survive. Under its former management it had been allowed to slip from being one of the top-ranking establishments in Paris; but it is now again headed by one of the most famous teams in France. Everyone is happy to see them there, for they are installed in beautiful quarters that are a worthy setting for Alain Senderens's genius; and Lucas-Carton has, in turn, been restored to its former glory.

Tarte Tatin aux Mangues

Tart Tatin with Mangoes

Serves 4
4 discs (circles) of puff pastry, cut from 250g/use ½ lb puff pastry (see below)
1 egg beaten with 1 tablespoon water (eggwash)
icing (confectioner's) sugar
2 large, bulbous mangoes
65g/good 2 oz (Br.)/¼ cup (U.S.) butter
140g/5 oz (Br.)/¾ cup (U.S.) sugar

Equipment:
1 or 2 tiny blini pans or ovenproof frying pans of about 8 to 10cm/3½ to 4in diameter

The pastry:
Have the pastry circles ready in advance. To make them, roll out the puff pastry just enough to be able to cut 4 discs the size of the diameter of your pan. Cut with a scallop-edged scone (biscuit) cutter and place on a baking tray. Freeze 10 minutes to ensure there will be no shrinkage during cooking, then brush with eggwash and bake in a 180ºC/350ºF oven for 20 minutes or until well risen and golden brown. Allow to cool. This is the conventional way of making the discs, and the easiest.

1. Alain gets an added glaze on his circle of puff pastry by dusting it with icing (confectioner's) sugar and caramelising the sugar with a lick of the flame of a blow torch. The pastry is then placed in the oven to reheat, ready to form the base of the mango tart.

2. Peel, halve and remove the stone (pit) from the mangoes. The mango halves are then cut into wedges so they can be re-formed into a circular shape to fit the pan for cooking.

3. Each little pan makes one tart at a time. Therefore, take the segments from one half mango, roughly divide the rest of the ingredients into four and proceed with each one as follows. Place about 15g/½ oz (Br.)/1 tablespoon (U.S.) butter in the base of the pan and

1

2

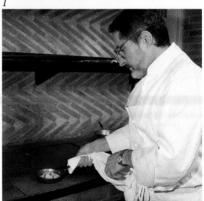
3

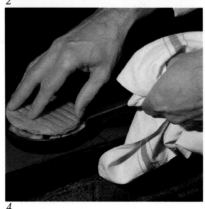
4

5

add a well-heaped tablespoon of sugar. Cook a moment until the sugar turns a light blonde colour, then place the mango segments carefully in the pan, filling the pan as well as possible for it to take on the rounded shape. Place the pan in the oven at 180ºC/350ºF for 15 to 18 minutes. If the mango is very soft and ripe, it is possible to pan fry it for about 3 minutes rather than bake it. In this time it will caramelise and take on the typically glazed top of a Tarte Tatin. If you have only 1 pan you will have to cook all the tarts separately and after unmoulding, reheat them in the oven before serving.

4. Firmly place the heated disc of pastry on top of the mango, without pressing hard enough to squash the mango.

5. Invert the tart onto the serving plate. The *Tarte Tatin aux Mangues* at Lucas-Carton is served with 2 tiny accompanying tartlets of fresh, un-cooked mango sitting in tiny pastry shells, and the dish is then served with a helping of fresh mango sorbet placed on a fresh raspberry coulis and decorated with 2 mint leaves.

250g/9 oz (Br.)/1¼ cups (U.S.) sugar icing (confectioner's) sugar to dust the tops of the soufflés

Melt the chocolate in a bowl over hot water. Allow to cool, but it must stay liquid and flowing. Stir in the cream and the softened butter and scrape out the powdery contents of the vanilla bean into the mixture. Finally stir in the egg yolks. Whip the eggwhites in a copper bowl to a firm snow, adding the sugar bit by bit to further firm the mass.

Now measure out 500g/1 lb 2 oz (Br.) of the base mixture (this should be about the entire quantity) and gently fold in the eggwhites. Transfer to buttered and sugared soufflé bowls and bake in a 200ºC/400ºF oven for 14 to 15 minutes. Sprinkle with icing (confectioner's) sugar and serve immediately, with the pistachio ice-cream on the side.

*Note from the picture, that Lucas-Carton serves extremely large portions and that the soufflé is served very creamy inside. Further cooking will firm the mixture more if you would prefer.

Glace Pistache

Pistachio Ice-cream

Makes about 1½ litres/a good 2½ pints (Br.)/6 cups (U.S.)
1 litre/35 fl oz (Br.)/4 cups (U.S.) milk
2 egg yolks
250g/9 oz (Br.)/1¼ cups (U.S.) sugar
1 tablespoon pistachio paste (available canned in specialist pastry suppliers)
2 tablespoons (Br.)/scant 3 tablespoons (U.S.) blanched, peeled, chopped pistachio nuts

Make a *crème anglaise* in the usual way by scalding the milk with half the sugar, and creaming the egg yolks with the other half of the sugar. Blend the latter with a little of the hot milk and then return it all to the saucepan, stirring vigorously until it thickens. Do not allow to boil or it will curdle. Allow this mixture to cool, then refrigerate until cold and churn in an ice-cream machine, adding the chopped pistachio nuts just at the last moment, to prevent them from crushing in the churn.

Soufflé au Chocolat Amer, Glace Pistache

Bitter Chocolate Soufflé with Pistachio Ice-Cream

*Serves 6 (10 in smaller moulds)**
The base mixture:
250g/use ½ lb dark (bittersweet) chocolate
1½ tablespoons (Br.)/2 tablespoons (U.S.) cream, preferably with 45% milk fat (heavy cream)
½ vanilla bean, split lengthwise
65g/good 2 oz (Br.)/¼ cup (U.S.) unsalted butter, well softened
5 egg yolks

The eggwhite mixture:
700ml/scant 1¼ pints (Br.)/scant 3 cups (U.S.) eggwhites (approximately 20)

Michel Roux

Waterside Inn
Bray, England

The two famous brothers Michel and Albert Roux were born in the Burgundy region of France, a fact that Michel assures us has a lot to do with his liking of good food. Although both began their careers with an apprenticeship in pâtisserie, it is Michel particularly who has kept up this aspect of his profession and he remains today a wonderfully skilled pâtissier. In 1976, he sat the masterly exams of the Meilleur Ouvrier de France Pâtissier, the most difficult of all the Meilleur Ouvrier exams, and won a gold medal. At the same time he entered for the Meilleur Ouvrier de France Cuisinier (Chef) award, mainly because nobody has ever managed to gain this inspiring ranking in both disciplines. He won a silver medal...missing by just one mark this never-yet-achieved duo.

The younger of the two brothers, Michel watched Albert set off overseas to work as the Chef at the French Embassy in London, while he himself worked at the British Embassy in Paris. Their careers ran parallel again when Albert went to work with Lady Astor and Michel began a seven-year term as Chef for Cécile de Rothschild. The Rothschilds paid well, but better still they expected and knew perfection. Salt and pepper were simply not allowed on the table. 'If we employ chefs, we don't expect to have to add salt to our food.' Michel recalls with a certain wry satisfaction at having completed such an apprenticeship, 'You could be brought out and rapped over the knuckles in front of everybody, but you learnt to strive for perfection and to accept only perfection. I can conceive of no better training.'

Michel's protégés are trained in the same way. 'Anybody can achieve mediocrity,' he constantly throws at them, 'that's no standard, not what we're here for at all.' Michel's a perfectionist, and sometimes he drives it home the hard way. To make his point in the pastry section one day, the commis saw him throw out three trays of uncooked pastry just because it wasn't aligned well. As he cried out, 'This is a three-star restaurant — in the oven, and in the dining room,' they learnt once and for all how the standards are set. Michel calls his brigade of between sixteen and twenty 'his boys', and he inspires enormous loyalty among them. He's a disciplinarian, for sure, but when he grabs them behind the neck and turns them around, looks them straight in the face and tells them what he expects of them, they'd swear he was interested in no one in the world but them. I've known a good many chefs who've done time under Michel, and they are all devoted to him. His skills are undoubted and he has an enormous capacity to communicate them.

Nowadays the Roux brothers own six restaurants, and even that number is destined to increase, for they often encourage their favourite former chefs by helping them set up on their own. Michel and Albert began together at Le Gavroche in the heart of London. It is now under the direction of Albert alone, while Michel maintains as his day-to-day responsibility the direction of their second restaurant, the Waterside Inn. Perched over the Thames at Bray, just forty minutes from London on the M4, the Waterside Inn has surely one of the loveliest restaurant settings in England. It is a spacious place with large rooms tastefully decorated in pastel greens and pinks, and large windows overlooking the river. The Inn seats up to 120, and is the more informal of the two restaurants. People can, and do, arrive by water, and there is a charming little wooden summerhouse out on the riverbank, where they can take their apéritif, or coffee and petits fours. With the Roux brothers at the helm, it was not surprising to see the Michelin award the Waterside

Tresse de Poisson au Gingembre

Inn with the second three-star accolade to be placed in the British Michelin Guide.

This sort of perfection, and the brother's high media profile (they are familiar faces on television and have written two books, one on their style of cuisine in general, and one specifically on pastry) have done much to improve restaurant standards in Britain as a whole. But their perfection is not easy to copy. They shop all over Britain, flying in salmon from Scotland, and the best Britain has to offer from all corners, and then, to ensure they lack for nothing, they even run their own truck twice weekly to the Paris markets at Rungis. To facilitate this expenditure, they have bought the celebrated old Château de Montreuil hotel and restaurant in the northern French province of the Pas de Calais, where one of their protégés is installed as chef and partner.

But lest I forget to pay them the compliment, let me also add, that no kitchens have more open doors in England than the Roux brothers' kitchens. Always ready to share their skills, they take in many itinerant chefs wanting to improve their skills. The 'kitchen French' tells it all. When the gutteral accents of the true French language call *'ça marche'* in the kitchens of Le Gavroche and the Waterside Inn, many an American, English or Australian-accented voice is raised in reply. One senses the Roux brothers have given to England more than they have taken from it.

And not only to chefs. While both their books are strong and detailed enough to interest and instill professional skills in practising chefs, they are also written clearly and concisely for home cooks. Michel's Australian wife Robyn has been indispensable in putting both manuscripts together, and each recipe was given to three different chefs to test.

Of the recipes Michel has chosen to cook below, he feels the concept of the 'chlorophyll' needs particular explanation. This purée of fresh herbs, with its unique pungency and colour kept intact in a non-gritty, concentrated, paste-like substance, is formed by blanching, clarifying and puréeing fresh herbs. The result is an essence which is unique in concept and adds an extraordinary strength of flavour to many dishes in the Roux repertoire. It is a preparation rarely seen in the modern restaurant, in fact, according to Michel, rarely seen outside private homes, for it is a time-consuming task. But it puts a marvellously earthy flavour of herbs into dishes, and offers a challenge. It's a very interesting concept to master, and one Michel doubts many will have seen.

The snail recipe is the most popular entrée on the menu at the Waterside Inn. Always practical, Michel won't be upset if you have to make do with canned snails — most restaurants do — however, perfectionist that he is, Michel would see no fault at all if I were to start the recipe, 'First catch your snails...'

1

2

3

Tresse de Poisson au Gingembre

Fish Plait with Ginger

The original English version of this Roux brothers' recipe was done with salmon and brill. Michel has demonstrated this dish often in his travels, replacing the white fish most often with a local substitute, and choosing between either salmon or trout for the pink fish. When deciding which white fish to use, remember to choose one with a firm, small-lobed flesh consistent with the flesh of the pink fish so that the cooking times of each are about the same.

Serves 8

Depending on the size of the substitute fish you will need **either** 8 individual trout or 1 large trout weighing about 1.5kg/use 3¼ lb **and either** 8 sole; 6 to 8 flounder, John Dory (*St. Pierre*) or whiting depending on size; or 1 large ling or salmon weighing about 1.5kg/use 3¼ lb. Use the larger fish only if you have **both** pink and white fish large, for the thickness of the sole, flounder, John Dory (*St. Pierre*) or whiting requires that it should be coupled only with the individual, smaller portions of trout or salmon.

550 ml/18 fl oz (Br.)/2¼ cups (U.S.) fish stock
160g/5½ oz (Br.)/¾ cup (U.S.) butter
2 firm, red, ripe tomatoes
2 zucchinis (courgettes)
30g/1 oz fresh root ginger
3 tablespoons (Br.)/3½ tablespoons (U.S.) cup cognac
3 tablespoons (Br.)/3½ tablespoons (U.S.) dry white wine
50ml/1½ fl oz (Br.)/¼ cup (U.S.) veal stock
500 ml/good ¾ pint (Br.)/2 good cups (U.S.) cream, preferably with 45% milk fat (heavy cream)
50g/scant 2 oz (Br.)/3 tablespoons (U.S.) butter, preferably clarified
salt

Equipment:
8 squares of cardboard 10cm/4in square, covered with foil, buttered

1.   To prepare the fish:
Using a filleting knife, remove the fillets from the fish, remove the skin, and then any tiny remaining bones. Trim any frayed edges, then slice the fillets into strips. If using large fish, they can be sliced in half lengthwise before cutting into the strips. You need 32 strips of each kind of fish cut to the length of the cardboard to make the plaits.

To form the plaits:
2.   Arrange 4 strips of fish of one colour vertically across the cardboard.

3.   Interweave 4 strips of fish the other colour horizontally through these 4.

4.   A finished plait showing the alternating coloured pattern. The fish should cover the foil almost entirely.

5.   Arrange the fish and foil-covered cardboard in a roasting pan or in 2 sauté dishes, and pour over 300ml/½ pint (Br.)/1¼ cups (U.S.) of the fish stock. Cover with lightly buttered greaseproof (parchment) paper and set aside.

Plunge the tomatoes into boiling water, then into cold water; peel and seed. Finely dice the flesh and set aside. Rinse the zucchinis (courgettes) and cut into fine matchsticks. Blanch in boiling water for 10 seconds, drain and set aside. Peel the ginger and reserve the peelings. Cut the root into fine, fine julienne and set aside.

6.   The sauce: Combine the ginger peelings, cognac, dry white wine, the remaining fish stock and the veal stock in a shallow pan. Set over high heat and reduce the liquid by half. Add the cream, lower the heat and cook gently for 20 minutes. Stir in 30g/1 good oz (Br.)/2 tablespoons (U.S.) butter, then pass through the sieve. Correct the seasoning, add the julienne of ginger and place in a bain-marie to keep hot until required.

To cook:
When needed, cook the fish in a 240°C/475°F oven for 3 to 4 minutes, basting with the fish stock to ensure that they are cooked right through.

To serve:
Coat 8 plates with sauce and slide a plait diagonally onto each plate. Place a little warmed, diced tomato at one point of the diagonal. Arrange a few matchsticks of zucchini (courgette) on either side of the point. Brush lightly with clarified butter and serve immediately.

4

5

6

Petits Flans d'Escargots en Habits Verts

Tartlets of Snails in Green Overcoats

Serves 6
36 snails (canned are acceptable)

The pastry:
80g/3 oz puff pastry trimmings
flour for rolling

The parsley purée:
70g/2½ oz rinsed and trimmed
parsley, or ½ large bunch
250ml/8 fl oz (Br.)/1 good cup (U.S.)
cream, preferably with 45% milk fat
(heavy cream)

The soufflé:
45g/1½ oz (Br.)/3 tablespoons (U.S.)
butter
1 heaped teaspoon flour
100ml/3 fl oz (Br.)/scant ½ cup (U.S.)
milk
1 egg yolk
10 egg whites
¼ teaspoon chlorophyll (see recipe
below)
2 tablespoons/scant 3 tablespoons
(U.S.) chopped chives
2 tablespoons (Br.)/scant 3 tablespoons
(U.S.) chopped tarragon
salt and freshly ground pepper

Equipment:
6 tartlet moulds (8 cm/3in diameter)

To make the pastry:
On a lightly floured marble or wooden
pastry board, roll out the pastry as thinly
as possible. Roll it round a rolling pin,
then unroll it over the 6 tartlet moulds.
Push the pastry into the depth of the
moulds and line them. Roll the rolling
pin over the edges of the moulds to
remove any surplus pastry. Prick with
a fork and refrigerate for 10 minutes.
Remove, line the pastry cases with a
circle of greaseproof (parchment) paper,
weighted with dried beans, and bake
in a 200ºC/400ºF oven for 10 minutes.
Remove, and unmould onto a cake rack.

To make the parsley purée:
Plunge the parsley into boiling water
for a few seconds, then drain. Pour the
cream into a saucepan and bring it to
the boil. Add the parsley and boil for

a moment. Purée in a blender or food
processor for 2 to 3 minutes, then rub
through a fine sieve using a pestle or
a plastic pastry scraper. Return the mixture to the pan and keep it hot. It should
have the consistency of a liquid purée;
if it seems thin, reduce it over a high
heat for a few minutes.

To make the soufflé:
Using a whisk and a small saucepan,
make a roux with a heaped teaspoon
of butter and a heaped teaspoon of flour.
Stir in the cold milk and bring to the
boil. Off the heat, blend in the egg yolk,
season to taste with salt and pepper and
keep warm while awaiting the beaten
egg whites.

1

2

To assemble the tartlets:
Divide the parsley purée between the
pastry cases. In a frying pan, heat 30g/
1 good oz (Br.)/2 tablespoons (U.S.)
butter and roll the snails in the butter
for a few seconds or they will toughen.
Drain them and put 6 in each pastry

case. Beat the egg whites until well risen, then fold them into the soufflé mixture, together with the chlorophyll, chives and tarragon. Heap a little soufflé mixture in a dome shape on top of each flan and smooth the surface with a palette knife. Bake for 3 minutes in a 220°C/425°F oven until golden and well risen. Serve immediately.

Chlorophyll

Chlorophyll (finely puréed green herbs used to add colour and a fine earthy flavour) is used for a multitude of purposes in the Roux cuisine, and Michel and Albert consider it well worth the long, rather tedious preparation. Put the chlorophyll into small individual ramekins and pour over a drop of oil to form an insulating film, and it will keep for about 2 weeks in the refrigerator. In hot weather, leave out the shallots, which may cause the mixture to ferment or may spoil the flavour after 4 to 5 days in the refrigerator.

*Makes 150g/about 6 oz (about 6 tablespoons or 1 small ramekin), but is **very** concentrated*
2 bunches parsley (approximately 4 to 5 cups when rinsed and trimmed)
1 bunch chives (about ¾ cup if chopped)
45g/1½ oz (Br.)/about ½ cup (U.S.) chervil
45g/1½ oz (Br.)/about ½ cup (U.S.) tarragon
1 kg/use 2 lb spinach (English spinach)
70g/2½ oz shallots
salt
2 litres/3½ pints (Br.)/scant 9 cups (U.S.) water

Rinse and trim the parsley, wash the chives. Wash the spinach and herbs and remove the stalks. Peel and wash the shallots. Place all the ingredients in a blender or food processor with the water and process for 5 minutes, slowly at first and then at medium speed.

Lightly stretch a muslin cloth over a saucepan and pour in the contents of the blender (picture 1). Let all the liquid drain through, then gather up the edges of the muslin and twist it extremely gently to extract as much liquid as possible. Discard the pulp and wash out the muslin cloth in cold water.

Season the green juice with salt and set the saucepan over a medium heat. Stir gently with a wooden spatula until the first trembling of the liquid — this will cause some of the ingredients to coagulate and will clarify the remaining liquid. Remove the pan from the heat immediately — do not allow it to boil.

Stretch the muslin over a bowl and, using a ladle, gently spoon out the contents of the saucepan (picture 2). Use a metal palette knife to scrape up the purée (the chlorophyll) from the muslin; discard the liquid. Store as above until needed.

Rillettes de Canard
Rillettes of Duck

Serves 12
If you can persuade the butcher to bone the duck for you, the recipe will be much easier; but boning is not as hard as you think if you go slowly, starting from the back and slowly working your knife around to the breastplate. Chop up the bones and carcass of the duck, freeze and use them later for gravy or stock.

1 x 2.75kg/6 lb duckling, or 2 smaller ones
400g/good 14 oz (Br.)/1¾ cups (U.S.) fresh pork fat from the belly pork (ensure it's as free of meat as possible)
1 medium onion
1 medium carrot
125g/4½ oz pork fillet, cut into 4 pieces
1 clove garlic
bouquet garni with the addition of a few sage leaves
1 teaspoon green peppercorns
350ml/11 fl oz (Br.)/1½ cups (U.S.) dry white wine
salt and freshly ground pepper

Lay the duckling breast side down and, using a sharp knife, bone it out through the back. Remove the skin from the flesh. Cut off 150g/good 5 oz (Br.)/⅔ cup (U.S.) fat from the fattiest parts; cut into small dice and reserve. Discard the skin. Remove the flesh from the bones and cut out the breast fillets and the flesh from the thighs. Cut into strips of about 4cm/1½ in. Do not use the flesh from the drumsticks. Discard all sinew.

Cut the pork fat into very small dice. Peel the carrot; cut in half. Peel the onion; cut in half horizontally.

Place the pork fat and the duck fat in the casserole; pour in enough water to barely cover it. Set over a medium heat, cover and simmer gently for about 30 minutes, stirring occasionally until all the water has evaporated. By this time the fat should have melted. Add the pork fillet and the duck flesh, the unpeeled garlic clove, onion, carrot and bouquet garni. Season with a little salt, pour in two-thirds of the wine and bring to the boil.

Cover the casserole and set it over a very gentle regular heat so that the mixture is barely trembling. Stir with a spatula from time to time to prevent the mixture sticking to the bottom of the casserole. Leave to cook for 3 hours. Leave the mixture in the casserole, but remove all the vegetables and aromatics. Pour over the remaining wine, add the green peppercorns and cover the casserole with a damp cloth, which must not touch the meat. Put the casserole in a cool, airy place.

To pot the meat:
When the mixture is lukewarm, work the meats together with your fingertips until all the shredded flesh and the fat are thoroughly mixed together. Correct the seasoning with salt and pepper. Put the *rillettes* into earthenware pots or terrines and cover them with greaseproof (parchment) paper. They will keep for 3 to 4 weeks in a cold place. Serve with plain or toasted bread.

Rillettes de Canard

Sablés aux Fraises
Strawberry Shortbread

Serves 6
800g/1 lb 12 oz strawberries
500 ml/good ¾ pint (Br.)/2 good cups
(U.S.) strawberry coulis (puréed
strawberries, sweetened to taste with
250g/9 oz (Br.)/1¼ cups (U.S.) sugar)
shortbread dough (1 quantity of recipe
below)
1 egg yolk, beaten with 1 tablespoon
milk, to glaze

The shortbread dough:
300g/ scant 11 oz.(Br.)/1¼ cups (U.S.)
butter
pinch salt
150g/6 oz (Br.)/1 scant cup (U.S.)
icing (confectioner's)sugar
2 egg yolks
375g/13 oz (Br.)/scant 3 cups (U.S.)
flour, sifted
1 drop vanilla or lemon essence

To make the shortbread dough:
Cut the butter into small pieces and place
on a marble or wooden surface. Work
the butter with your fingertips until very
soft. Sift the icing (confectioner's) sugar and add to the butter with a pinch
of salt. Continue to work the mixture
with the fingertips until the ingredients
are thoroughly blended, then add the
egg yolks and mix in lightly. Only then
amalgamate the flour evenly into the
mixture. Rub the pastry gently 2 or
3 times using your palm; do not over-
work. Roll into a ball and flatten it out
lightly. Wrap in greaseproof (parchment)
paper or a plastic bag or film and chill
for several hours.

Note: Unlike most chefs, Michel always
adds the flour to a shortbread dough
at the last minute so that the pastry
remains crumbly and short. This makes
an excellent but very delicate pastry, and
it must be carefully and quickly dealt

with when transferred to the baking
tray or moulds, as it can soften very
quickly. Once the flour is added, the
pastry must never be overworked, but
mixed only until the ingredients are
amalgamated; overworking will ruin it.

To make and bake the shortbread:
On a lightly floured marble or wooden
surface, roll out the pastry to a thickness of about 3 mm/1/8 in. Cut out
the 18 circles with a 10cm/4 in scallop-
edged pastry cutter and arrange them
on a baking sheet. Brush with the eggwash. Decorate them as you like or draw
lines with the back of a small knife or
fork. Place all the shortbread circles in
a preheated 200ºC/400ºF oven for about
8 minutes. When cooked, allow them
to cool slightly, then use a palette knife
to transfer them to a wire cake rack,
and keep cool.

Wash the strawberries only if necessary,

hull and either halve them or leave them whole, depending on their size. Roll them in two-thirds of the strawberry coulis, then keep them in the refrigerator.

To serve:
Place an unglazed shortbread base on each plate. Over each spread a few strawberries, then on top, balance a second layer of shortbread base and garnish it likewise. Top with a glazed circle. The top may be dredged with 200g/8 oz (Br.)/1 good cup (U.S.) icing (confectioner's) sugar or not, as desired. Spoon a little of the remaining coulis around each serve.

Jacques Torrès

Le Chantecler, Hôtel Negresco Nice, France

The brigade at the Negresco numbers twenty-seven, of which ten are the inner core, without whom Jacques Maximin, the Executive Chef, says he could not manage. With an average age of twenty-five, young, enthusiastic and totally inspired by their leader, they are an exciting group of able chefs, each aspiring to attain the same sort of perfection Jacques has shown them.

Among the most dedicated and already a name in his own right while in his twenties is the self-effacing pastryman, Jacques Torrès. Were he the type to lay claim to his fame, he could already tell tales of an illustrious career.

Nicknamed Jacqui, to differentiate him from his boss in the requisite yellings in the kitchen, he is the youngest ever Meilleur Ouvrier de France Pâtissier. Jacqui was awarded the rank at only twenty-six years of age but, as he tells it, it was only Jacques Maximin's encouragement that made this happen.

Born in Algeria, Jacqui came back to France in his youth and was apprenticed in a pâtisserie shop in Bandol. He worked his way up the ranks until his military service was over and his ship threw him out in Marseilles. Wandering along the Riviera in a holiday mood, he says his life changed when he simply walked into the Negresco and said to Jacques Maximin, 'I like the climate of the south, and I hear you're a great chef . . . do you need a pastryman?' Within the hour he had on an apron, with a warning that, 'If you're no good, you won't last.' Within two months Jacqui was Jacques's chief pâtissier.

As well as doing the desserts and pâtisserie for Le Chantecler, the luxury restaurant of the Negresco, Jacqui also furnishes the banquet rooms, bars and coffee shops, and provides room service with croissants and fresh bread. To top it all, the grand salon serves high tea and cakes between 5 and 7pm each day. All are Jacqui's domain and, although so young, he is held in tremendous esteem by most pâtissiers of more than twice his age.

For the desserts of Le Chantecler, Jacqui often works in conjunction with Jacques, taking direction and adding his own pâtissier's finesse in finalising the results. Once Jacques realised Jacqui's potential, he allowed him the time he needed to prepare and sit for the gruelling round of examinations that make up the accreditation for Meilleur Ouvrier de France. To attain this qualification in the field of pâtissier is said to be the hardest of all among the food-related professions. Even chefs grudgingly admit this is so. The examinations are held only every four years and are competed for and judged by the elders in the profession. Applicants need to have a high level of historic and general knowledge on their subjects and have usually had a solid experience of many years in the industry. Aside from the technical and menial skills taken for granted at this high level, they must also have the touch of creativity that is necessary for their peers to elevate them to join the few who at any one time hold this title.

Here Jacqui shows you a dessert in the innovative style that has attracted such attention. The desserts may be formed in metal egg rings, like those used in hamburger bars, which should be available in hardware or commercial cookery shops. However, for fear of discolouring the dessert, especially if you choose to vary the fruit and work with acidic fruits such as raspberries, Jacqui suggests obtaining some heavy white plastic 'plumber's' tubing, as it is easily cut into the shape required. It is a mould, just the right size for individual portions. An inventive cook will find many uses for it.

Crème Chiboust Gratinée au Citron Vert

1   2   3   4

5   6   7   8

Crème Chiboust Gratinée au Citron Vert

Grantinéed Lime-flavoured Cream Chiboust

Serves 6

The lime cream:
75ml/2¼ fl oz (Br.)/⅓ cup (U.S.) lime juice
60ml/scant 2 fl oz (Br.)/3 tablespoons (U.S.) cream, preferably with 45% milk fat (heavy cream)
25g/¾ oz (Br.)/1 tablespoon sugar
10g/2 teaspoons cornflour (cornstarch)
3 egg yolks
2 leaves or 2 teaspoons granulated unflavoured gelatine

Meringue italienne:
3 egg whites
60g/2 oz (Br.)/scant ⅓ cup (U.S.) sugar mixed with 5 tablespoons (Br.)/6 tablespoons (U.S.) water, dissolved over heat and brought to 120°C/235°F

The orange sauce:
3 tablespoons (Br.)/3½ tablespoons (U.S.) sugar
juice of 4 oranges

250g/use ½ lb (Br.)/1 good cup (U.S.) unsalted butter
dash of Grand Marnier

The garnish:
crystallised green lime zests for décor

Equipment:
4 metal rings about 10 x 1.5cm/4 x 5/8 in deep. It is possible to fabricate heavy cardboard strips covered with foil and stapled together for the purpose; in the photographs, we used heavy plastic 'plumber's' tubing, sliced (see note in introduction).

The lime cream:
1. The lime cream is a sort of *crème pâtissière* in which the familiar milk is replaced with cream and lime juice. Thus, place the egg yolks with the sugar in a bowl and stir, then stir in the cornflour (cornstarch). Meantime, combine the lime juice and cream in a saucepan and bring to the boil.

2 Pour the hot cream into the egg yolk mixture, blend well and return to the saucepan, stirring over heat until the mixture comes to the boil.

3. Soften the gelatine in a little cold water, then stir into the finished cream to dissolve.

The *meringue italienne*:
4. Heat the sugar and water until the soft ball stage (temperature registers 120°C/250°F). Meantime, whip the egg whites to a firm peak with an electric mixer. Remove the sugar syrup from the heat and pour it in a steady stream into the egg whites, continuing to beat until the mixture is completely cold (about 15 minutes). The meringue Italienne is a very stable type of pâtissier's meringue, capable of keeping its shape well into the next day.

5. Take about a cup of meringue Italienne and stir well into the lime-flavoured cream, then return all the cream to the meringue bowl, and fold in carefully and lightly.

6. Place the rings on a large piece of greaseproof (parchment) paper on a baking tray. Spoon the lime cream into the rings, flattening the tops as best you can with a metal spatula. Place in the freezer for about 3 hours to aid the

transfer later to the individual serving plates.

7. Release the moulds by running a knife around the edges, sprinkle them liberally with sugar, and gratiné (glaze) them under a salamander, a very well-heated grill (broiler), or with a blow torch. When well coloured, transfer to the serving plates.

8. The orange sauce: Place the sugar in a small saucepan with nothing else, and gently shake it over the heat until it goes a pale caramel. Add the orange juice and slowly (it spatters at first) bring it to the boil so that it reduces to half its volume and becomes syrupy and sauce-like. Mount by whisking in the cold, chopped tablespoons of butter. Skim before using, and spoon around the lime cream.

To decorate:
Finish by decorating with a few strands of lime zest julienne.

Terrine au Chocolat et aux Fruits
Chocolate and Fruit Terrine

Serves 5 to 6
The *crème anglaise* base:
4 egg yolks
250ml/8 fl oz (Br.)/1 good cup (U.S.) milk
50g/scant 2 oz (Br.)/¼ cup (U.S.) sugar
5 leaves or 4 teaspoons granulated unflavoured gelatine
25g/1 oz (Br.)/1 heaped tablespoon canned praline paste
40g/1½ oz dark (bittersweet) chocolate, grated
1 tablespoon icing (confectioner's) sugar
1 tablespoon grated fresh coconut
2 bananas, mashed well with a fork
1 leaf or 1 teaspoon granulated unflavoured gelatine
500ml/good ¾ pint (Br.)/2 good cups (U.S.) cream with 35% milk fat (whipping cream)

The sauce:
You may use extra banana purée, with lemon juice to keep it from browning.

Equipment:
small china or glass rectangular terrine of about 1.2 litres/good 2 pints (Br.)/5 cups (U.S.) capacity

Scald the milk. Place the egg yolks in a bowl and whisk in the sugar. Pour on a little of the milk, whisking to blend well, then return all to the saucepan over heat and stir continuously until it thickens into a custard with enough body to coat the back of the spoon.

Meantime, soften the larger quantity of gelatine, then stir it into the custard. Strain the mixture into a bowl, then divide it equally into 3 separate bowls. Into 1 bowl, quickly stir the grated chocolate and the tablespoon of icing (confectioner's) sugar; into another the praline paste; and into the third the grated coconut. The bowls may be stood in hot water while stirring to aid incorporation, but do not allow them to overheat.

Allow the custards to cool to room temperature and begin to thicken while you prepare the banana pulp. Mash the bananas very finely. Soak the single leaf of gelatine in water, squeeze the water out, and then place in a tiny saucepan and shake over low heat until melted. If using granulated gelatine, place directly in the saucepan with about 1 tablespoon of water, and when swollen shake over heat until it dissolves. Pour the gelatine, stirring well, into the banana pulp in a fourth bowl.

Whip the cream and divide it equally between the 4 bowls. Fold it into the cooled, but not yet set, mixtures so that it blends into each smoothly.

Into the terrine, spoon a layer of chocolate, coconut, praline and banana in turn, being careful not to mash each layer into the one below. It may help to place each layer in the freezer for about 5 minutes. Do not refrigerate the waiting mixtures or they will set too much. Freeze the terrine for about 3 hours.

To serve:
Turn the mould out while still frozen and slice while firm. The slices are served cool, not frozen. Serve 2 thin slices per person, with a little sauce.

The Photographers

Anthony Blake:
The most respected of all London's food photographers, Anthony works mostly on books and occasionally editorial work. His book *The Great Chefs of France* was a landmark in style for books on food.

His photographs include Michel Roux's *Tresse de Poisson au Gingembre*, and *Rillettes de Canard*.

Mark Chew:
Born in Africa and educated in England, Mark had no formal education in photography. He started his career assisting in advertising studios in London and went on to work with some of the better advertising photographers, including Nic Tompkin, Byron Newman and, after arriving in Australia, celebrated food photographer John Street. Having spent a year travelling to get to know his new country, Mark started as a staff photographer for *Home Beautiful* and *Epicurean* in 1987 and, along with Gary Chowanetz, began to do much of my food photography for both magazines.

His photographs include Stephanie Alexander's Rockpool Revisited, and Macadamia Nut Tart step by steps; Iain Hewitson's Indian Marinated Fish with Pickled Vegetables; Ken Hom's Warm Peach Compôte with Basil Leaves, and Sun-dried Tomato Spring Rolls; Madeleine Kamman's *Aiguillettes* of Lamb Mechoui Style; Antony Worrall-Thompson's Fresh Summer Fruits with Cassis Granita, and Trio of Beef Salads.

Gary Chowanetz:
After graduating with a Diploma of Photography from the Royal Melbourne Institute of Technology (Australia), Gary became a dark-room operator at Brian Brandt Studios and then worked at the Audio-Visual Workshop. He joined the magazine *Home Beautiful* in 1977, working mainly on house and interior design photography and only incidentally on the food pages, and then started work as well on the food magazine *Epicurean*. After six years he withdrew to run his own studio. He filmed three major cookbooks in this time, but returned to *Home Beautiful* and *Epicurean* full time in 1987. I have been proud to have done much of my work with Gary over the past ten years.

His photographs include Stephanie Alexander's Mussels; Mogens Bay Esbensen's Lamb with Tamarind; Lyn Hall's Terrine of Fresh Fruit with Raspberry Coulis; and the dishes of Marcella Hazan; Ken Hom (except Warm Peach Compôte with Basil Leaves); Madeleine Kamman (except *Aiguillettes* of Lamb Mechoui Style); Prue Leith (except Hearts and Flowers Pudding); Jean-Pierre Lemanissier; Jacques Maximin; Anton Mosimann; Gérard Pangaud; Jacques Torrès.

Michael Cook:
An exceedingly well-respected food photographer from Sydney, Australia, Michael works often for *Vogue*, the *Vogue Entertaining Guide* and *Epicurean* magazine. He has many cookery, art and photography books to his name.

His photographs include Berowra Waters Inn's Tuna Braised in Olive Oil; Mogens Bay Esbensen's Baby Chicken with New Season's Garlic, Banana Prawns and Crab in Coconut Sauce, and Coconut Custard in a Pumpkin.

John Hay:
Trained in Melbourne, Australia at The Royal Melbourne Institute of Technology, John gained his Diploma of Illustrative Photography in 1974. He has since worked in 35mm colour doing corporate audio-visual

work; he worked for one year for the magazine *Home Beautiful*; and then got the chance to work for Australia's best known cookbook photographer John Street. John now works freelance, doing both editorial and food photography for books, and works often with us at *Epicurean* magazine. Considered by many to be the best new-generation food photographer in Australia, John also does a lot of commercial and business photography from his studio Penny Lane.

His photographs include Berowra Waters Inn's *Crépinette* of Pheasant with Pigs' Trotters and Truffles, and Orange Bavarian Cream with Caramel Sauce; Giuliano Bugialli's *Pere al Mascarpone*; John Desmond's *Soufflé aux Poires d'Alsace, Soufflé Glacé au Liqueur Sauce Caramel*, and *Pannequets au Citron*.

John Hollingshead:

English-born John spent his youth in Perth, Australia, moved to Melbourne to study photography at the Prahran Institute of Technology and graduated in 1975. He soon found a position assisting in the studios of veteran food photographer John Street, and from there became a staff photographer for *Home Beautiful* and *Epicurean* magazines from 1983 to 1985. In November 1985 we worked in France, Italy and England together. John moved to London where he has since been freelancing, mainly doing editorial work for interior design magazines, the Condé Nast group, and the food magazines *Taste* and *A la Carte*.

His photographs include the dishes of Joël Bellouet; Paul Bocuse (except *Rougets en Ecailles*); Dominique Bouchet; Gérard Boyer; Giuliano Bugialli (except *Pere al Mascarpone*); Alain Dutournier; Jane Grigson; Iain Hewitson's Ballotine of Chicken; Gualtiero Marchesi; Damien Pignolet's Grilled Guinea Fowl Breast with a Râgout of Wild Mushrooms, Grilled Scallops with Cider Vinegar Butter Sauce, and Tartare of Scallops; Albert Roux; Roger Vergé; Alain Senderens; Michel Roux (except *Tresse de Poisson au Gingembre*, and *Rillettes de Canard*).

My thanks also to:

Bill Anderson: Stephanie Alexander's Macadamia Nut Tart (except the step by steps); François Minot.

Victor Budnik: Alice Waters.

Georges Guiot: Paul Bocuse's *Rougets en Ecailles*.

Ray Jarratt: Damien Pignolet's *Boudin Blanc* of Chicken, Sweetbreads and Cèpe Mushrooms.

Guy Lamotte: Antony Worrall-Thompson's Cream Soup of Mussels and Saffron, and Minestrone of Shellfish and Vegetables Perfumed with Fresh Basil.

John Lee: Lyn Hall's Leek Terrine with Hazelnut Vinaigrette, and Hong Kong Steamed Prawns.

Tony Miller: John Desmond's *Feuilletés de Coquilles Saint Jacques*.

Peter Myers: Prue Leith's Hearts and Flowers Pudding.

Andrew Payne: Jeremiah Tower.

E.K. Waller: Wolfgang Puck; John Sedlar.

Bibliography

Alexander, Stephanie.

Stephanie's Menus for Food Lovers. Methuen Haynes, Sydney, 1985.

Stephanie's Feasts and Stories. Allen and Unwin/Haynes, Sydney, 1988.

Bertolli, Paul with Waters, Alice.

Chez Panisse Cooking: The Nature of the Feast. Random House, New York, 1988.

Blake, Anthony and Crewe, Quentin.

The Great Chefs of France. Mitchell Beazley, London, 1978.

Bocuse, Paul.

La Cuisine du Marché. Flammarion, Paris, 1976.

British edition: *The New Cuisine.* Granada, London, 1978.

Bocuse dans Votre Cuisine. Flammarion, Paris, 1982.

British edition: *The Cuisine of Paul Bocuse.* Granada, London, 1985.

Bocuse à la Carte. Flammarion, Paris, 1986.

British edition: Oram Press, London, 1987.

Bugialli, Giuliano.

The Fine Art of Italian Cooking. Times Books, New York, 1977.

Giuliano Bugialli's Classic Techniques of Italian Cooking. Simon and Schuster, New York, 1982.

Giuliano Bugialli's Foods of Italy. Stewart, Tabori and Chang, New York, 1984.

British edition: *The Taste of Italy.* Conran Octopus, London, 1984.

Bellouet, Joël.

Apprenez l'Art du Sucre Tiré. Paris, 1982.

Apprenez l'Art du Sucre Soufflé et Coulé. Paris, 1983.

La Pâtisserie. Traditions et Evolution. Paris, 1987.

(All self published and available from Bellouet at I Square Bernard Palissy, Fontenay-le-Fleury, France, 78330.)

Desmond, John.

Ma Cuisine. Minneapolis, 1979.

Ma Cuisine 2. Minneapolis, 1981.

Ma Cuisine d'Aujourd' hui. Minneapolis, 1984.

(All self published and available from Desmond at 5 Square Lamartine, Paris, France 75116.)

Dowell, Philip and Bailey, Adrian.

The Book of Ingredients. Michael Joseph, London, 1980.

Esbensen, Mogens Bay.

Thai Cuisine. Thomas Nelson, Melbourne, 1986.

A Taste of the Tropics. Viking O'Neil, Melbourne, 1988.

Grigson, Jane.

Charcuterie and French Pork Cookery. Michael Joseph, London, 1967.

Good Things. Michael Joseph, London, 1971.

Fish Cookery. Michael Joseph, London, 1973.

English Food. Macmillan, London, 1974.

The Mushroom Feast. Michael Joseph, London, 1975.

Jane Grigson's Vegetable Book. Michael Joseph, London, 1978.

U.S. edition: Atheneum, New York, 1979.

Food with the Famous. Hollen St. Press, London, 1979.

The Observer French Cookery School (with Anne Willan for the *Observer*). Macdonald, London, 1980.

Jane Grigson's Fruit Book. Michael Joseph, London, 1982.

U.S. edition: Atheneum, New York, 1982.

Jane Grigson's Book of European Cookery. Michael Joseph, London, 1983.

U.S. edition: Atheneum, New York, 1983.

Hazan, Marcella.

The Classic Italian Cookbook. Alfred A. Knopf, New York, 1976.

More Classic Italian Cooking. Alfred A. Knopf, New York, 1978.

Marcella's Kitchen. Alfred A. Knopf, New York, 1986.

British edition: Macmillan, London, 1987.

Hazan, Victor.

Italian Wine. Alfred A. Knopf, New York, 1982.

British edition: Penguin, London, 1984.

Hom, Ken.

Chinese Technique (with Harvey Steiman). Simon and Schuster, New York, 1981.

British edition: Ebury Press, London, 1981.

Ken Hom's Chinese Cookery. BBC Publications, London, 1984.

U.S. edition: Harper and Row, New York, 1986.

Ken Hom's Asian Vegetable and Pasta Cookbook. BBC Publications, London, 1987.

U.S. edition: William Morrow, New York, 1987.

Ken Hom's East Meets West Cuisine. Simon and Schuster, New York, 1987.

British edition: Macmillan, London, 1987.

Kamman, Madeleine.

The Making of a Cook. Atheneum, New York, 1978.

When French Women Cook. Atheneum, New York, 1982.

In Madeleine's Kitchen. Atheneum, New York, 1984.

Leith, Prue.
Leith's Cookery Course, (3 volumes). Fontana. London, 1979.
Leith's Cookery School (with Caroline Waldergrave). Macdonald, London, 1985.
Entertaining with Style (with Polly Tyrer). Macdonald, London, 1986.
Marchesi, Gualtiero.
La Mia Nuova Grande Cucina Italiana. Rizzoli Editore, Milan, 1980.
   French edition: *La Cuisine Italienne Réinventée — les Recettes Originales de Gualtiero Marchesi*. Editions Robert Laffont, Paris, 1983.
Maximin, Jacques.
Couleurs, Parfums et Saveurs — les Recettes Originales de Jacques Maximin. Editions Robert Laffont, Paris, 1984.
   British edition: *The Cuisine of Jacques Maximin*. Arbour House, London, 1986.
Montagné, Prosper.
Nouveau Larousse Gastronomique. Librarie Larousse, Paris, 1938.
   (Regularly revised and updated. Regularly appears under the imprint of various international publishers.)
Mosimann, Anton.
Cuisine à la Carte. Northwood Books, London, 1981.
A New Style of Cooking. Macmillan, London, 1983.
Cuisine Naturelle. Macmillan, London, 1985.
Shellfish (with Holger Hofmann). Hamlyn, London, 1987.
Anton Mosimann's Fish Cuisine. Macmillan, London, 1988.
Olney, Richard.
The French Menu Cookbook. Simon and Schuster, New York, 1970.
Simple French Food. Atheneum, New York, 1974.
   (Richard Olney was also chief consultant for *The Good Cook* series of 21 cookbooks for Time-Life International, Amsterdam, 1979–1982.)
Ten Vintage Lunches. Ebury Press, London, 1988.
   Australian edition: Allen and Unwin, Sydney, 1988.
Puck, Wolfgang.
Modern French Cooking for the American Kitchen. Recipes from the Cuisine of Ma Maison. Houghton Mifflin, Boston, 1981.
The Wolfgang Puck Cookbook. Recipes from Spago's, Chinois and Points East and West. Random House, New York, 1986.
Root, Waverley.
The Food of France. Alfred A. Knopf, New York, 1958. Random House, New York, 1977.
The Foods of Italy. Atheneum, New York, 1971. Random House, New York, 1977.
Food. Simon and Schuster, New York, 1980.
Roux, Albert and Michel.
The Roux Brothers New Classic Cuisine. Macdonald, London, 1983.
The Roux Brothers on Pâtisserie. Macdonald, London, 1986.
Senderens, Alain et Eventhia.
La Cuisine Réussie. Editions Jean-Claude Lattès, Paris, 1981.
   British edition: *The Cuisine of Alain Senderens*. Macmillan, London, 1986.

Sedlar, John.
Modern Southwest Cuisine. Simon and Schuster; New York, 1986.
Shere, Lindsey Remolif.
Chez Panisse Desserts. Random House, New York, 1985.
Smith, Michael.
Fine English Cookery. Faber and Faber, London, 1973.
Terrail, Claude.
Ma Tour d'Argent. Stock, France, 1974.
Tower, Jeremiah.
New American Classics. Harper and Row, New York, 1986.
Vergé Roger.
Ma Cuisine du Soleil — Les Recettes Originales de Roger Vergé. Editions Robert Laffont, Paris, 1978.
   British edition: *Cuisine of the Sun*. Macmillan, London, 1979.
Les Fêtes de Mon Moulin. Flammarion, Paris, 1986.
   British edition: *Roger Vergé's Entertaining in the French Style*. Webb and Bower, Exeter, 1986.
   U.S. edition: Stewart, Tabori and Chang, New York, 1986.
Von Welanetz, Diana and Paul.
The Von Welanetz Guide to Ethnic Ingredients. J.P. Tarcher. Inc., Boston, 1982.
Waters, Alice.
Chez Panisse Menu Cookbook. Random House, New York, 1982.
Chez Panisse Pasta, Pizza, and Calzone Cookbook (with Patricia Curtan and Martine Labros). Random House, New York, 1982.
Chez Panisse Cooking: The Nature of the Feast (with Paul Bertolli). Random House, New York, 1988.
Worrall-Thompson, Antony.
The Small and Beautiful Cookbook. Secrets of the Ménage-à-Trois Restaurant. Weidenfeld and Nicolson, London, 1984.

All books have been credited in their original editions. Where known, other editions have also been noted.

Glossary

Aspic: Jelly, commonly of meat or fish, used to set and/or give a sheen to cold meats.

Bain-marie: Tray of hot water in which food in moulds (custards, pâtés, etc.) is stood to prevent rapid penetration of heat when baking.

Blanch *(blanchir)*: To bring to the boil in cold, unsalted water for the purpose of:
(a) removing bitterness (cauliflower, witloof, turnip)
(b) removing saltiness (bottled olives)
(c) firming flesh for easy skinning (brains, sweetbreads)
Commonly, but erroneously, used to mean to drop into a pot of boiling water for part cooking (this usage applies particularly to vegetable cookery).

Blender: Modern electric appliance with small base blade designed to liquefy soups, purée, chop or blend foods together. Preferred uses are soups or very fine mousse-style pâtés. It has a tendency to aerate too much for blending other compositions.

Boudin blanc: A classical sausage of finely ground meat, usually pork, known sometimes in English as 'white pudding'.

Bouquet garni: Small bundle of herbs used to flavour simmered dishes. Comprises at least parsley, thyme and a bay leaf. Other herbs or a piece of celery are common additions. The fresh flavour is essential; prepared dried sachets are musty.

Butter: The word butter in this book refers to salted or lightly salted butter unless qualified. Unsalted butter, however, is regularly specified, particularly with the European chefs, and in pâtisserie and dessert recipes, where salted butter would add an unwanted saltiness. In a hollandaise sauce or *beurre blanc*, take care when seasoning if using salted butter.

Caulfat (French, *crépinette*): A membrane, thin and lacy in appearance due to an erratic ribbing of fat; part of the amniotic sac of animals and human beings. The membrane from pork is available in butchers in most countries, although sometimes only specialist butchers sell it to the public. In France, it is readily available and typically used to envelop a popular pork rissole, by extension also called a *crépinette*.

Champignons: Not to be confused with forest or other dark mushrooms, champignons are cultivated mushrooms bred to be tiny, white and closed.

Chinois: Conical strainer, efficient in straining from a large vessel to a small one. Can be either fine wire mesh, or stainless steel with holes punched over the entire surface.

Clarify: To render a liquid clear and brilliant. Stock is clarified to remove impurities left by meat, vegetable particles or blood. Butter is clarified to remove milk solids for better frying.

Coral *(corail)*: The orange part of a scallop is referred to as the coral. It is sometimes detached and puréed to enrich scallop sauces.

Coulis: An unthickened purée, commonly of fresh fruit and vegetable, used as a sauce. A coulis can be hot or cold, cooked or uncooked.

Crépinette: see Caulfat.

De-glaze *(déglacer)*: To lift meat sediment from the bottom of the pan by adding liquid. The term includes bringing it to the boil, stirring to blend all flavours.

De-grease *(dégraisser)*: Literally, to remove grease from a substance. (a) To de-grease a stock, soup or other liquid, allow the substance to settle, and the grease to rise; then spoon the grease off the top carefully so only the grease is discarded. If small drops remain, e.g. in a plated consommé, they can be absorbed by brushing small pieces of paper towelling across the surface. (b) To de-grease a roast dish after baking, tip the juices to one corner and spoon off only the grease that sits on top.

Dégustation: Literally, a tasting. The *dégustation* menu in vogue in large French restaurants is a menu designed to give the diner a taste of a chef's style, and thus comprises many small courses.

Demi glace: Demi (half) glace is made by heavily reducing a well-made stock (usually veal or beef) to a strongly flavoured and syrupy consistency for use in sauces. To induce stronger flavours, while it is condensing, the stock is most often enriched with further (and fresher) flavouring, by the addition of new meat and vegetables.

Détrempe: Name given to the flour and water dough used at the beginning of puff pastry making, to differentiate this dough from the later stages, in which the butter is already incorporated.

Duxelles: Classical mixture which combines extremely finely chopped onions and champignons (baby mushrooms) by frying them, seasoning and reducing all liquid. Used most often as a stuffing for poultry and winged game.

Feuilleté: Puff pastry case of any shape.

Food mill: Designed to purée soups and softened solids by pressing them through a perforated disc. Handheld versions are cheap and better than a food processor for anything containing skin, bones, seeds, pips or strings, as these elements cannot pass.

Food processor: Modern electric appliance designed to blend, purée, chop, grate and mix, depending on the application of various attachments. With the exception of the task of liquefying soups, it outperforms most blenders.

Gratiné *(gratiner)*: To pass an element, usually a precooked dish, under a salamander or domestic griller (broiler) in order to brown and glaze the surface. A very hot oven can sometimes gratiné but there is a great risk of curdling a delicate sauce through overheating. Note: To gratiné does not imply the addition of breadcrumbs, butter or any additional ingredient, although these additions are sometimes added to enhance the colour. If required,

they have been specified in the ingredient list and the method.

Julienne: Small matchstick-sized pieces. Method of cutting vegetables, peel and garnishes, such as ham.

Jus: Traditional French light (unthickened) gravy made by de-glazing the sediment on the base of a roast dish. Built only with stocks, wine and flavourings, it differs from a traditional British gravy, in that it is unthickened.

Lardons: Bite-sized pieces of thickly sliced bacon used as a garnish, particularly in casseroles and vegetable dishes. The French use uncooked *lard fumé*; failing that they are best made from strong smoked bacon, available from continental butchers and good delicatessens.

Macerate: To bathe in alcohol; a term usually applied to fruit.

Marinade: The wine and vegetables etc., in which meat is marinated.

Marinate: To bathe in liquid, usually wine and flavouring ingredients. The intention is to flavour and soften the texture of the tougher cuts of meat or game.

Mesclun: Term given to mixed salad greens, notably the dwarf varieties of cress, radicchio, cos, endive, lamb's tongue lettuce (*mâche*), chrysanthemum leaves and various small Japanese-style salad greens. The term designates a mixture of the various types.

Mirepoix: Diced vegetables, notably carrots and onions, fried to give added flavour to the gravy of baked meats, casseroles and sauces.

Mincer: Originally a hand-held appliance clamped onto the bench, but now an attachment to a variety of comprehensive electric applicances, the mincer grinds meat to two or three different consistencies for stuffings, pâtés, hamburger meats and even ultra-fine ground sausage meats. The various consistences are made by changing the perforated grill through which the meat passes. Much more efficient in the job than a food processor, since the processor cannot guarantee an even texture or sizing in the particles.

Mousseline: Commonly, a mixture of puréed fish, eggs and/or eggwhite and cream. Used as a forcemeat for fish or poached in moulds. Chicken and veal mousselines exist also.

Pâte feuilletée: see Puff pastry.

Paupiette: Rolled meat or fish fillet, usually stuffed.

Poach: To cook gently at a temperature under boiling point to avoid damaging delicate foods, e.g. eggs. Optimum temperature is around 90°C/190°F.

Puff pastry (*pâte feuilletée*): Traditionally a flour, water and butter pastry in which the butter is rolled between layers of the flour and water dough in a series of six 'turns', producing a succession of 1459 separate layers (leaves) of pastry in which the butter is trapped between the layers of flour. With the application of heat, the butter swells and the steam hits the layer above, thus forcing it to rise. The secret is in preserving these layers intact right to the oven.

Quenelle: A sausage-shaped dumpling, usually of fish but also of chicken or veal. Quenelles of the Lyonnaise area are chou pastry based; modern recipes require only puréed fish, eggwhite and cream.

Rind: The peel of a citrus fruit. It contains both the zest and the pith (white portion). Although sometimes employed in cooking this way, the white part is usually considered too bitter, and for most recipes only the zest is used. (see also Zest)

Roux: The combination of butter and flour basic to most sauces. Traditional recipes use equal quantities of butter and flour; the modern trend is to slightly undercut the quantity of flour, thus rendering slightly thinner sauces.

Salamander: A professional grilling (broiling) element, usually of gas, capable of excessive heat; used in a restaurant to gratiné (glaze) the top of dishes.

Salsa: A combination of chopped ingredients, most often but not necessarily uncooked, to serve as a (chunky-style) sauce or accompaniment. cf. Chutney, an English relish.

Sauté: To toss an ingredient in butter, oil or other grease. Ingredients are sautéed both to soften and grease them, and to colour them. The word itself does not imply colouration. (see also Sweat)

Scald: To bring to the boil; term most often applied to milk.

Score: To make shallow incisions to aid penetration of heat or liquid, e.g. fish for cooking under a griller (broiler), pork rind to help crackling blister, the fat of a leg of lamb when placed in a marinade.

Shallots: The little brown cluster onion that is the real *échalote* of French cuisine, used to give depth of flavour to sauces and casseroles. In some countries or regions, it is confused with the spring onion, a light, tubular little green vegetable that looks like an overgrown chive with a white onion-flavoured tip, or a very thin member of the leek family. Scallion is another term often used for the more bulbous form of the spring onion, or even green onion. Neither of these is a shallot as these chefs mean it. To substitute: The pickling onion, or dwarf brown onion is a better substitute for the shallot than a spring or green onion. Substitute with the latter only when the shallot is to be eaten raw e.g. when chopped and scattered over a salad. Spring (green) onions are not strong enough to give depth of flavour in cooked dishes.

Shortcrust pastry: A blend of flour, butter and water, sometimes sweetened with sugar, incorporated with as little kneading as possible to ensure a friable dough for pies, tarts and other elements requiring pastry crust. The balance of the ingredients varies depending on the skill and intention of the cook, and often the delicacy of the product it is surrounding. Generally, the more friable, the crisper and lighter the taste, if the composition of the dish allows it (cf. a dessert tart or a hefty pâté requiring a hardy pastry encompassing it).

Shuck: To remove from shell; term usually applied to seafood.

Stock: Flavoured water derived from cooking meat, poultry or fish with vegetables. Used to enrich soups, casseroles or sauces.

Sweat: To cook a vegetable slowly in butter, oil or other grease (very occasionally without grease if the vegetable contains a lot of liquid). Sweating a vegetable will soften it and also bring down, and potentially evaporate its juices. Vegetables that are sweated usually become translucent, but should not colour.

Vinaigrette: Mixture of oil, vinegar and seasonings, sometimes herbs. Also known as French dressing.

Zest: The outer part of orange or lemon peel, or oil squeezed from it, used as a flavouring. In grating zest, only the outer skin is taken; the white part being bitter is not used. (see also Rind)

Index